ROCK
ON FILM

Books
DELILAH

DISTRIBUTED BY G.P. PUTNAM'S SONS
N E W   Y O R K

DAVID EHRENSTEIN & BILL REED

ART DIRECTION BY ED CARAEFF

Special thanks to:

Academy of Motion Picture Arts and Sciences, David Alper, Danny Benair,
Jonathan Benair, Lise Bloch-Morhange, Meredith Brody, Joan Cohen, Anne Collier,
Jim Di Giovanni, Pearl Ehrenstein, Hilda Goldsmith, Walter Goldsmith,
Wes Goodwin, Marguerite Howe, Andy Hughes, Richard Meltzer, Karen Moline,
Jonathan Rosenbaum, Virginia Rubel, Jeannie Sakol, Michael Sragow AND, our
editor, Martin Torgoff.

Back cover and all inside posters from the Alan Betrock Collection.

PHOTOS
Culver Pictures: p. 22
Michael Ochs Archive: p. 11, p. 13, p. 30, p. 46
MOMA Film Stills Archive: p. 21, 74, 93, 207, 211, 223, 252
Reed/Ehrenstein Collection: p. 12, p. 85, p. 152, p. 194
P. Spheeris: p. 140

Book and Cover Design by ED CARAEFF

For Fred Ceely

C O N T

E   N   T   S

FOREWORD(S)

I SAW *ROCK AROUND THE CLOCK* the very first day it opened in 1956 (on a double bill with *Over-Exposed,* starring the late, great Cleo Moore), and I've been hooked on rock and roll movies ever since.

Just last week I stayed up until three a.m. to catch Neil Sedaka singing "Do The Waterbug" in a 1970 Canadian exploitation thriller called *Decoy For Terror.* (Truly one of the all-time stinkers. I loved it!)

The co-author of this book, David Ehrenstein, grew up at the movies. (*Meet Me in St. Louis* proved especially traumatic.) If it's got sprocket holes he's all for it, be it Carl Dryer's *Gertrud* or Vittorio Cottafavi's *Hercules Conquers Atlantis.*

One day not too long ago (but which now seems more like *years*), I suggested to him that we do a book on rock and roll movies—with David being FILM and me being ROCK. After all, there definitely was a desperate need for just such a book.

Five minutes later we were hard at work on *Rock on Film.*

BILL REED

TWENTY-FIVE YEARS AGO ROCK AND ROLL was just another "dance sensation sweepin' the nation," but today it seems as if every third film that comes along falls back on rock for some sense of support—if only as musical glue. Until we began work on this book we didn't realize just how very *many* films involving rock and roll there were. Consequently in order to put things into focus certain lines had to be drawn.

For example, Bill initially wanted to include short promotional films. But to emphasize just how many of these items there are, I showed him a recent Warner/Reprise record catalogue which lists over 150 *currently available* items. Clearly these 3 to 5 minute shorts require a book all to themselves.

Then there was the problem of certain foreign films—French "ye ye" musicals with only tenuous connections to rock, obscure "shoestring" German productions. We decided not to rack our brains too much over this area, realizing it would take a massive research team years to ferret out all these very marginal celluloid goods.

Likewise we found it impractical to make note of each and every time so much as *one bar* of rock and roll music was used as dramatic background. If rock was used in any way that was important to the action you're sure to find mention of it here.

What we *have* done in *Rock on Film* is to provide both the casual movie and music lover *and* the more committed fan with solid perspective on both the historical and esthetic evolution of rock, its performers, and the films that featured them. Along the way we've also included insights, arcana and assorted bits of trivia that we hope will both inform and amuse.

The field of rock film is wide open for study, and while our book isn't intended as the *absolute* final word on the subject, we're sure it will more than help fill the informational void that has existed up to now.

DAVID EHRENSTEIN

INTRODUCTION

by Michael Sragow

EARLY ROCK AND ROLL HAD A COCKSURE SPIRIT. It gave off the feeling that a new sound was being forged on dirt roads and city streets, and that any teenager with enough gumption and talent could put that sound into his music and turn it into a best-selling record. Even now, people who came of age in the 50's and 60's dream of recapturing the collective euphoria of that era. They flock to oldies concerts, or to movie revival theaters showing *The Girl Can't Help It,* hoping to recharge their grown-up pulses on a teenage beat.

That same crowd should grab up copies of this book, for rock and roll's youthful anarchic energy bops and rebops through its pages. This chronicle of rock's conquest of the movies covers everything from teen ''problem'' films like *Blackboard Jungle* to beach movies, Beatles films, ''rockumentaries'' like *Woodstock,* and even movies that have rock only on the soundtrack. It's an octopus of a subject, yet writers David Ehrenstein and Bill Reed have managed to wrestle each tentacle to the ocean floor without losing their enthusiasm. They carefully note the flaws and virtues of almost every film they write about—nothing cinematic is alien to them. And despite their affection for the good old days, they aren't crippled by nostalgia. They're as up-to-date as *URGH!,* a punk rock epic filmed in 1980 but yet to be released. *Rock on Film* is in part a testament of faith that the spirit of rock is alive and kicking in the 80's, no matter how strange or foreign its new forms.

Ehrenstein and Reed are serious about frivolity. Savvy about industry trends and formulae, sensitive to the quirks of movie art, they're the children of Roland Barthes and Rona Barrett. What makes the book funny is the authors' bemused attitude towards their often absurd subjects. Their good-humored tolerance makes the chapter on the slapped-together ''jukebox musicals'' of the 50's and early 60's especially amusing. They nail down the narrative flaw in all these movies—that the filmmakers had no inkling of how to connect the story organically with the rock acts. Their notation of 1961's *Teenage Millionaire* reaches heights of whimsicality: ''All the writers could come up with was the device of having the film's singing protagonist, played by Jimmy Clanton, *imagine* the musical acts.'' But the authors aren't merely derisive, even towards *Teenage Millionaire.* They list the movie's musical acts (Chubby Checker, Jackie Wilson, Merv Johnson and Dion) and also come up with the following jaw-dropping piece of info: that the film featured Zasu Pitts, ''co-star of TV's *Oh Susanna,* star of Eric von Stroheim's masterpiece *Greed,* and author of the only posthumously published combination autobiography and candy cookbook, *Pitt's Hits* (1964).''

This combination of critical/historical zeal and a fan's enthusiasm has always been rare in writing about rock movies, because many of the best film critics have been terribly condescending to rock. There was probably no more entertaining or lucid film columnist writing regularly in the early 60's than *Esquire's* Dwight Macdonald, but re-reading his opening paragraph to an other-wise right-on rave for *A Hard Day's Night* amounts to pop-culture shock. Writing in January '65, he calls the Beatles ''cult-fetishes of adolescent hysteria, related to their audience on about the same level as an African witch doctor to his clients, indeed on a lower level in some ways since the rhythmical beat that is their specialty is less sophisticated than the intricately varied rhythms of many tribal dances.'' He sounds like nothing more than a refugee from 1956's *Shake, Rattle and Rock* in which a spokesman for the SPRACAY—''the Society for the Prevention of Rock and Roll Corruption of American Youth''—uses footage of African tribal dancers to show the ''source of this so-called cultural form, rock and roll.''

Rock on Film is partly a chronicle of how rock *movies* tried to defend the *music* against charges of immorality and mindlessness. Pursuing this theme leads Ehrenstein and Reed to some major discoveries. Who before them, for example, had fully appreciated the role that beach movies played in making rock and roll seem wholesome? It was movies like *Beach Party* (the writers suggest) that softened the American public up for the Beatles' onslaught, and the social-cultural revolution that followed.

Unlike many rock and movie commentators, Ehrenstein and Reed don't feel defeated by the ebbing of the counterculture; they're able to go with the flow of reggae, punk and Bette Midler. Their eclecticism suits their subject; if in rock history ''the early clue to the next direction'' has turned up in places as unlikely as Lubbock, Texas and Liverpool, who's to say where it'll pop up next? By the end of the book you're convinced that new rock sights and sounds are sure to come—and they're apt to break out anywhere.

I

IN THE BEGINNING

THERE NEVER WERE any two less likely bedfellows than rock and roll and Clare Booth Luce. Yet it was Luce in 1955 who landed the first blow that helped move rock and roll movies into the spotlight for the very first time.

As late as the previous year, sweet n' soothing forties-style music by the likes of Patti Page and Perry Como still held sway at the top of record sales charts, with rock and roll still thought of as only a passing fad. By early '55, though, this new of, by and for the kids music was front page news thanks to, of all people, Ms. Luce—popular playwright, Ambassador to Italy and wife of *Life Magazine* publisher, Henry Luce.

What happened was that Ambassador Luce got an advance peek at MGM Studio's *Blackboard Jungle*, which contained the first use of rock and roll as part of a film soundtrack, Bill Haley's "Rock Around The Clock." Since *Blackboard Jungle* was the official U.S. entry that year at the Venice Film Festival Luce hit the ceiling over what she saw, for the Richard Brooks film painted an especially bleak and disturbing picture of juvenile gang activity in the New York City public school system.

In the film Glenn Ford portrays a dedicated high school teacher totally unprepared for the violent scene he meets up with on his first day at his new slum school assignment. After the film's 101 minutes of running time has elapsed the situation resolves on a relatively cheery note.

Clare Booth Luce called *Blackboard Jungle* a degenerate film, even in spite of the fact that the film contained a typical Hollywood upbeat ending. In turn, Luce's detractors accused her of being a self-appointed censor and a snob. Luce finally pulled rank with a vengeance over the film, for she announced that if *Blackboard Jungle* was screened at Venice she'd boycott the fest.

By the time that announcement was made, broadcast and print media were full of charges and countercharges arising from Luce's tactics. Even MGM's maneuver of placing a disclaimer at the beginning of the film saying that the actions depicted in *Blackboard Jungle* were atypical of U.S. schools failed to mollify Luce. She finally got her way for the film was withdrawn from Venice to be replaced by *Interrupted Melody*, an innocuous weepie about a crippled opera singer.

The center of all this controversy was a modest black and white film in the same vein as *The Wild One* (1954) and *Rebel Without A Cause* (1955) and other "hard hitting" fifties films which dealt with the subject of juvenile delinquency. In terms of column inches generated by the Luce fracas, though, the furor caused by these other films was mild by comparison.

The upshot of all the publicity about *Blackboard Jungle* was an enormous amount of curiosity, especially on the part of teens, to see what all the shouting was about. So while anti-censorship crusaders lost their battle with Luce in regard to the Venice Fest, the makers of the film, MGM, won a great victory at the box office.

Teenagers attended the film in droves, at first no doubt because of the lure of the forbidden—views of gang rumbles and a steady flow of images of such emerging sub-cultural phenomena as switchblade knives and ducktail haircuts. After viewing the film the young viewers marched right out of the theatres and snapped up millions of copies of "Rock Around The Clock," a tune which had only been a minor hit prior to its inclusion in *Blackboard Jungle*. The film was not just a movie, but a phonograph record as well—*two media experiences for the price of one!* This movie industry/music biz sort of hybrid was not really that new, for nearly every major swing era star had made films. *Blackboard Jungle*, however, represented the first time that rock and roll and film had come to each other's mutual aid.

Even while *Blackboard Jungle* was causing so much controversy (the film was banned in several big U.S. cities) the music scene was still dominated by conventional "adult" sounds. Still, early forms of rock and roll were making inroads, mostly in the form of recordings aimed at a white teen market, performed by Fats Domino, Joe Turner, The Clovers, Ruth Brown and other black rhythm and blues stars. No longer were musicians like these selling to a strictly all black market as they had been previously. Around the early 1950s, a white audience, dominated by teenagers, began listening as well.

This embracing of black music by white adolescents was viewed with alarm by most parents and other adult authority figures, (just like when jazz came on the scene several decades earlier). The rise of rock was seen by most grownups as a threat to decency, and as (perhaps) part of a "commie" plot.

The increasing popularity of rock remained unchecked and by early 1956 numerous young white performers had jumped on the bandwagon and were recording big beat hits equal in quality to those by blacks. Sanford Clark, Carl Perkins, Buddy Holly and Jerry Lee Lewis were just some of the young white rockers who were now sharing rock honors with The Platters, Frankie Lymon, Bill Doggett, Chuck Berry and other black stars who were now selling records by the millions. Foremost among the young white stars was, of course, Elvis Presley—who would go on to become a major force in rock on film.

Prior to the rise of the other young white rock and rollers Bill Haley was, for a short while, the undisputed king of rock and roll. The music they all made wasn't really all that new, however. As Robert Palmer pointed out in an essay in *The Rolling Stone Illustrated History of Rock and Roll*, "each of (the) early rock and rollers was firmly rooted in the music of earlier years. The white rockabilly stars groomed by Sun Records' owner Sam Phillips (Presley, Perkins, Lewis et al) were raised on white country music, country and western and hillbilly boogie. It was Phillips who urged them to listen to black bluesmen and to affect black singing styles, though Presley at least had already been listening to bluesmen like Arthur Crudup."

In essence, then, early rock music by both blacks and whites, sounded like everything, and yet *nothing*, that teenagers of the 1950s had heard before.

Teens, in the mid-1950s, were experiencing a new sense of autonomy that previous generations had never had. To express this new freedom a music all their own was called for, and rock and roll filled the bill perfectly. With its concerns of sex and speed, instead of the "June, moon and spoon" of their parents' music, rock was a perfect music for the atomic era—its goading orgiastic sound made all the more poignant by the possibility of oblivion's imminence. Everytime a parent got unnerved over phonographs blaring out "that noise" their offspring could well have reminded them of an even bigger noise that was totally an adult responsibility. The Big Beat may have seemed dangerous to mom and pop, but it couldn't hold a candle to the Big Bang.

All of these social, cultural and economic considerations played a large part in *Blackboard Jungle*'s turning out to be a major international movie hit, and Haley's "fox trot" (the description of the song on the initial Decca label release) became the first authentic number one rock and roll single—none of which was lost on veteran Hollywood quickie producer, Sam Katzman.

In the scheme of corporate filmmaking in the 1950s Katzman was the cinematic equivalent of tabloid journalism. The sort of films the producer specialized in bore titles like *Spotlight Scandals, Siren of Bagdad* and *The Tiajuana Story*. Before he died in 1973, Katzman acted as producer on well over a hundred sub-"B" movies like these. If there was one quick buck (literally "one"') to be made from exploiting news headlines about dope and crime, or from cheaply cashing in on a current movie fad, producer Katzman was *the* man for delivering the goods. But with his film *Rock Around the Clock* in 1955, Katzman finally invented a sub-genre all his very own—the rock and roll movie musical!

Though no David O. Selznick, Katzman's participation in the evolution of rock on film was carried out with all the cunning and calculation he'd learned while working, since the early 1930s, on Hollywood's "B" picture assembly line. In the instance of *Rock Around the Clock* Katzman reasoned that if

X-amount of kids would shell out so many dollars only to hear rock music on a movie's soundtrack, as with *Blackboard Jungle*, think how many more would be willing to pay not only to hear but to *see* the music performed on screen.

To that end, in late 1955, Katzman secured the services of the off-screen star of *Blackboard Jungle*, Bill Haley (and his Comets) to appear in the movie named after Haley's hit single, *Rock Around The Clock*—also starring The Platters and influential rock dee-jay Alan Freed.

The plot of *Rock Around The Clock* was as safe as safe can be. In fact, the film's storyline consisted of nothing more than the one used over and over again in most of the big band swing musicals of the forties, i.e., struggling band with a "new" and "daring" sound finally gets the "big break" after battling through a predictable series of hard knocks. Instead of Tommy Dorsey or Artie Shaw, though, this trailblazing Katzman effort presented The Platters singing "Only You" and "The Great Pretender," and Haley and his Comets miming their way through nine big hits, including the title tune, plus "See You Later, Alligator," "Mambo Rock," among others. The film also contained some other musical acts of no rock consequence.

Even though erstwhile country and western singer Haley in this film touted as "the whole story of rock and roll" comes off as almost offputtingly middle-aged and square (with nary a hint of sexuality evident), the fact of this didn't detract from the film's popularity. It cleaned up, becoming one of the better grossing films of 1956. Further, shortly after *Rock Around The Clock* opened it went on to establish a controversy similar to the one caused by *Blackboard Jungle*. Teen theatre riots even flared up in some cities where the Haley film was shown. *Rock Around The Clock* was banned in several locales, thus further insuring publicity for it.

In England, the brouhaha over *Rock Around The Clock* was even greater than in America. Katzman's basically harmless little movie, across the ocean, generated front page banner headlines because of the riots that took place almost *everywhere Rock Around The Clock* was shown. No less than the Queen of England and parliament were swept up into the fray, and the banning and debating over the film continued on for some time. (Shortly after the flames subsided, Haley and his band swept through the British Isles on a monumentally successful tour.)

Films similar in tone and construction to *Rock Around The Clock* began to be turned out by Hollywood with relentless regularity, like Katzman's 1956 followup to "Clock," *Don't Knock The Rock*, starring Haley and Little Richard, *Shake, Rattle and Rock* (1956) which featured Fats Domino and Joe Turner, *Mister Rock and Roll* (1957) and *Go, Johnny, Go* (1958) with the latter two both starring dee-jay Alan Freed hosting an almost non-stop vaudeville parade of musical acts like Frankie Lymon, Eddie Cochran, Richie Valens, Chuck Berry and Little Richard—in these virtually identical musical entries. Although all of these later jukebox musicals were hits to one degree or another, none hit paydirt the way *Rock Around The Clock* did. (See chapter three for further, in-depth discussion of these variety musicals.)

Teenagers, both in America and abroad, were invariably loyal to the *Rock Around The Clock* knock-offs, for these quickly-made, double-bill-styled star parades served as clear evidence that a musical and social phenomenon had come along that was uniquely their own, something very nearly illegal—ROCK AND ROLL!

Soon pop sociologists rushed the phrase, "rock and roll," into operation as a buzz word to toy with alongside rock music's supposed end result, JUVENILE DELINQUENCY. It began to become clear that rock and roll was here to stay, if but only for a little while. The new sound, and the films trafficking in it were not just a passing fad, after all.

Ironically, none of these rock musicals had much to do with the real life concerns of American teenagers. Most of the kids in them would've seemed stuffy even in Louisa May Alcott's time. But this didn't really bother the films' young attendees, for no one paid much attention to the plot. The sole purpose of movies like *Rock Around The Clock* and *Go, Johnny, Go* was only to squeeze in as much music as possible into their ninety minutes (or less) of running time —with the "dramatic" filler consisting of such will-o-the-wisp concerns as the havoc wreaked by a teen vamp, a band's struggle for stardom or being allowed to attend the big dance.

It was this very sort of music/plot clash that inspired writer-director Frank Tashlin when he set out to out-Katzman Katzman with the very first major studio, big budget rocksploitation musical, *The Girl Can't Help It* (1956). What Tashlin affected with *The Girl Can't Help It* was simply the replacement of the white bread plot that Katzman and his like had used to sandwich the music, with his own brand of wry rye. Squarely facing the accusation that rock and roll was merely a gimmick that even the totally talentless with the right kind of promotion could parlay into big bucks, Tashlin devised a situation to exploit the ultimate gimmick, namely Jayne Mansfield.

The blonde comedienne's overstuffed proportions were a perfect foil for Tashlin's cartoonist sensibility. A parody of the Marilyn Monroe phenomenon while *that* phenomenon itself was just getting under way, Mansfield was the ideal antidote to the rock-plot predictability of the first quickie rock musicals. Neither adult, nor child, Mansfield's bubbly enthusiasm and total lack of self-pretense complemented the spirit of rock and roll to a tee. Tashlin establishes the film's flip tone by casting this starry-eyed Amazon as the girlfriend of a gangster (Edmund O'Brien) who wants to make Mansfield into a rock star because he can't face marrying "a nobody." Already, in *The Girl Can't Help It*, the conventions of most rock musicals are set on their heads, for Mansfield is dead set against O'Brien's scheme. Who had ever heard of a film where the central character *resists* stardom?

Tashlin cast Tom Ewell as the agent drafted into Mansfield's service who discovers that while she can't sing, she *can* emit a piercing scream—the perfect sound effect for a song her fiance wrote while in jail for income tax evasion, "Rock Around The Rock Pile." The film's conclusion finds Mansfield and Ewell, with O'Brien's approval, walking off into the sunset together, but only after an impressive array of rock greats have been allowed massive amounts of screen space and time for performing some arresting musical numbers. The visual inventiveness of Gene Vincent's rehearsal studio number (where he and his Blue Caps flip off their hats in unison while singing "Be Bop A Lula") and the lush colors offsetting such performers as Eddie Cochran ("Twenty Flight

Rock''), Fats Domino (''Blue Monday'') and The Platters set standards that wouldn't be reached again until Richard Lester's *Hard Day's Night*.

Most astonishing of all is Tashlin's use of Little Richard. The residual racial prejudice that has always lain beneath the surface of rock's opposition had left its mark on rocksploitation films prior to *The Girl Can't Help It*. Black performers always were shown at their most docile, and never were incorporated into the plot any further than an emcee's introduction. But in *The Girl Can't Help It* Little Richard, one of the most sexually volatile rockers of them all, appears in a central scene. (In the sort of posh nightclub he'd never have been so much as allowed inside the doors of in real life—but, here he's the headliner!) During the Little Richard section of the film, under Tom Ewell's instruction, Mansfield is attempting to capture the attention of the assembled swells by undulating her leaning tower charms across the nightclub's floor. Little Richard keeps pounding away throughout all of this, and as Tashlin cuts between the mountainous movements of Mansfield's whiter-than-white form and Little Richard's jet black lascivious response, racist paranoia is dealt the satiric *coup de grace*. Tashlin's adaptation of Sergei Eisenstein's notion of montage-as-collision in this scene produces an image that's pure rock and roll. Tashlin seems to be asking, Which figure is more fearful, Little Richard's aroused Abyssinian, or Mansfield's Aryan Avatar?

Finally, what Tashlin is sending up in this genuinely funny film, though, isn't just racism and sexuality; it's the Sam Katzman brand of quickie promotion. And in sharp contrast to the flat, backgroundless settings of those first few black and white rock films, the director unleashes all of Twentieth Century Fox's color and Cinemascope resources. The studio lavished a good deal of money on the project and when *The Girl Can't Help It* was released Fox's faith was justified by strong moviegoer approval.

Fox leant a further vote of confidence to the rock movie in 1956 by producing Elvis Presley's first film, *Love Me Tender*. The only movie companies who had gone out on the limb for rock movies, prior to Fox, were small independent outfits like Directors Corporation of America (DCA), American International Pictures (AIP), plus minor ''major'' studios such as Columbia Pictures.

Since *The Girl Can't Help It* was the first big budget rock film, it laid down a whole new set of rules for rock and roll movie projects. It was, in words used in another landmark film a decade later (*Hard Day's Night*), ''an early clue to the new direction.'' While Fox didn't pull out all the stops, a la *The Girl Can't Help It*, for its second rock project, *Love Me Tender*, the approach the company took with Elvis's screen debut was, at least, offbeat.

Just a scant quarter of a decade after Elvis Presley's ascendance as the single most influential figure in pop culture since Charlie Chaplin, his myth has become almost too frighteningly fixed and locked in. Even pre-teens of today are likely to know a good deal of Presley lore, but what they cannot sense is the tenor of hysteria and all-pervasiveness accompanying Elvis' arrival on the scene. Presley-mania laid the groundwork for Beatlemania in later years, but since in the instance of Presley the focus was on just one person, not four, the impact of Presley's initial appearance was, in a way, even greater than that of the Beatles. Eldridge Cleaver, in *Soul On Ice*, wrote of the impression first made by the singer: "Elvis, with his *unfunky* (yet mechanical, alienated) bumpgrinding, was still too much Body (too soon) for the strained collapsing psyches of the Omnipotent Administrators and Ultrafeminines." Translated, "the Eisenhower era." But whereas Cleaver's assessment of Elvis from the vantage point of the sixties was cool and clinical, response to him in the fifties was anything but analytical and detached. Typical of the heated writing concerning Presley was a critique of his first film, *Love Me Tender*, that appeared in *Films In Review*: "Presley is a pied piper who could lead his followers to an end more socially deleterious than their permanent disappearance in a cave."

Fox tried everything it could to defuse the possibilities of reactions like these when it signed up Elvis, the act of which stunned a lot of people. Why would prestigious and conservative 20th Century Fox have anything to do with a hot potato like Elvis Presley, they wondered? What would they do with him? The more dispassionate only wondered how the singer's sexually charged talents could be captured and contained on film without tampering with his teen appeal.

What the studio did to keep criticism over their signing Elvis down to a dull roar was to drop their bonus baby into the midst of an already scheduled, distinctly non-contemporary Civil War melodrama, originally titled *The Reno Brothers*. A *dramatic* part! "Don't worry," this move on Fox's part suggested, "he's not going to sing very much and get the kids all riled up."

Then the studio proceeded to surround Elvis with a stock company of reputable actors like Richard Egan and Mildred Dunnock, thus lending some much-needed "legitimacy" to the rocker's dramatic debut. If it turned out the kid couldn't act, maybe having these and other seasoned troopers around would deflect away from that fact. Further conservative measures on Fox's part included their filming their novice star in discreet and *cool* black and white, and having him warble his first conventional adult ballad, "Love Me Tender," which replaced *The Reno Brothers* as the film's new title. Also, Elvis got killed off nine-tenths of the way through his first film. Having Elvis serenade his movie audience with a decidedly non-rock song could only broaden the age range of his fans, Fox decided; and by having him die in *Love Me Tender*, the idea might have been subliminally telegraphed to grownups that Presley was gone, nevermore to agitate their highly excitable young. (The kids, of course, knew differently.)

Fox's tactics worked perfectly. Even the billing that superstar Elvis received—the discreet and down-played "and introducing Elvis Presley" (which prompted one wag to note "that's like saying 'and introducing Dwight David Eisenhower'")—was a clever touch. Thus the tone of most of the public scrutiny, naturally, turned away from the moral question to, merely, "CAN HE ACT?" The answer to which was mixed.

In its review of *Love Me Tender*, *Time Magazine*'s film critic asked of Presley, "Is it a sausage? It certainly is smooth and damp looking, but whoever heard of a 172-lb. sausage, six feet tall? Is it a Walt Disney Goldfish? It has the same sort of big, soft beautiful eyes and long curly lashes, but whoever heard of a goldfish with sideburns? Is it a corpse? The face just hangs there limp and white with its little drop-seat mouth, rather like Lord Byron in the wax museum." (*Time*, 11/26/56)

Regarding the Elvis/*Love Me Tender* question, less sophisticated, more hysterical quarters than *Time* still rumbled with moral degeneracy aftershock, with reports about Elvis' "coition-simulating movement of primitive negroes." Luckily, though, reviews for Presley's debut generally were favorable, and Fox and its star were off the hook.

Movie audience response to Elvis and his first film outing was almost 100% positive: with the star's every utterance in *Love Me Tender* being greeted by clamorous cheers. All Elvis had to do was say "You ain't got no right to do this," or "Yeah! What about it?" and audiences for *Love Me Tender* went wild.

In this first Elvis Presley film the definitive characteristics that would typify later rock films began to take shape: what was going on at theatres showing *Love Me Tender* was something more than the ardor ordinarily expended by film fans. Even Valentino's followers couldn't compare with this audience's ravenous desire to literally *devour* the images and sounds coming from the screen. Their squeals and cries of approval turned the theater into a revival meeting. It was nothing less than the discovery of a new use for film: movies were no longer something to be seen in quiet passivity and calmly remarked upon later. Instead, the experience would be dealt with in the here and now. Rock film was an experience to *eat*.

While the kids now were ready to sit down to a rock and roll movie feast, the adult filmmaking chefs were uncertain about what to serve them—not so much because of ethical jitters (i.e., all that pubescent energy unleashed by rock sights and sounds), but mostly because of reasons having to do with the staying power of such films. The success of *Rock Around The Clock* and *The Girl Can't Help It* could, after all, just have been a fluke arising out of a fad. After the months-long staying power of *Love Me Tender*, producers of films who'd only been partially committed to rock movies began to feel a good deal less uncertain. For the Presley film recouped its negative cost in a little over two weeks' time, and it continued to do big business for many months to come.

While legions of teen Presleyites formed the core of the audience for *Love Me Tender*, what finally put Elvis' debut film over the top was the hordes of curious adults who also turned out to see what all the shouting was about. Elvis was fast assuming the position of not just rock films', but *rock's* pivotal make-or-break figure. Now, since Elvis was such a smash his first time on the giant screen, it was beginning to look like rock and roll *and* rock and roll films were going to become a permanent part of the movie scene.

II

THAT'S THE WAY IT WAS

WELCOME BACK!
ELVIS PRESLEY
YOU'RE THE GREATEST!

METRO-GOLDWYN-MAYER
presents

Jailhouse Rock

in CinemaScope · An Avon Production

CO-STARRING Judy Tyler · WITH Mickey Shaughnessy · Dean Jones · Jennifer Holden · SCREEN PLAY BY Guy Trosper

DIRECTED BY Richard Thorpe · PRODUCED BY Pandro S. Berman · An M-G-M Re-Release

WHILE ELVIS PRESLEY wasn't exactly a threat to Laurence Olivier in his film debut, even some of his detractors conceded that in his first dramatic performance, Elvis did a respectable job. He could read lines competently, and this ability in turn suggested that with the proper coaching Elvis could develop into a solid leading man. But even more than mere acting ability, Elvis displayed in *Love Me Tender* that seldom suitably defined "something extra" of *presence*.

Elvis' face *held* the screen. When he smiled his face glowed with the grateful innocence of a 4-H Club prize winner; and when he frowned, his face clouded over like a sky before a storm—the eyes went dark and come-hitherish in a manner guaranteed to send chills down little girls' spines.

Playing the odd man out in a tragic western love triangle, *Love Me Tender* gave Elvis the opportunity to brood romantically in the grand Valentino manner. As "Clint Reno," married to the fiancee (Debra Paget) of a brother (Richard Egan) presumed dead in the just concluded Civil War, Elvis portrayed a character caught between noble intentions and personal passions. For with the brother turning up alive and his wife unable to conceal her amorous ambivalence, "Clint," marooned on the sidelines, finds that his own personal happiness has become an inadvertent force of destruction.

Paget's vacillations between Presley and Egan may have seemed strange to Elvis' female fans at the time, but it made for good drama, providing them, through close-ups, with a most intense examination of their idol.

"Clint" may have lost in the end—inadvertently shot down by his brother in the final gun battle—but Elvis had already *won* in the film's musical numbers ("Poor Boy," "We're Gonna Move," "Let Me" and the title tune) staged in a quasi-concert manner with on-screen females squealing just like the ones in the movie audience.

In order to maintain this pitch of erotomania however, something more than the low-key *Love Me Tender* was needed—something that would fix and center Elvis' film persona in a much more definite way. His next film, *Loving You* (1956) provided the perfect vehicle.

Cleverly concocted by veteran producer Hal Wallis, and directed in business-like fashion by Hal Kantor (from a script by Kantor and Herbert Baker), *Loving You*, in effect, *is The Elvis Presley Story*, but gussied up with traditional Hollywood glamour and pop mythology.

In *Loving You*, flanked by established Wallis stock-player/stars like Lizabeth Scott and Wendell Corey, Elvis is led like Alice-in-Wonderland through a topsy-turvey looking-glass reflection of his own life and career. As good old country boy "Deke Rivers," Elvis is plucked from the the crowd at a hoe-down to sing a song. Reluctantly he does so, and scores a big hit. As luck would have it, "Deke" is spotted by a sharp-eyed music promoter (Scott), and the rest is—as they say—musical history.

Instantly recognizing his appeal, Scott pushes the somewhat rueful and hesitant "Deke" into show business. After a series of predictable backslides and obstacles, "Deke" finally becomes a Presley-like star through Scott (playing, in essence, Elvis' real-life Svengali, Colonel Tom Parker.)

Loving You is a light, good-natured film, not above even kidding itself to some degree (though it nowhere approaches the audacious spoof style of *The Girl Can't Help It*), but there's a slightly eerie overtone to it all. With so many scenes in *Loving You* duplicating actual events from Elvis' life, watching it can almost be likened to seeing a production of *The Passion Play*—only with Christ playing himself. Just three scant years prior to starring in *Loving You* Presley, just like "Deke" in the film, had been barnstorming throughout the Southwest U. S. doing a series of juke joint one night stands. One scene of young, local toughs getting unhinged over the effect "Deke" is having on their girlfriends, is taken from actual Presley lore, for from the very beginning Presley had the capacity to turn virginal Southern belles into sex-crazed tigresses right before their boyfriends' disbelieving, horrified eyes.

Further "Deke"/Elvis parallels crop up in the film. Just as (as has been rumored) Parker paid local oldsters to complain over early Presley concerts so does Scott as "Deke's" manager, in *Loving You*. After having established "Deke" as "controversial," Scott then proceeds to play off both ends against the middle, for "Deke"/Elvis is not just a truly gifted performer, but a gimmick to exploit a la Mansfield in *The Girl Can't Help It*. Things finally reach such a state in the film that the very right of "Deke" to exist becomes the basis of a national television referendum on rock and roll. (A touch of Elvis' *Ed*

Sullivan Show controversy creeps in around the edges of this particular scene.) Needless to say, rock wins out, with Elvis offering up as pro-rock musical evidence, "Teddy Bear," Gotta Lot of Livin' To Do," "Mean Woman Blues," "Hot Dog," plus the title tune and several more songs.

While the question of "Deke's" right to rock wins out in *Loving You*, the film still manages to leave one important dramatic loose end hanging in the breeze—the problem of Elvis' sexual allure. For while ingenue Dolores Hart has been on hand throughout the film as a suitable romantic projection substitute for Presley's teenage fans, the older Lizabeth Scott is *Loving You*'s real feminine "love interest." With her whole approach to managing "Deke" always verging on sexual come-on, Scott serves as a touchstone for the more adult female viewers. In the nick of time, Wendell Corey (Scott's ex-husband) steps in to claim her, leaving Elvis to the less volatile demands of Dolores Hart. But the bittersweet aftertaste of Elvis' unconsummated affair with Scott lingers on.

All things considered, *Loving You* is the sort of perfectly entertaining affair you'd expect from Elvis at this point in his career, and just as predictably the singer's next two ventures reworked *Loving You*'s rise-in-the-music-business formula, only in a more serious dramatic context.

Jailhouse Rock (1957) and *King Creole* (1958), both black and white cinemascope productions, could be described as musical *film noirs*. These rock melodramas cast a harsh light on the show business big time before succumbing to the usual love-conquers-all panacea in their finales. The darker "lower class" aspects of the real life Presley persona were highlighted in these two films, with a manslaughter conviction landing him in prison at the start of *Jailhouse Rock*, while *King Creole* (loosely based on Harold Robbins' *A Stone For Danny Fisher*) had New Orleans gangsterdom for a backdrop.

Both films contained good musical numbers, with the title tune production spectacular of *Jailhouse Rock* looming as large in Elvis' legend as the Odessa steps sequence in *Potemkin* does in Eisenstein's. The curl-over-the-forehead hairstyle Elvis sported in *Loving You*, and that film's lush and lively technicolor were absent—and sadly missed— from these two films. A welcome addition, however, was the new sense of acting authority Elvis brought to them. His compulsive clinch with Judy Tyler in *Jailhouse Rock* is a memorable moment in an otherwise standard series of dramatic events. "It's just the beast in me, honey!" Elvis explains to Tyler by way of apology for his presumptuousness, and his fans everywhere cheered in gleeful assent.

Just as Elvis' movie career was going full speed, the U.S. Army came along to throw a wrench in the works. The star was drafted in 1958, and while this caused concern, in the long run it worked to Elvis' benefit. Two years later when Elvis was discharged with a spotless record, this once controversial figure had become a respected vet. (Ironically, there is reason to suspect that Elvis' introduction to "speed" began while he was in the service.) But two years' absence from recording and performing had taken its toll.

G.I. Blues (1960) finds Elvis in an onscreen role connecting him with the off-screen life he'd just left. This was to be expected, and that the film was a frothy musical was par for the course. For the first time, though, Elvis was cast not as a super-talented diamond-in-the-rough, but only as an ordinary Joe who *just happened* to be able to sing. This sort-of remake of forties musical *The Fleet's*

In, co-starring dancer Juliet Prowse, effected a turnabout in Elvis' screen image, for all of a sudden he was presented as mythically scaled down (a trend that would continue in nearly all of his movies over the next decade). Also complicating matters is the fact that none of the tunes in *G.I. Blues* had the snap of the musical material from Elvis' previous films.

One could compile a convincing greatest hits package from the singer's first four films, consisting of songs like "Jailhouse Rock," "Loving You," "Love Me Tender" and "Teddy Bear," whereas most of the material in *G.I. Blues* was on the totally forgettable side, i.e., the title tune, "Pocketful of Rainbows," "Wooden Heart" and "Tonight Is So Right For Love" and more along those same lines—clearly a forecast of the even worse titles to be heard in Elvis' future movies with tunes like "Pioneer Go Home" (*Follow That Dream*, '62) and "Queenie Wahine's Papaya" (*Paradise Hawaiian Style*, '66).

The two films Elvis followed *G.I. Blues* with, *Flaming Star* (1960) and *Wild In The Country* (1961), are dramas where onscreen music is either eliminated (the former film), or soft-pedalled, as with the 1961 movie. Both are moderately ambitious efforts, but neither works as well as did the earlier of Elvis' films. Most of the blame for this must be laid at the feet of the managerial forces behind Elvis, who simply couldn't make up their minds as to which direction his films should go.

Directed by Don Siegel, *Flaming Star* presented Elvis in his first non-musical dramatic role, the fact of which formed the basis of the film's publicity campaign. Elvis, however, looks bewildered here, evidencing a sense of confusion far more extensive than should have arisen from the relatively simple demands of portraying an Indian half-breed torn between white and native American cultures. Perhaps part of the problem was that Elvis, while in the army, had lost his intuitive sense of acting.

In *Wild In The Country* Elvis fares better but, apparently, 20th Century Fox messed things up. With a script by no less a writer than Clifford Odets , the artistic outlook for the film seemed good. Elvis played a troubled youth with a literary bent who is in a constant state of sexual conflict with *three* different women: nice girl, Millie Perkins; sexually frustrated older woman, Hope Lange; and hellcat, Tuesday Weld.

The film's director, Phillip Dunne, recalls in his autobiography, *Take Two*, the various front office snags that negatively affected the promising project. These included Fox's demands for budget cuts, insistence by the studio that songs—however unnecessary for plot development—be inserted into the film, and a rushed shooting schedule. All of these considerations contributed to the disappointing end results of a film that Dunne (and Presley) had hoped would establish Elvis once and for all as a serious dramatic performer.

While Elvis' work in *Wild In The Country* is competent, an uneasiness shows through. This is all the more unfortunate, for with Tuesday Weld (with whom Elvis was romantically linked around the time the film was made) as his co-star one could have reasonably looked forward to some real fireworks. But Elvis looks as out of it in *Wild In The Country* as does his other co-star, the noticeably discomfitted Hope Lange in a part originally slated for Simone Signoret. Only Weld walks away with any acting honors in this tepid *Peyton Place*-styled soap opera.

"*Wild In The Country* fell between two stools," writes Dunne of Elvis' eighth film. "Audiences who might have liked Clifford Odetts' drama wouldn't buy Elvis and his songs; Elvis fans were disappointed in a Presley picture which departed so radically from his usual song-and-sex comedy formula."

Even without front office apprehension, Fox *still* might not have known what to do with Elvis, as evidenced by the fact that by 1961 his musical appeal had begun to simmer down a bit. (None of his recordings were in the top ten that year.) Musical tastes had begun to shift toward softer sounds, and Elvis' material rapidly started to jettison its rock underpinnings so that a lot of the time his new recordings were neither ballad nor boogie, fish nor fowl.

By the early 1960s, the interests behind Elvis' movie career, both the studios and Colonel Parker, began to realize that audiences *would literally pay to see Elvis Presley in almost anything*—even the confused *Wild In The Country* was a moderate hit. As it became clear to these forces that Elvis should be regarded not just as a short term, but a long range film phenomenon, an assembly line approach began to emerge.

Blue Hawaii (1961), Elvis' next vehicle, set the pace for twenty-five-odd films to follow. The "king of rock and roll" was unconvincing, cast as the son of a pineapple plantation owner. Elvis still carried his guitar, but what came out of his mouth was no longer rock, but rather lightweight up-tempo swing and ballads. Accordingly the romantic "Hawaiian Wedding Song" was the film's show-stopper, instead of something like the frenetic "Jailhouse Rock."

At least as far as his further viability as a celluloid rock and roller was concerned, the show *had* stopped for Presley now. There would be few more dramatic challenges for him to face, fewer athletic actions of any consequence for him to perform—nothing much for him to do but show up, stand on his mark, open wide and . . . croon. Audiences that before had paid to see films *with* Elvis were now content to settle for seeing pictures *of* him—faded reprints of the lively rock-infused colors of the original.

After *Blue Hawaii* only fleeting fugitive moments suggested the Elvis of yore—the man who according to critic/philosopher Richard Meltzer ". . . invented the 20th Century as a concrete something-or-other for cryin' out loud!" Meltzer's stinging diatribe against Elvis' later film output, appearing in the magazine *Take One* (v.4, no.2), was felt to be unduly harsh by many Presley fans. But it's hard not to concur with the writer's view that "of all the singer-turned-moviestars, there were *none* of 'em ever made as many stinkers as Elvis."

In *Follow That Dream* (1962), Elvis is cast in a country boy role, more like a hick, that's almost a parody of his real down-home self. In real life Elvis had travelled so far by now from his simple beginnings that it's doubtful that he gave this irony much of a thought. By now it seemed that Elvis had abdicated rock and roll as surely as Edward VII had turned his back on England. Whereas once Elvis was an axiom of the cinema, now he'd gone on to become only a mere mechanism of it.

Elvis on screen now meant a guaranteed box office return—and little else. The once-unique phenomenon was trimming his sails to play such routine parts as that of a boxer (*Kid Galahad*, 1962), a fisherman (*Girls, Girls, Girls*, 1962), a tour guide (*It Happened At The World's Fair*, 1963) and a lifeguard (*Fun In*

Acapulco, 1963). The scripting and directing in such as these entries may have been B-movie, but the production values continued to be Grade-A, all the way.

Soon, however, even this aspect of Presley's films gave way as the Colonel turned to the services of Sam (*Rock Around The Clock*) Katzman to oversee Elvis' next movie, *Kissin' Cousins* (1964). No doubt Parker had been impressed by Katzman's overall handling of 1964's *Your Cheatin' Heart*, the story of singer Hank Williams, and a movie in which Elvis would've been ideal in the title role.

This next chapter in the Elvis movie saga, which featured the singer in a dual role, was yet *another* routine musical, but with Katzman at the helm the high gloss that was a standard fixture in Presley films up until then, was now gone. Katzman didn't produce all of Elvis' future films, but the ideas and attitudes he brought to *Kissin' Cousins* left their mark. Katzman's cost-cutting methods were appropriate when applied to the featherweight fare he'd turned out in Hollywood for over three decades; but Elvis was, well, Elvis, and deserved something better.

Attention to detail and film craftsmanship made their last appearance in an Elvis movie *Viva Las Vegas* (1964). Even though the film had a Katzman-like budget it was directed by George Sidney, a veteran of movie musicals, and a firm believer that low-budget need not necessarily be synonomous with low quality.

Ann-Margret, then just another starlet-on-the-rise, clinched her ascendancy by impressively fulfilling her co-star duties in *Viva Las Vegas*. Here, she is just as capable a rock and roller as Elvis; and the Elvis/Ann-Margret duet on "C'mon Everybody" is a standout, with A-M's lips curling suggestively in a manner remindful of Presley.

After this winning interlude, though, it was back to business as usual in such tatty, low-overhead frolics as *Roustabout* (1964), *Girl Happy*, *Tickle Me* and *Harum Scarum*, all 1965.

From the mid-sixties on, Elvis ran mostly on two movie speeds: SLOW, for when he was supine and crooning, and FAST—though not like before in animal fashion, but rather as a cyborg (i.e., part-man, part-machine), only able to suggest thrust and drive when placed behind the wheel of a car as in *Spinout* (1966), or *Speedway* (1968) or a boat, as in *Clambake* (1968). (And then usually in front of rear screen projections.) It finally didn't matter what Elvis did, for it all turned out the same way—Boy Meets Girl frothy romances with songs now reduced to the level of "Do The Clam" (from *Girl Happy*). By now, even "The Hawaiian Wedding Song" looked good.

As the sixties came to a close, Elvis turned to dramatic roles once again as if in a last-ditch effort to regain cultural respectability and ensure continued financial success. But neither the western *Charro* (1969), nor the social drama *Change of Habit* (1970) were up to the level of even *Wild In The Country*. Production values on these two films that proved to be Elvis' acting swan songs had sunk to a sub-television plateau.

Returning to live performance on the night club and concert stage—and in documentary films of these appearances (*Elvis—That's The Way It Is*, 1970 and *Elvis On Tour*, 1972)—Presley staged a "comeback" (though he'd never really been away) that gave his career a much needed boost. Still, things would never again be the way they were before Elvis jumped on the Hollywood treadmill.

Vocally, Elvis had never lost his muse, managing over the years to turn out solid, valid hits like "Return To Sender," "Burnin' Love" and "In The Ghetto." But for whatever reason, he never completely found his way to applying such art to screen drama. The simple fact of the matter was that Elvis as a musical performer was ever so much more than the sum of his parts than Elvis the dramatic actor—a truth brought home forcefully in both concert documentaries and the recent biographical documentary *This is Elvis* (1981).

Written and directed by Malcolm Leo and Andrew Solt (with Colonel Parker serving as "technical advisor"), *This is Elvis* neatly charts the course of the singer's life through television and film clips, newsreels and home movies. Marred by contrived imitation documentary passages using actors (mostly non-speaking and in long shot) to stand in for Presley, his family and friends, the film features a spoken narration (vocal imitations of Elvis and his mother Gladys primarily) that lends a sticky-sweet fan magazine air to Elvis' far from sugar-coated life.

Out-takes from *Elvis—That's The Way It Is* and *Elvis On Tour* touch briefly on Presley's raunchy side, but what really makes up for the film's "mom's apple pie" wet blanket atmosphere is Elvis himself belting out "Hound Dog," "Heartbreak Hotel" and his other greats in kinescope and videotape-to-film transfers of his numerous television appearances. It's these clips that testify to the enduring strength of the Presley legend.

Amiably skipping his way through "Witchcraft" with Frank Sinatra on a special celebrating the end of his military service or letting loose with "Don't Be Cruel" on his 1968 *tour de force* spectacular, Elvis' sexuality—and talent—blast through unmistakably. Moreover, his vocal ability was with him right up to the very end as shown at the close of *This is Elvis* in a harrowing excerpt from his last television show taped only weeks before his death.

Sweaty and bloated, his face showing the effects of some sixteen odd years of high-flying, superpowered show biz debauchery, Elvis' voice (singing "Are You Lonesome Tonight") is as clear and true as ever.

Subjects for further research:
Frankie and Johnny, Easy Come Easy Go, Stay Away Joe, Double Trouble, Live A Little Love A Little, The Trouble With Girls, Bye Bye Birdie, Sing Boy Sing, Hound Dog Man, Elvis (D: John Carpenter), *Touched By Love.*

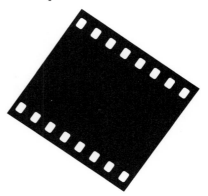

HOLLYWOOD HOTWAX

THE KINGS OF **ROCK**
ARE ROLLIN' BACK TO THE SCREEN...
IN THEIR
BIGGEST!

BILL HALEY
AND HIS COMETS

Don't Knock The Rock

MADE BY THE
PRODUCERS OF
"ROCK AROUND
THE CLOCK"!

ALAN DALE

ALAN FREED

THE TRENIERS
LITTLE RICHARD
DAVE APPELL
AND HIS APPLEJACKS

with JOVADA and JIMMY BALLARD
Written by ROBERT E. KENT and JAMES B. GORDON · Produced by SAM KATZMAN
Directed by FRED F. SEARS · A CLOVER PRODUCTION · A COLUMBIA PICTURE

T O GET A HANDLE on the kind of rock movies being turned out around the time of Elvis' first cinematic splash, a look at American-International's *Shake Rattle and Rock* (1956) provides some clues. . . . .

Dick Clark-ish dee-jay, Gary Nelson (Touch Connors), and his *American Bandstand*-like TV show, *Rock, Roll and Shake*, have just come under fire—because of "vulgar lewd rock and rolling"—from a group of local bluenoses, SPRACAY (The Society for the Prevention of Rock and Roll Corruption of American Youth).

Undaunted, Nelson and the kids from his TV show stage a benefit, starring Fats Domino and Joe Turner, to raise funds for a "Teen Town" club house; during which a Faginlike thug and his sidekick start a brawl in a wayward try at re-recruiting reformed juvenile delinquents away from the clutches of do-gooder, Nelson.

The next day's "Clarion" headlines read "Teenage rioters on rampage. Local disc jockey faces possible arrest charges for complicity in rock and roll orgy." (Only a few days earlier the newspaper had printed a pro-rock editorial—"In the final analysis youth *must* express its overabundance of energy; better around the jukebox, than the pool table.")

Then the unexpected happens. Nelson (and rock and roll) come to trial, which is televised, and at just the point when one of the old poops is showing films of African natives dancing ("You see," he says, "the *disgusting* source of this so-called cultural form, rock and roll."), Nelson counters his tack by showing an ancient clip of people dancing the black bottom (to illustrate *his* contention that "the youth of today is no more corrupt that it has ever been" and "that the times we live in determine the tempo at which we live" (?!). Suddenly someone spots one of SPRACAY's members doing a wicked turkey trot in Nelson's film. A meaningful dialogue ensues between both sides, and rock and roll wins the case. Then ALL (SPRACAY, the kids, Nelson, the thugs et al.) boogie off into the sunset to the strains of Fats Domino, piped into the trial on tv, singing his big hit, "I'm In Love Again." The end titles read "THE MOST TO SAY THE LEAST."

Shake, Rattle and Rock was neither the most nor the least, but it was one of the first in a long line of quickie jukebox musicals that began flooding the nation's theatres during the middle-1950's. The recipe for most of these films (aside from petty cash budgets) consisted mainly of de-sexualized petting-above-the-neck sub-plot romances between boy and girl ingenues (often involving a triangle); a parallel storyline of authority figures attempting to tar-and-feather rock and roll out of town AND, most importantly, lots and lots of musical footage parachuted into the films at random junctures every few minutes.

Fortunately, plot plausibility in movies like *Shake, Rattle and Rock*, and others like it such as *Let's Rock* (1958) and *Rock, Rock, Rock* (1957), was so shaky that the kids who attended these films hardly ever felt thwarted when the story made way for the musical interludes. Besides, the intrusion of the dopey plot provided the moviegoers a perfect opportunity to prowl the theatre, chat with friends and make dates for after the show. But when the music eclipsed the bubble-gum story, socializing ceased and the cheering began.

The musical action that grabbed their attention doesn't qualify as *performance*, in the strictest sense, for all that Bill Haley, Fats Domino, Joe Turner and the other rockers were doing on the screen was going through the motions, miming their old recordings. The occasional fervor, though, displayed by someone like Chuck Berry mouthing the lyrics, "Hail, Hail Rock and Roll," or just the sight of youthful Frankie Lymon (no older than the kids themselves) athletically bounding back and forth across the screen was more than enough to cancel out the lack of "live" authenticity.

As for the question asked by some of these films as to whether rock music was *good* or *bad*, the makers of these first primitive musical parades tended to waffle. The standard answer provided by the films was yes AND no. "Yes", this new music probably was damaging to the morals of youth, but it was also concluded that cause for alarm existed *only* if these leaders of tomorrow allowed their rock and roll impulses to remain unchanneled toward loftier, nobler goals. So, guided lovingly but firmly, by wise grownups in such films as *Don't Knock The Rock* (1956) or *Don't Knock The Twist* (1962) the kids took their music and used it as a tool for social good. In the latter film rock becomes a useful force when pro-rockers and performers (Chubby Checker, Gene "Duke of Earl" Chandler and The Dovells) in the best Andy Hardy tradition, stage a TV special to raise money for sending orphans to summer camp. (This film was a sequel to producer Sam Katzman's profitable twist entry of the previous year, 1961's *Twist Around The Clock*, which also starred Checker.)

The rapidity with which these musicals were assembled is typified by the shooting schedule of *Don't Knock The Twist*, for it began actual production on January 30th, 1962, and by the following February 23rd it was on its way to the nation's movie houses. The assembly line methods that were used for films like these resulted in their having highly disreputable reputations with the critics. But these productions got the rent paid (with a little bit left over for starting up the next quickie), and, therefore, Uncle Sam Katzman and his imitators turned out half-a-dozen of them a year well into the early 1960's.

Such fly-by-night delights as *Mister Rock and Roll* (1957) and *Teenage Millionaire* (1961) suggest that they actually *could have* been made by teenagers. Although concocted by ''adults'', the time frames governing production of juve-rockers such as these, made for a ''look'' that a first glance just might pass muster as youthful energy, childlike innocence and, on the other hand, NEAR anarchy. In these numerous ''Sons'' and ''Brides'' of *Rock Around The Clock*, such traditional and time-honored film requisites as dramatic suspension of disbelief, creditable acting, complimentary lighting and attractive set decoration became frills and unaffordable luxuries. All these ''quaint customs'', and more, fell by the wayside as producers clambored over one another to hurriedly cash in on what they thought might still be only a passing fad. (Rock's possible transitoriness loomed so large that one enterprising item, *Bop Girl Goes Calypso* (1957), posed the musical question of whether Big Beat would give way to Bongo and Ba-Ba-Lu.) As often as not, the net result of these quickies was a trifle on the surrealistic side.

For example, a whole Sorbonne-full of semiologists could not exactly detect the rhyme and reason of *Let's Rock* (1958). And what, exactly, did its producers have in mind when they made it? Why, for instance, did they cast post-teen, forties-styled baladeer Julius LaRosa as the star of this juve-rocker? And how can they account for the casting of Phyllis Newman, a strictly Broadway musical comedy performer, as his romantic foil? Were the makers of *Let's Rock* only out to add a little class to their act; or were they reaching for a more ''adult'' audience; or was it all simply a case of sheer accident brought about by the harried production schedules that went with the territory? *Let's Rock* ends up looking like ''The Frank Sinatra Story''—only turned inside out.

LaRosa plays crooner Tony Adano, who is experiencing a mid-career slump brought on by recent inroads made by ''the new sound.'' Much like Sinatra at the time (and LaRosa too) Adano's recordings are going gold only *after* they're shipped *back* from the record stores. Following a predictable series of personal awakenings (laid in between some, soggy conventional pop tunes alternating with an equal amount of genuine enough rock from Danny and The Juniors and The Royal Teens), Adano sees the light and lays down an ersatz rock and roll track that rockets him to the top all over again. (It's okay to rock and roll, but only if you're *not* a teenager, seems to be the message here.) The Sinatra figure, Adano, sells his soul to rock and roll, and not only lives to tell about it but, cops a gold record as a reward for his daring—unlike Sinatra who daringly eschewed rock.

No such complex plot machinations are evident in the next year's *Go,*

Johnny, Go (1959), a rock and roll scrapbook item which strictly adheres to the regulation jukebox formula. As such, this feature contains one of the most impressive lineups of any rock film up to that time. Here dee-jay, Alan Freed, once again essays the role of safe, older, neutral guide to teenland, just as he had in *Rock Around The Clock* and *Don't Knock The Rock* and, as before, he acts as arbiter and translator between teens and old fogeys. However, as *Go, Johnny, Go* unfolds, Freed doesn't get a chance to do much more than run through some emcee chores, for plot is thrown almost entirely to the wind. No wonder, for this feature is a 75-minute affair that manages to wedge in a solid hour of music into its short running time. The come-on for "Johnny" included promises of "10 Great Rock and Roll Stars and 17 New Rock and Roll Hits!"—something of an improvement over the seminal *Rock Around The Clock*, so topheavy with plot and resolution it could only find time to deliver up Haley and The Platters, plus a handful of non-rock acts.

Go, Johnny, Go marks the only screen appearance of Richie Valens (singing "La Bamba"), who shortly after completion of the film was killed in the infamous plane crash which also claimed Buddy Holly and The Big Bopper (J.P. Richardson). The film's ads billed the singing star as "the late Richie Valens," and in James Dean-like Hollywood fashion the Chicano rocker went on to become even more a major figure in death than in life. (Much of the musical footage appears to have been lensed at the same time as other musical clips cropping up in another film from Director's Corporation of America, the same studio that made the previous year's *Rock, Rock, Rock*, which also featured Freed. D.C.A., incidentally, was the distributor of the notoriously bad "Golden Turkey" winner, *Plan Nine From Outer Space*, by Edward D. Wood, Jr.)

Go, Johnny, Go also offers glimpses of singer Jimmy Clanton; Chuck Berry doing three numbers ("Maybelline," "Johnny B. Goode" and "School Days") and Jackie "Lonely Teardrops" Wilson. Vocal groups from the doo-wop hall of fame like the The Moonglows and The Cadillacs also turn up and, additionally, the film features another soon-to-be-deceased favorite, Eddie Cochran.

This film and *Rock, Rock, Rock* present a nostalgic spectacle to viewers of today, for aside from the aforementioned "dead-before-their-time" stars, Cochran and Valens, two other now-dead musicians are on hand in *Rock, Rock, Rock*—rockabilly mainspring Johnny Burnette and 13-year-old Frankie Lymon (with The Teenagers). Here Lymon's sly and cynical rendering of "I'm Not a Juvenile Delinquent" is a masterpiece of understated irony. Acts returning to *Go, Johnny Go* from the other D.C.A. release include Berry, The Moonglows and The Flamingos. Since the musical numbers for these two films were shot at the same time, which performer appeared in which film was, in all likelihood, determined by a flip of the coin. Plots—or what passed for them—were then built around these musical fillings.

Viewed with the hindsight of two decades, *Rock, Rock, Rock* is especially memorable for the lunatic devices used for fitting numbers into the storyline. Worthy of a surrealist essay is one scene in which a character enters the vicinity of a poolside at a country club only to stumble upon four fully clothed men (with unseen and massive orchestral backing), breaking into song without any provocation whatsoever. Elsewhere in the film, a highly-charged argument between parent and child is underway when a television set is suddenly turned on.

The show it's playing features Alan Freed introducing what amounts to a four-song interlude. This not only interrupts the living room fracas, it stops it dead cold.

Cost-cutting and out of kilter lip sync-ing weren't the only reasons these films were frowned upon by all but the kids who doted on them. For most such quickies contained musical casts which featured an unprecedentedly large number of blacks. That an almost exclusively white army of American teenagers in the almost totally segregated United States should spend their Saturday afternoons at the Bijou watching movies with ''nee-grows'' in them, caused more than a few eyebrows to be raised. Small matter that the films' black musical principals hardly ever uttered a word and that they were cast exclusively in outsider roles, the fact that despised blacks were actually taking center screen was what disturbed these white parents.

In entries like these, whites could dance and sing and, on occasion, actually deliver lines of dialogue, but blacks (until the Chubby Checker twist musicals) were seldom, if ever, utilized as dramatis personae. This is a perfect example of filmdom's fear of blacks. As in daily American life (then and now), blacks came to work at the (film) factory, did their (musical) jobs, and then returned to the mysterious outskirts of town.

The focus of the action was still white teenagers—like Tuesday Weld, all of thirteen years old, making her screen debut in *Rock, Rock, Rock*. With her singing voice ghosted by Connie Francis, the be-sweatered Weld early on in the film impresses as yet one more capable young performer in the Lolita mold. But when the character is called upon to exert guile, the actress begins to give off early glimmers of the quality that reached its first flowering when Weld, a few years later, portrayed the ultimate 50's teen vamp, ''Thalia Menninger'' on the *Dobie Gillis* TV series.

Besides previewing players like Weld, who were on their way up in Hollywood, these quickies often served as a kind of character actor's burial ground. *Shake Rattle and Rock* (discussed at the opening of this chapter), provided a day or two's work for many notable bit players. Directed by cheapie veteran Edward L. Cahn, this A.I.P. programmer conveys such a cheesey look there's little doubt it was rushed into production only days after the first box-office returns for Columbia Picture's *Rock Around The Clock* were made known. Yet the film does muster sporadic amusement thanks to the work of such vets as Sterling Holloway, Douglas Dumbrille, Clarence Colb, Percey Helton, Frank Jenks and—Groucho's old nemesis-amour—Margaret Dumont. Fully aware of the script's moldiness, these players camp it up like crazy—Dumont going so far as to let fly with a mean funky chicken at the film's conclusion.

But such lively moments were few and far between in a sub-genre that was quickly beginning to show signs of strain. Soon all manner of musical acts were being dropped into these formerly all-rock productions. Why this came about isn't entirely clear. Was it a conscious attempt to reach a broader audience? Non-rockers subbing for rock acts that were no-show? Whatever the reason, jazz, calypso, schmaltz and sub-Como crooning were now being included in films that were essentially still being advertised as rock and roll movies. Universal's *The Big Beat* (1958) tried to get away with such anomalies as swing 'n' sway bandleader, Russ Morgan, *alongside* of two superior rock groups, The Del

Vikings and The Diamonds.

Even more of a smorgasbord is *Jamboree* (1957), from Warner Brothers. Nominally a tale of two insipid teen pop stars, "Honey" and "Pete", this cut-and-paste job features not only Fats Domino and Jerry Lee Lewis, BUT jazz greats, Joe Williams and Count Basie as well. Other musical disparities on display in this film include a motley tenor looking for all the world like something left over from the entre-act at the dog fights in Tijuana. He yowls out "Male-guena" only moments after rockabilly kingpin Carl Perkins has just polished off a set. Also on hand in *Jamboree* to provide cross-stylistic seasoning are *Louis* (not Frankie!) Lymon and The Teen Chords (not Teenagers), pop thrush Jodie Sands and (from late night TV commercial fame) Slim Whitman. Soaring above all this, you get the treacly solos and duets of YUCH! "Honey" and "Pete"—who have about as much to do with rock and roll as do Jeanette Mc-Donald and Nelson Eddy.

Of course, there are just so many ways you can skin a cat. By 1961, in *Teenage Millionaire*, things were getting so hard-pressed in the music-plot integration department that all the writers could come up with was the device of having the film's singing protagonist, played by Jimmy Clanton, *imagine* the musical acts. And so at random intervals in this United Artists release, Clanton relaxes in a chair, flutters his closed eyes and in an unprecedented example of suspension of disbelief, the viewer shares Jimmy's musical reveries of Chubby Checker, Jackie Wilson, Marv Johnson and Dion parading across the screen, each singing one or two of their respective chart hits. Zasu Pitts, co-star of TV's *Oh, Susanna,* star of Eric Von Stroheim's 1923 masterpiece, *Greed*, and author of the only posthumously published combination autobiography and candy cook-book, *Pitt's Hits* (1964), is also on hand in *Teenage Millionaire* for comic relief, in one of her last screen appearances.

That the jukebox mode of rock movies was running out of steam is evident in the poverty stricken *"Millionaire."* Rock music, also, was moving out of a watershed era into a temporary creative impasse. The tunes at the top of the sales charts were beginning to give off a glow of *deja vu*, being remarkably similar in some instances to the type of songs that were popular prior to the advent of rock and roll. These early sixties hits included such retrograde recordings as "Theme From Exodus," "Calcutta" and "Wonderland By Night." Even the successful sides cut by bonafide rockers around this time tended to be somewhat on the soft side, with Rick Nelson's "Travelin' Man," Dee Clark's "Rain-drops" and Ray Charles' "I Can't Stop Loving You" being typical of the smoother sounds teenagers were beginning to listen to. Hard-driving rock (prior to the Beatles-Stones invasion) had finally painted itself into a corner. In turn, the business end of the recording industry had also gone sour on unadulterated rock.

Even Sam Katzman had lost the faith. In 1964, rattled and confused, he turned to crafting a little quickie in order to cash in on what he saw as the next big dance craze to supplant the twist—The Watusi! But the handwriting was already on the wall—the watusi was so short-lived that by the time the film was released its original title, *Watusi A Go Go*, had to be changed to *Get Yourself a College Girl*. Only a couple of valid rock acts appear in this film, but their casting proved especially far-sighted, demonstrating that "Sam the Man"

YOU KNOW... LIKE I MEAN—
IT'S WAY OUT!

JIMMY ("JUST A DREAM") CLANTON

SANDY ("ROCK, ROCK, ROCK") STEWART

CHUCK ("MARACAIBO") BERRY

The Late RITCHIE ("DONNA") VALENS

JACKIE ("LONELY TEARDROPS") WILSON

EDDIE ("COME ON EVERYBODY") COCHRAN

HARVEY of the ("TEN COMMANDMENTS") MOONGLOWS

SEE!
10 GREAT ROCK 'N ROLL STARS!

HEAR!
17 GREAT NEW ROCK 'N ROLL HITS!

STARRING
ALAN FREED
The King of ROCK 'n' ROLL!

"GO, Johnny GO!"

THE ("SPEEDO") CADILLACS

JO ANN ("WAIT A MINUTE") CAMPBELL

The ("LOVERS NEVER SAY GOODBYE") FLAMINGOES

starring ALAN FREED · JIMMY CLANTON · SANDY STEWART · CHUCK BERRY
SPECIAL GUEST ARTISTS:
The Late Ritchie VALENS · Jackie WILSON · Eddie COCHRAN · HARVEY of the MOONGLOWS · The CADILLACS · The FLAMINGOES · JoAnn CAMPBELL
EXECUTIVE PRODUCER: HAL ROACH, JR. · PRODUCED BY ALAN FREED · DIRECTED BY PAUL LANDRES · A HAL ROACH DISTRIBUTION CORP. RELEASE
59-154   PRINTED IN U.S.A.

wasn't entirely asleep at the switch, after all. While the intrepid producer couldn't possibly afford the services of the already skyrocketing Beatles, he *did* manage to sign up two outfits that *were* perfectly acceptable examples of the burgeoning British invasion: The Dave Clark Five and The Animals. It proved an uphill struggle for the two bands, for the remainder of the musical cast in *Get Yourself a College Girl* consisted mostly of pseudo-jazz and "Vegas-rock", as exemplified by Freddie Bell and The Bell Boys. This group's appearances in Katzman musicals were almost *de rigueur,* and years later this fact still puzzles, since the outfit had almost no noticeable public following.

Katzman's association with the previously mentioned Chubby Checker twist musicals, *Twist Around The Clock* and *Don't Knock The Twist* is further evidence of the confused state rock films were in around the turn of the decade. While these two did contain *some* provisionally acceptable examples of rock music, neither project had musicians of the Chuck Berry or Gene Vincent caliber. Yet those two releases did turn a profit, and so Paramount Pictures entered the sweepstakes with their own twist entry, *Hey, Let's Twist* (1961), starring co-twist king, Joey Dee. Still, Paramount's film didn't even bother to insert any musical antidotes to the twist in their film, while the two Columbia/Katzman twisters did: The Marcels and Dion in "Clock" and Gene Chandler and The Dovells in "Don't."

Even after The Beatles and Richard Lester rang the death knell for music/ plot/music (etc.) programmers with *A Hard Day's Night* in 1964, a few diehard examples of them still managed to straggle into the theatres well into the mid-sixties. Topical/milkshake by way of jukebox best describes a confusing 1968 release, *C'mon Let's Live a Little*. Featuring two capable *pop* performers from the Liberty Records fold, Jackie DeShannon and Bobby Vee, the film attempts to compensate for its limited appeal by patching in a Mario-Savio-esque free speech sub-plot. But the seams show woefully, and the flat lighting, static camera work and the ridiculous sight of DeShannon lip-sync-ing to an overdubbed recording of herself only drag matters down all the more.

Perhaps part of the problem with *C'mon Let's Live a Little* is that while it commenced filming in 1966, it wasn't actually completed until two years later due to massive legal snags encountered by its producers. When it finally did reach the screen, audiences faced with the exhortation to "c'mon and live a little" wisely decided not to and stayed away in droves. *The Cool Ones* (1967), featuring Glen Campbell and Mrs. Miller, was a similar last gasp jukebox effort.

For ten years or so, filmdom's poverty row had successfully mined the jukebox-vaudeville approach to rock film since (with the exception of the lavish *The Girl Can't Help It*) the negative costs for each of these juve-rockers seldom exceeded $300,000. (With the profit return generally turning out to be many times the original investment). But by the mid-sixties the ballgame was just about over. What finally killed these films off wasn't just the gauntlet flung down by The Beatles' film, for television shows like *American Bandstand* and *Shindig* had now come along to showcase the sight of rock acts lip-sync-ing their hit recordings—with better production values, and *minus* the goopey storylines. (With 1964's *The Tami Show* and documentaries like *Woodstock* (1970) something even more exciting was on display—rock stars actually singing and performing "live.")

Viewing these films today it's hard to believe that anyone actually skipped school, blew their allowance, fought with their parents or made dates to see any of them. From the plateau of the eighties, films like *Rock Around The Clock* and *Mister Rock and Roll* appear like quaint artifacts of some long lost civilization rather than what they were—the fantasy fodder of the budding imagination of 50's American youth.

Subjects for further research:
Be My Guest, Sing and Swing, Hold On, Mrs. Brown You've Got A Lovely Daughter, Just For Fun, Play It Cool.

IV

BAD GIRLS AND OTHER LEADERS OF THE PACK

RUNNING ALONG A parallel track to the juve-rockers, another kind of movie was feeding the fantasy appetite of 50's rock and rollers—the Youth-Runs-Wild melodrama. In sharp contrast to the Good Clean Fun of the sock hop specials, productions like *Rock All Night* (1956) and *Platinum High School* (1960) embodied all the horrors that adults felt rock music would unleash upon the young.

The indisputable high priestess of this sub-genre was bargain basement sex bomb, Mamie Van Doren. While herself scarcely a teenager, Van Doren served in numerous films as a perfect example of the end results of post-A-bomb youthful confusion. Originally manufactured by Universal Pictures as an even lower-budgeted version of Fox's Jayne Mansfield, (who in turn was a cut-rate answer to that studio's Marilyn Monroe), Van Doren trashily sashayed her way through numerous bleak troubled-adolescent epics during the late 1950's. The platinum-haired, ample-bosomed actress was a standard fixture—in every sense of the word—in such "explosive" penny-dreadfuls as *Untamed Youth* (1957), *High School Confidential* (1958) and *Girl's Town* (1959), usually playing the part of a young, misunderstood hellion who was, in the immortal words of The Shangri-La's "Leader of the Pack", "good-bad, but *not* evil."

These volatile Van Doren films, and others just like them, often secured the services of rock stars like Eddie Cochran and Paul Anka not just to make music, but for acting chores as well—in teen *noirs* that were pitched to their audience with advertising copy along the lines of "the social ills of America's youth ripped from today's (and tomorrow's) headlines!" The films themselves didn't always contain overt rock music, but so pervasive was the use of thumping 4/4 underscoring that invariably the message telegraphed was one of rock and roll's being inextricably bound up with, and responsible for such recent and unprecedented social phenomenae as youthful drug addiction, pre-marital sex and gang wars.

These cheapened version of more artful forerunners like *Rebel Without a Cause* and *Blackboard Jungle* featured rock's throbbing beat not only in steamy love scenes, but in more action-filled sequences like drag races and rumbles. These juxtapositions of rock and plot couldn't help but convey the underlying notion that where rock went, trouble followed.

Typical of this more downbeat rock film was *High School Confidential* (1958), a crazy-quilt of a yarn directed by Jack Arnold and supposedly representative of the prevailing teen temperament. In the face of attacks on his film when it was first released, producer Albert Zugsmith defended it as a cautionary tale that, among other things, preached against the evils of marijuana. His detractors, however, saw the film (and others like it) not so much as a solution to the problem, but a part of it.

Still-in-all the sight of Jerry Lee Lewis in the opening shot of this film, seated at his "pumping piano" atop a moving flatbed truck while he belted out the title tune, is one of the most memorable images in all of rock film—an overture comparable to the unleashing of the furies in Murnau's *Faust*.

Mamie Van Doren, in *High School Confidential*, is cast as the over-sexed "aunt" of an undercover cop (Russ Tamblyn) who's been sent in to smash a high school drug ring. Unfortunately, it is never really made clear anywhere in the film whether Van Doren really is Tamblyn's aunt; and if she *is* his aunt why is she always coming on to him sexually. Further, she appears to be a moll of the dope ring, but at other times it seems as if she could be another undercover cop whom Tamblyn isn't aware of. Oh! it's all too confusing as to who and how and why. All that really matters is that Mamie V.D. is on hand to vamp it up and add some sexual spice.

Aside from these and other joyous script incongruities, Zugsmith's film is fun because of the staggeringly large cast of has-beens and never-wases culled from offspring of the truly famous, i.e. Charles Chaplin, John Barrymore and William Wellman, JRS—all in a motion picture whose moral seems to be that sexual promiscuity is a gas (!) and that a trip to the slammers is more fun than a high school diploma.

The spectre of teenage drug addiction rears its ugly head not just in this film, but also in a number of other youth-in-turmoil releases from around the same period as *High School Confidential*, including *The Tijuana Story* (1957) and *Daddy-O* (1959). Ironically, though, contrary to the fictional evidence advanced by these films, drug use really wasn't a big part of fifties middle-class adolescent behavior. And so, as hinted at by Zugsmith's critics, the suspicion lingers? As American males doffed their undershirts to copy *en masse* the Clark Gable of the

1930's *It Happened One Night*, there isn't a case to be made for films like these actually spurring adolescent interest in drug experimentation, i.e. you've seen The Movie, Heard The Music, NOW Try the Drug!

If the possibility of out-front rock and roll is what lured many to go and see *High School Confidential* or *The Tijuana Story* and *The Cool and The Crazy* (1958), another dope drama, in the case of the latter two they ended up disappointed. For there's no real on-screen rock in either of them, but ersatz big beat in these and all the other youth-on-the-loose fare *does* permeate the soundtrack coming forth from car radios, juke joints, etc. "Ersatz" because in the main this sort of music was a Hollywood studio orchestra's *idea* of rock and roll.

One of the current behind-the-scenes stars of the Hollywood soundstage, composer John *Star Wars* Williams (in the spirit of "everyone has to start *somewhere*") wrote the score for an especially tatty 1959 film, *Daddy-O*. This affair does have rock in it, of sorts, in the person of the title role portrayed by real-life accordionist, Dick Contino. Although "Daddy-O's" musical forte isn't exactly the old decidedly square accordian standby, "Lady of Spain," when he isn't busy smashing teenage drug rings he whiles away the hours away singing the likes of the almost equally doubtful (gulp) "Rock Candy Baby." His aide in these endeavors is energetically played by the now long-forgotten Sandra Giles who is, ironically, an almost dead ringer for Blondie's Debbie Harry.

Hot Rod Gang (1958) is but one more youth-gone-bad release, but with a significant difference in that it featured the actual singing (and acting) of a name rock and roller—Gene Vincent. While faithful to the themes of many of the other teen *noirs* from around the same time, the resolution of generational conflicts is atypically mild and low-key, being more like the neatly tied-up conclusions of the jukebox musicals. John Ashley, here portraying a young heir with a decided flair for drag racing and guitar strumming, became a familiar face in teen films of the 50's and 60's, along with others who came to constitute a virtual revolving comany of stock players for this kind of a hypertense quickie. This group includes Yvonne Lime, Edd Byrnes and Fay Spain, who in Roger Corman's *Teenage Doll* (1957) uttered the immortal line, "I'M GONNA CHANGE MY NAME, MOVE TO PHOENIX AND LEARN TO SCUFFLE!"

The titles of films in this cycle mostly held out the promise of lurid thrills, for example: *Hot Rod Rumble, Motorcycle Gang, Reform School Girl, Riot in Juvenile Prison* and *Explosive Generation*. It would seem as if almost no possible combination of words that connoted speed, sex and anarchy eluded the producers of these stormy double-bill features.

What *did* elude their makers was almost any sense of reality when it came to dealing with these films' ostensible subject matter. Instead, most of them were cockamamie mixtures of *imagined* threats to white, middle-class culture *and* highly fanciful estimates of the potential of youth to rock the status quo, (with occasional dollops of accurate renderings of teen-appropriated beatnik slang thrown in for verisimilitude's sake.) Here, Main Street, USA was depicted as a powder keg ready to explode. And the detonator was always rock and roll.

It would seem that movies dealing with such matters and concerns should've been strictly a Hollywood specialty, but Britains, too, were adept at turning out films covering much the same ground as the likes of *Teenage Doll*

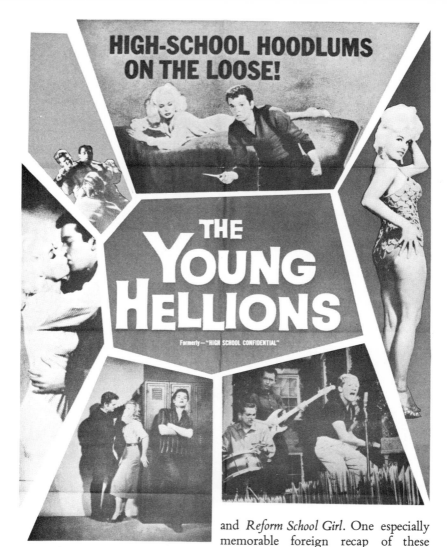

and *Reform School Girl*. One especially memorable foreign recap of these seemingly (strictly) American themes was *Wild for Kicks* (1962), originally titled *Beat Girl*.

Made in England by French "B" movie director, Edmund T. Greville, the tone of this film is standard Hollywood teen-problem-pic, but the ending is strictly *No Exit* (doubtlessly affected by breezes of existentialism wafting in from France), with a fade-out even more unresolved than James Dean's classic *Rebel Without a Cause*.

The film's harsh anti-conclusion comes as a shock, for the preceeding action consists more-or-less of quaint notions of adolescent anguish such as getting upbraided for playing the phonograph too loud and not getting on with one's parents.

Reality intrudes in "Beat Girl's" life when she discovers that her hated step-mum was once a stripper. Soon she herself is involved in the sordid Soho underworld, becoming enmeshed in the murder of her step mum's slimy paramour, played by Christopher Lee. This melodramatic shift is both affecting *and* believable—in no small part thanks to a sub-plot enlivened by the performance of British Presley rival, Adam Faith. For while "Beat Girl" (Noelle Adam) pouts and struts like Fay Spain, wreaking havoc in standard teen temptress fashion, the alienated character of her boyfriend, given life by Faith, strikes a real chord. The acting talent Faith early-on displayed here would be used to even greater effect in films the singer-actor worked in later, like *Stardust* (1975) and *McVicar* (1980).

The score for *Wild For Kicks* by The John Barry Seven while not *exactly* rock does manage to work itself up, from time-to-time, to a kind of Preston/Epps/Johnny and The Hurricanes frenzy, even to the extent of pre-figuring much of the surf-punk sound of the B-52's.

Punk attitudinizing itself (in an early form) can be spotted in Greville's film, for it's a very short step from Adam Faith's dead-ended alienation to The Sex Pistols' Johnny Rotten's punk battle cry of "No Future."

Teenagers, both in America and England, regularly attended these dramas with a rock and roll backbeat, even though few of them had much to do with their experiences and real-life considerations. All that mattered to the kids was that these films *purported* to be about teenagers.

Even when the music faltered almost entirely in some youth movies, these films still operated as grist for pubescent fantasy mills. For example, Pat Boone's starring vehicles at Fox such as the highly-laundered *April Love* and *Bernardine* (both 1957) didn't even contain any real rock music, inasmuch as their star was Boone. Nor did Universal's *Rock, Pretty Baby* (1956) and *Summer Love* (1958), the former starring Sal Mineo and John Saxon, the latter with Saxon only. Just the sight of heart throbs Boone, Mineo and Saxon trying to pass themselves off as rock and rollers was enough to satisfy the females in the audience. The hint of rock in a film, especially in the title, was adequate for acceptance by an audience starved for role models and situations with which they could identify.

Even the mildest of these various musicals and dramas dramatized a world of teenagers demanding their place in the sun, even if it only meant cinching the right to do the latest dance craze without adult intervention. And the wildest of these films weren't *all* that pessimistic and cynical, for after the body counts had been taken and the damage assessed at their conclusions, the various depicted "shenanigans" were generally dismissed as but latter-day proof that "youth must have its fling."

As the sixties rolled into view, however, something new was in the air, for many teenagers of the fifties had entered post-adolescence without ever assuming the values identifying them as "responsible adults." This was new on the American scene. And at the same time, their younger brothers and sisters were also entering *their* teen years—newer rebels with even newer causes.

Together, these two groups would form what would come to be called the Youth Culture Explosion, the emergence of which would demand its own unique filmic responses—always with more and more rock music. Films that would ultimately leave Bill Haley and Mamie Van Doren trailing behind in the dust.

Subjects for further research:
Carnival Rock, College Confidential, Platinum High School.

V

BEACH BLANKET BOXOFFICE

CONNIE FRANCIS! . . . a seminal figure in the evolution of rock movies? Occasionally she visited the *Billboard* charts with a vaguely rock-ish hit like "Stupid Cupid" or "Lipstick on Your Collar," but the main *forte* of this New Jersey-born songstress was torpid balladry—exemplified by her mixed-metaphor smash "My Heart Has A Mind Of Its Own." Schmaltzy warblings like this worked perfectly with the image Francis projected—a scaled-down, younger, more "ethnic" (i.e. Italian) Doris Day.

That this anti-Mamie Van Doren ruled for a short while as media mistress of responsible American teen womanhood isn't so surprising in view of the tenor of her times. The first wave of teen self-consciousness had ebbed, and rock around 1960, for whatever esthetic and/or sociological reasons, had fallen into a post-Elvis/pre-Beatles slump.

Happily Francis—a holdover from the past—became a portent of better things to come when prestigious MGM cast her in the first grander-scaled ($3,000,000) movie designed exclusively for teens and young adults—*Where The Boys Are* (1960). While this glossy comedy-melodama can't by any stretch of the imagination be regarded as a rock and roll movie (save for some background sounds) it *can* be said with a fair degree of certainty, that had it not appeared (and succeeded), the next wave of rock and youth oriented films might not have come about so easily.

A sort of teen remake of *How To Marry A Millionaire* (1953), *Where The Boys Are* recounts the adventures of four female collegians (Dolores Hart, Yvette Mimieux, Paula Prentiss and Connie Francis) off on their first adventure away from home. Based on Glenn Swarthout's novel of the same name, *Where The Boys Are* capitalized on newspaper coverage of college student hi-jinks during Easter vacation in Ft. Lauderdale, Florida. A minor national rite of youthful passage had turned, according to press accounts, into an out-of-control bacchanal. However, filtered through the lenses of MGM's cameras, whatever disturbing elements may have been there, all came out looking like typical teen movie merriment.

Still, unlike youth-aimed entertainments of the Mickey Rooney and Judy Garland era, *Where The Boys Are* did manage to grapple quasi-realistically with such matters as alcoholism, pre-marital sex and (very daringly), rape. The Dolores Hart, Paula Prentiss and Connie Francis characters go through the usual ups and downs of young love Hollywood style. In Yvette Mimieux's case however, total licentious abandon (or as much of it as a 1960 major studio release was willing to show) was the order of the day. This Good Girl/Bad Girl formula was scarcely a new thing in Hollywood, and neither was adolescent hell-raising (ie. Mamie Van Doren). What was new about *Where The Boys Are* was that this material was being given the full MGM gloss, and being pitched at the largest possible audience.

The upshot of the success of *Where The Boys Are* was a spate of films where, against the grain of tradition, teens took center stage with adults shunted off toward the fringes of the action. *Ride The Wild Surf* (1964), with music by Jan and Dean, *Girls on The Beach* (1964) with the Beach Boys, and *Swingin' Summer* featuring Gary Lewis and the Playboys, were among the first of this new subgenre promising sun, salt air, sand and ocean in their titles. Budgets for these films were not much higher than those of the first primitive fifties rockers, but they did partake of a new sense of outdoorsey abandon—albeit leaving the more "serious" concerns of a *Where The Boys Are* by the wayside. The main thing these films had going for them was rock music. But unlike *Shake Rattle and Rock* and other jukebox jamborees of yore, rock was never seen here in terms of a pressing social issue. No specter of "juvenile delinquency" cramped the style of these new oceanside frolics—everything was clear skies, green lights and *good times* all the way. In no time a series of films from a single studio emerged to form a rallying point for this new surf hedonism—the *Beach Party* series from American International.

When the original *Beach Party* was made in 1963, probably all the studio was reaching for was a pseudo and cheaper *Where The Boys Are*. What finally reached the screen, however, in this and the other AIP beach epics that followed—*Muscle Beach Party, Bikini Beach* (both 1964), *Beach Blanket Bingo* and *How To Stuff A Wild Bikini* (both 1965)—was more along the lines of a *Mad Magazine* parody of the MGM film. These AIP "Looney Tunes" proved more adept at capturing turn-of-the-decade teen *zeitgeist* and the spirit of rock music than any other Hollywood fabrication up to that time.

As AIP's answer to Connie Francis, ex-Mousketeer Annette Funicello starred in the series as "Dee-Dee," whose long-suffering devotion to her boyfriend "Frankie" (established teen heartthrob Frankie Avalon) served as the nominal center for some lightweight musical romping. Instead of traveling to far-off Ft. Lauderdale, the denizens of these sandy frolics found they could raise just as much "heck" in their own beach backyards. While there aren't any overt sexual goings-on, the constant display of nubile flesh twisting and frugging to the big rock beat, more than compensates for the erotic constraints of the script.

When the scantily-clad inhabitants of this beachworld aren't otherwise engaged in spouting "True Romance" comic strip dialogue, They're bumping and grinding their cares away to the all-pervasive surfin' sound of (principally) Dick Dale and the Del-Tones, Little Stevie Wonder (who appears at the close of both *Muscle Beach Party* and *Bikini Beach*), The Hondells, The Pyramids and The Kingsmen. The mere *sound* of rock and roll was always more than enough of an excuse for the principals of these Coppertone capers to abandon their weightiest worries and dance up a storm.

Just as in *Where The Boys Are*, there's no parental supervision to these proceedings. Still, various oldsters show up in the form of sympathetic writers doing research on teen tribal customs (Bob Cummings in *Beach Party*), or as unsympathetic old poops (Keenan Wynn in *Bikini Beach*) who in the course of things are won over to the kids' boogalooing ways.

The only trouble in paradise comes in the form of a biker gang—a sort of loyal opposition to the surf and sand set—whose Brando-parody of a leader, Erick Von Zipper (Harvey Lembeck) tirelessly tries to undo All That Good Clean Fun in ways that inevitably backfire on him "Roadrunner" fashion.

Further support to the antics of "Frankie" and "Dee Dee" are provided by such stock players as dancer *extraordinaire* Candy Johnson (who like "L'il Abner's" "Stupefyin' Jones" has a wiggle that can make men crash into walls), and "surfer bums" "Deadhead" and "Johnny"—Jody McCrae and John Ashley. Besides the aforementioned Wynn and Cummings, Dorothy Malone, Martha Hyer, Mickey Rooney and Buster Keaton are among the other visitors from the world of more "respectable" filmmaking who lent an air of class and professionalism to what otherwise might have come off only as an endless series of car crashes, chases and slapstick interleaved with rock music. It's a mark of the new status the burgeoning rock culture had achieved, that by the mid-sixties such mainline players could appear in films like these without doing *too* much damage to their careers.

The "Beach" series may not have sported the satirical "smarts" of *The Girl Can't Help It*, but there's a low-brow infectiousness to them that has held them in good stead. The duets and solos of Avalon and Funicello are the only elements to have aged badly in these films that have otherwise come to be regarded as a small but significant slice of "Pop" Americana.

With the success of the *Beach Party* approach secured, AIP went on to impose the wacked-out formula of that series on other teen oriented efforts including two James Bond-ish spoofs, *Dr. Goldfoot and The Bikini Machine* and *Dr. Goldfoot and The Girl Bombs* (both 1966), a comedy-thriller *Ghost In the Invisible Bikini* (1966) and a comic sci-fi affair called *Pajama Party* (1965). These last two were closest in spirit to the "Beach" films, but neither had nearly as much rock music in them.

The idea of placing "Beach" and horror or fantasy elements together as this group of AIP programmers did was nothing new. As early as 1964, *The Horror of Party Beach*, the first rock and roll monster movie, appeared as if in response to the experience to be had viewing a typical AIP double bill—usually pairing a *Beach Party* entry with a Roger Corman variation on Edgar Allan Poe like *Masque of the Red Death* (1964). A Saturday afternoon at the Bijou consisting of such emotional push-me-pull-you double bills was doubtless an unsettling semi-surrealist experience to many. But the big pay-off for such programming practices came years later when *Horror of Party Beach* found its apotheosis in Steven Spielberg's *Jaws* (1975), a hybrid monster vs. surfers epic that is, in a way, the *ultimate* "beach" movie.

Before the wave of "beach" films washed out to sea, many others tried to cash in on the AIP formula with less than felicitous results. Comic-turned-producer/director Lennie Weinrib, for example, illustrated just how fatal the impulse to copy can sometimes be with *Beach Ball* (1965), *Out of Sight*, and *Wild Wild Winter* (both 1966). In contrast to the AIP films, the musical talent lineup for these quickies represents a partial who's who of rock in the sixties. The

Supremes, The Righteous Brothers, The Walker Brothers, The Four Seasons and The Hondells all appear in *Beach Ball*. But these performers are so ill-served, lumped together as they are in a climactic execrably-filmed vaudeville turn, that viewing today is a grueling chore for all but the most dedicated.

The kind of scorn generally heaped by the ill-informed upon the amiable and harmless AIP "beach" rockers is much more fittingly reserved for the likes of *Beach Ball* or its follow-up *Out of Sight*. Here Weinrib tries even harder to be AIP-wacky, but it's hard to do when bad scripts and cut-rate budgets are compounded by directionless direction. The Turtles, Gary Lewis and The Playboys, and Freddie and The Dreamers are the acts on hand in this one, and they're just as poorly treated as the performers in Weinrib's first opus.

Weinrib wasn't alone in the sub-B level of sixties "beach" rockers. Director Maury Dexter's wares—*The Young Swingers* (1963), *Surf Party* (1964) and *Wild On The Beach* (1965)—were every bit as misbegotten as Weinrib's. What both these "beach" entrepreneurs failed to realize was that it takes more than getting name acts like Sonny and Cher (who appear in Dexter's *Wild On The Beach*) to do a "turn". The acts should be properly filmed, *and* surrounded by an hour's worth of action that at the very least *aspires* toward comedy. Plot-wise, Weinrib and Dexter were stuck in the same groove as fifties jukebox musicals—which in turn were derived from "big band" musicals of the forties. The "beach" cycle from AIP had transformed this formula into a looser free-form approach to storytelling.

But even AIP occasionally missed the target as in *Ski Party* (1965) when it

it's where the **HE**s meet the **SHE**s on **SKI**s and there's only one way to get warm!

FRANKIE and **DEBBIE**... they've found a way to put love on ice!

AMERICAN INTERNATIONAL'S

Ski Party

IN **PATHÉCOLOR** AND **PANAVISION**

Hear **LESLEY GORE** and **JAMES BROWN** sing their newest HITS!

DWAYNE'S in the hands of **YVONNE** ...the exper 'SHE instructor

STARRING				GUEST STAR
FRANKIE AVALON	DWAYNE HICKMAN	DEBORAH WALLEY	YVONNE CRAIG	ROBERT Q. LEWIS

JAMES **BROWN** AND THE FAMOUS FLAMES · AND **LESLEY GORE**

CO STARRING · ARON KINCAID · BOBBI SHAW · PATTI CHANDLER · MARY HUGHES

PRODUCED BY **GENE CORMAN** · DIRECTED BY **ALAN RAFKIN** · WRITTEN BY ROBERT KAUFMA

©1965 American International Pictures

tried to bring the beach to the ski slopes. For this crucial change of venue, the producers took along the "beach" series' songwriting team of Gary Usher and Roger Christian—as well as certain of the "beach" company players, like Frankie Avalon and Dwayne Hickman. Also included for extra added insurance was an unusually high (for AIP) number of "name" recording talents—James Brown, Leslie Gore, and The Hondells. Perhaps because it lacked the touch of "beach" series director William Asher (replaced here by Alan Rafkin), or simply because "beach" antics don't "play" with a fully-clothed cast, *Ski Party* misses the "snap" of the other AIP's (though things do momentarily pick up when James Brown zipps into view).

Oddly enough, the major popularizers of surf music, The Beach Boys, appeared in only one of the dozens of films made in the sixties to exploit the surf scene—the aforementioned *Girls On The Beach*. They may have been holding out for something a little more than run-of-the-mill, but if so they didn't hold out quite long enough. Their only other film appearances were in Walt Disney Productions' *The Monkey's Uncle* (1965), a *Son of Flubber*-type comic fantasy in which they sing the title tune with Annette Funicello,* and in the same year's *The T.A.M.I. Show.*

Gauging the ultimate esthetic value of the "beach" films is, in the last analysis, beside the point. To be a teenager in America—even as late as the mid-sixties—was tantamount to near non-personhood; and viewed from that perspective even such last gasp/gurgles as the profoundly dreadful *It's A Bikini World* (1967) had *something* positive to offer in the way of social identity.

By the time that little surfside *schlagger* (featuring The Animals and The Gentrys) waded into view, the "beach" musical had become firmly established in "pop" mythology. *Lord Love A Duck* (1966), George Axelrod's satirical near-masterpiece, draws heavily on "beach" movie ambiance both in terms of atmosphere (hundreds of bikini-ed teens twisting in the opening credit sequence) and character construction. Tuesday Weld as the fame-obsessed "Barbara Ann Green" embodies every girl's desire to *be* Annette Funicello, and in Axelrod's dark designs she gets her chance in an epic called *Bikini Widow*!

The most "beach" influenced film of them all however is George Lucas' *American Graffiti* (1973). This episodic day and night in the lives of small town California teenagers finds all the old "Frankie" and "Dee Dee' archetypes shoved into cars and given more realistic lines to read, turning their formerly trivial concerns into the stuff of meaningful drama.

But before this final evolution of *Beach Party* took shape, *another* major film development came along—The Beatles debut in *A Hard Day's Night*—that took the lightheartedness of the "beach" world into new areas that would change the face of rock films for all time.

Subjects for further research:
Almost Summer, Because They're Young, Gidget, More American Grafitti, The Hollywood Knights, Cooley High.

---

*Beach Boys leader Brian Wilson can be spotted—if you look *real* close—as a background player in *Muscle Beach Party* and one or two other films in the AIP "beach" series.

THE BEATLES
TO THE RESCUE

IKE *Love Me Tender*, *A Hard Day's Night* (1964) was made primarily as a celluloid celebration of its stars' status as a worldwide pop music phenomenon. But to the surprise and delight of both the mass public and the critical establishment, *this* rock movie wasn't just an entertaining vehicle tailored to the talents of a particular musical group, but a first rate piece of filmmaking regardless of genre.

When critic Andrew Sarris called *A Hard Day's Night* "the *Citizen Kane* of jukebox musicals," he wasn't being glib or clever, just *accurate*. The Beatles and director Richard Lester had managed through this one film to move the lowly rock programmer up onto a plateau of unprecedented respectability.

On one level, *A Hard Day's Night* simply does for the Beatles what *Loving You* did for Elvis Presley—create a fictional format for the purpose of mass media personality consumption. Unlike the Presley film however, *A Hard Day's Night* isn't concerned with an examination of the rise to fame so much as it is with contemplation of already achieved success. Moreover on a moviemaking level, the most important aspect of that success—even more than their singing—was the image of goodnatured youthful iconoclasm that The Beatles projected.

The Beatles—in contrast to all the pop performers that preceeded them—seemed unperturbed by sudden fame, answering reporters' queries with a quick flipness that slyly sent-up the whole notion of show-biz achievement. Alun Owen's script—a 48 hours in the life of the "Fab Four" as they prepare for a television appearance—never missed an opportunity to showcase this amiable "cheekiness." Whether twitting a stuffed shirt ("We fought the war for your lot!," "Bet you're sorry you won!") or deflating a pop music rival ("She's a drag, a well-known drag. We turn down the sound on the telly and make rude remarks."), The Beatles always appear to be *themselves*.

Verbal irreverence is only part of the film's success however. With the supple light-weight camera equipment that had been developed for *cinema-verite* documentary films, director Lester records real Beatle fans in action, hotly pursuing their idols at various points along the film's course. This virtual reality (in contrast to *Loving You*'s use of actors to squeal in ersatz Presleymania) works well alongside the carefully constructed version of the Beatles' lives the film presents, which while not corresponding to *literal* truth forms a valid rendering of a fan's fantasy expectations.

The Beatles' wives and girlfriends are kept out of the picture not just to avoid blocking a Beatlemaniac's access to pure uninterrupted idolatry, but as part of a broader effort to give the group the appearance of belonging to a lower age-bracket. Instead of Beatles' manager Brian Epstein, two bumbling music hall types, "Norm" and "Shake" (very well played by Norman Rossington and John Jukin) are seen shepherding these musical charges about like teachers managing a class outing. The Beatles in turn react like mischievous kids, shirking "homework" (fan letter answering) and skipping out to play "hookey" whenever possible (e.g. racing across a field like a class on a recess break in the "Can't Buy Me Love" number). Ringo even "runs away from home" in one sequence (to the tune of an instrumental version of the Beatles' hit "This Boy") when he's told he'd be better off leaving the group.

This nearly ruinous development is brought about by the film's other important character, "Paul's grandfather"—Wilfred Brambell star of the popular British television series "Steptoe and Son." Troublesome as a devilish six-year-old, this "clean old man," as the lads call him, rounds out the film's topsy-turvy view of age and responsibility. While "Norm" and "Shake" constantly nag the boys to "keep in line," it's "granddad" who really "needs looking after."

None of this action, however, gets in the way of *A Hard Day's Night*'s chief attraction—its brilliantly staged (and later widely imitated) musical numbers. Not since *On The Town* (1949) have music and movement meshed as infectiously as in this film. Lester makes no attempt at trying to pass the Beatles off as trained dancers. Instead he creates a *sense* of dance movement in the "Can't Buy me Love" number by quickly cutting between the four of them as they pose, gesture and jump about a field in rhythm to their music. In the "I'm Happy Just To Dance With You" sequence, the same free-spirited visual *feel* is created in a confined space. Sitting in a fenced off area of a baggage compartment on a train, The Beatles play cards, and as the song rises on the soundtrack, musical instruments suddenly appear in their hands. The rocking of the train is counterpointed by their rocking back and forth to the music. The whole scene *sways* in a way that at first glance would scarcely seem possible in light of the setting.

While critics analyzed Lester's technique, audiences were caught up by the force of the personalities that this director helped put on display. It was impossible to realize it at the time, but The Beatles came along to be embraced by a (not exclusively rock oriented) public looking for a way to fill the gap left in the wake of the deaths of Marilyn Monroe and John F. Kennedy. These two larger-than-life mythic personalities (linked romantically in gossip after their passings) were fixed in mass media consciousness as embodiments of Strength and Grace who had "died before their time" Who and what they *really* were became a subject for constant speculation at a point simultaneous to The Beatles' rise. What the rock group added to this thickening pseudo-sociological stew was an interrogation of the concept of personality itself.

When the Maysles brothers trained their *cinema verite* cameras on The Beatles for *What's Happening* (1964), their film about the Britishers' arrival in New York, it was with the sense of irony all such documentary works are made. The "knowing" filmmakers' record (in Jean-Luc Godard's words) "truth 24 times a second" about their famous subjects (producer Joseph E. Levine and actor Marlon Brando figure among the many that have been before the Maysles' cameras) providing an "insider's" view of what these noted figures are "really" like. But in the case of The Beatles this approach backfired for there was no "inside" or "outside" in the usual sense. So aware were they of camera technique that there was no way to "catch them with their guard down."

The Maysles film style is, to a large degree, parodied by Lester in the press party sequence of *A Hard Day's Night*. To reporters armed to the teeth with questions about the "meaning" of Beatlemania, The Beatles answer back with a grin and a giggle. George, for example, when asked what he "calls" his haircut, replies "Arthur." Ringo, when questioned about being either a "mod" or a "rocker," claims to be a "mocker."

Mockers were exactly what the Beatles were to their fans. With their Liverpudlian accents, they brought a whole sense of exoticism to rock and roll style in America, while shaking up class attitudes in their native England. To an uptight Britain here were "commoners," not only thoroughly at ease in chatting up the Queen at Court, but eager to use their newly-won social mobility to forge a royalty all their own.

A Hard Day's Night paved the way for the creation of this new rock dynasty, for its success made The Beatles not simply musically omnipotent, but international culture forces as well. That all this would emerge from England in the sixties couldn't have been forseen in advance on either a musical or cinematic level, for prior to The Beatles, what represented rock music in Britain lagged well behind most of what was available in America.

Musical vaudevilles, on a level matching the flimsiest of U.S. pop quickies, were ground out for such British stars as Cliff Richard, Tommy Steele and Billy Fury—all of whom vied at one time or another for the crown of "British Elvis." These largely American-styled opuses—for extra added box office insurance—frequently featured such American performers as Gene Vincent, Jerry Lee Lewis, Ray Charles and Bobby Vee along with British stars.

The talent-line-ups look and feel of most pre-Beatle rockers—like *Play It Cool* (1962) with Billy Fury and Helen Shapiro and *Just For Fun* (1963) featuring

Dusty Springfield—were heavily influenced by such popular British television shows as *Ready Steady Go* and *Top of The Pops*. Tilt-angled photography and finger-snapping choreography set the tone for these efforts.

Even the man who did the most to bring this kind of filmmaking to an end—Richard Lester—made his contribution to the British pop norm with *It's Trad Dad* (1962)—known as *Ring-A-Ding Rhythm* in the U.S. With knowledge of *A Hard Day's Night* to come it's possible to spot many a Lester touch in this Helen Shapiro/Craig Douglas starrer—in every other way typical of British pop product—about kids overcoming adult resistance to not just rock, but dixieland jazz (!).

Featuring Gene Vincent, Gene McDaniels, Del Shannon and Gary U.S. Bonds, it had these stars keeping up paces that were par for the musical course. Other sequences in *Trad* managed to go a bit further. Acker Bilk and his band, for example, were shot through a dot-like grid resembling newspaper photos (or, more to the Lester Pop Art point, Roy Lichtenstein paintings). Another scene with the Brook Brothers, placed this musical pair alongside huge blown-up photographs of themselves—a multi-image approach that became common later in the sixties on both film and television. Best of all, however, was a scene featuring the Temperance Seven, with members of that group changing places with one another with every change of shot—a technique that became Lester's trademark as in the previously mentioned "I'm Happy Just To Dance With You" number in *A Hard Day's Night*.

After the success of *A Hard Day's Night* numerous British musicals began to affect an approximation of the Lester "look." But there's a difference between real visual sophistication and shots of performers leaping about a lot. Freddie and the Dreamers worked out in two such affairs, *Seaside Swingers* (1964)—known as *Every Day's A Holiday* in England—and *Cuckoo Patrol* (1965). Gerry and the Pacemakers were involved in a similar effort, *Ferry Cross The Mersey* (1964). *Ghost Goes Gear* (1966)—a feature-length film cut down to the level of a short for its release—found The Spencer Davis Group and Stevie Winwood thrust into an equally wanting post-Lester context.

Meanwhile, Lester himself had gone off in an even more experimental direction with his next Beatles feature, *Help* (1965). Since the Beatles' personalities had been firmly established in their first film, Lester and scriptwriter Charles Wood felt free to explore other approaches. Shot in brilliant color, this *Goon Show*-inspired variation on Wilkie Collins' mystery-adventure *The Moonstone* was about as far from the relative simplicity of *A Hard Day's Night* as it's possible to go.

The plot revolves around a ring a Beatles fan has sent to Ringo, which turns out to be a sacred artifact of an obscure eastern religious cult, the "Kahili." The lads soon find themselves pursued from the Alps to the Bahamas by these comic "thugs" (led by Elinor Bron and Leo McKern) *and* by a "mad" scientist (Victor Spinetti who played the neurotic television director in *A Hard Day's Night*) who suspects that the ring may have powers that will allow him to "Dare I say it? Rule the world!"

Visually and dramatically, *Help*'s a cinematic "Hellzapoppin" with director Lester cleverly converting the spirit of Mack Sennett farce into the style of sixties "pop" art. But while the film doesn't shortchange on its musical numbers—"Ticket To Ride" and "I Need You" surpassing even "Can't Buy Me Love" in visual inventiveness—a feeling of awkwardness arises from the Beatles being something less than the center of attention.

It's easy to see what Lester had in mind from the way he integrates the group into the slapstick pratfalls set up by the other members of the cast who, in their comic villain roles, *instigate* the film's action in a way that The Beatles don't. The Beatles are never less than competent in going through these physical paces—and Ringo somewhat more than that—but it's clear that this sort of comic playing isn't quite their *forte.*

When *A Hard Day's Night* first appeared, more than one critic drew parallels between The Beatles and The Marx Brothers, but while it's possible to see the wisecracking John Lennon as Groucho and Ringo as a sort-of Harpo, furthering the analogy to see Paul McCartney and George Harrison as Zeppo and Chico wouldn't be apt. The group didn't function as a comedy "team" so much as a loose assembly of friends, all of whom sang, some of whom did "funny business."

As far as Beatle fans were concerned, distinctions like this really didn't matter. *Help* may not have had the novelty or excitement of *A Hard Day's Night*, but it was in many ways funnier and its musical set pieces were far from disappointing. "Ticket To Ride" found the lads playing high on an Alpine slope and romping through the snow as the notes to the song appeared on a piece of telephone wire, turning the screen into a sheet of music. "I Need You" set the group on the Salisbury plain surrounded by an army for protection—which sprang into action when the "Kahili" attacked at the song's end.

All these visual arabesques and dramatic absurdities were there for the delight of Beatle fans, but by the time of *Help*'s appearance there was a fast growing Richard Lester cult to cater to as well. For just as The Beatles' casual *cheek* became part of social style, so Lester's casual *chic* set fashion in film culture. His bright colors, fast pacing, fragmented scenes and all-around "cool" approach became a sixties hallmark in films as varied and diverse as *Blow-Up, Modesty Blaise* (both 1966), *Two For The Road* and *Point Blank* (both 1967).

Having A Wild Weekend (1965), *Good Times* (1967) and *Head* (1968) tried to do for their respective performers (The Dave Clark Five, Sonny and Cher, and The Monkees), what Lester did for The Beatles. All these films failed for reasons having as much to do with their performers less-than-charismatic appeal, as well as any deficiencies on the part of their directors—John Boorman, William Friedkin and Bob Rafelson—all of whom went on to "better things" in the non-rock field.

In the case of *Good Times*, a modest low-key affair in contrast with Friedkin's later expensive blow-outs (*The Exorcist, Sorcerer*), it was simply that at this stage in their career Sonny and Cher weren't ready to set the world on fire. A movie about all the possible movies that these singing sweethearts *could* make, *Good Times* has Sonny and Cher bouncing in and out of numerous costumes and sets. Unfortunately the edgy patter they later developed for their successful television series doesn't even begin to take shape here. They *smile* a lot.

Having A Wild Weekend (known as *Catch Us If You Can* in England) involved an entirely other set of problems. Suffering under the mistaken notion that The Dave Clark Five were going to be The Next Big Thing, producer David

Deutsch set young tv-trained turk Boorman and writer Peter Nichols about to quickly whip up something along the lines of *A Hard Day's Night*. Two stumbling blocks became immediately apparent. (1): The Dave Clark Five, engaging as they were, weren't The Next Big Thing—The Rolling Stones were. (2): Dave Clark (who was to shoulder most of the dramatic chores) had rather severe limitations as an actor.

The plot involved Dave, the group and actress Barbara Ferris as show biz fringe types whose try at "getting away from it all" gets converted into a publicity stunt. Starting out looking like imitation Lester, the film eventually managed to forge a style of its own—a sad grey lyricism coupled with a more wary view of the pop scene than shown in *A Hard Day's Night*. Instead of embracing commercialism as The Beatles did in their films, Dave and the boys were shown trying to escape it.

It was a tack that, not surprisingly, failed to find favor with the public, but many critics did cotton to Boorman's off-beat approach. Pauline Kael in her collection of essays, *Kiss Kiss Bang Bang,* wrote, "It's as if pop art had discovered Chekhov—the 'Three Sisters' finally set off for Moscow and along the way discover that there isn't any Moscow."

No such lofty comparisons inspired critics of *Head*. A series of loosely written shenanigans (by of all people actor Jack Nicolson), involving the self-confessed "plastic pop group" The Monkees—Columbia Pictures' shameless attempt at manufacturing an imitation Beatles—it featured a whole grab-bag of supposedly "with-it" oddities. Annette Funicello, cult B-movie bad guy Timothy Carey, and female impersonator T.C. Jones all make appearances, registering as little effect as the old movie clips (Bela Lugosi, Rita Hayworth) that crop up whenever the action flags—which is often. In once scene, this less-than-fab four (Peter Tork, Mickey Dolenz, Davey Jones and Michael Nesmith) are seen as dandruff romping over the *head* (get it?) of guest star Victor Mature. Film viewers quickly reached for the "Head & Shoulders" on this item. It wasn't enough to create disorienting camera angles and run around in funny outfits anymore—it had to be done with specific ideas in mind.

Only Frank Zappa (who had appeared briefly in *Head*) in his and Tony Palmer's *200 Motels* (1971) managed to capture—and even expand upon—the Lester spirit. Shot on videotape and later transferred to film stock, *200 Motels* featured a number of visual experiments (distorted imagery, "bleeding" of one shot into another) that Jean-Luc Godard would later use in his semi-video efforts *Numero Deux* (1975) and *Comment Ca Va* (1976). A series of semi-improvised scenes about an imaginary tour by Zappa and his band The Mothers of Invention (featuring Mark Volman and Howard Kaylan, formerly of The Turtles and later to be known as Flo and Eddie) *200 Motels* often worked itself up into an acid/slapstick frenzy very much in keeping with the spirit of that most overused of terms, surrealism.

In many ways, *200 Motels* was the sort of film one would have expected The Beatles to make at this stage of their careers. Ringo does, in fact, turn up in it, but the other Beatles are nowhere to be seen, for by 1971 they no longer existed as a group. Their spirit saw its last *full* screen flowering in the all too infrequently seen television film *Magical Mystery Tour* (1967).

Outrageous in its refusal to be merely accessible, this attempt at surrealism for

the masses is almost wholly undeserving of the bad reputation that has built up around it over the years. It's easy to understand why American television executives refused to air it at a time when The Beatles couldn't have been hotter. They must have been expecting a straightforward all-singing, all-dancing variety show. Instead, what The Beatles dumped in their laps was a television anathema—a personal, thoughtful and artful film statement.

Victor Spinetti and Bonzo Dog Band lend the Beatles support to what might be described as a "hippie" pastorale (with a nod to Lindsay Anderson's similarly fey "guided tour" featurette The White Bus made one year earlier) in which such hits as "I Am The Walrus" and "Fool On The Hill" get quasi-Lester production number treatment.

After American television passed on it, Magical Mystery Tour eventually made its way to the giant screens of movie revival houses—but for some reason, the prints are generally botched, chopped, third generation "dupes" of what was originally a lovely looking little jewel. The Beatles could have gone on to produce similar gems—and get them shown to a larger public—but ever since the success of the Rubber Soul, Revolver and (most important of all) Sgt. Pepper's Lonely Hearts Club Band albums, recordings took over their careers in a new way. No longer were the Liverpool lads to be thought of as mere entertainers. Now they were to be placed right alongside Stravinsky and Sartre—serious musical and artistic forces.

Ironically, this incredible burst of creative energy came at a moment when The Beatles were starting to come apart as a group. Speaking in a television interview many years later, John Lennon pointed out that while fans saw their time together as brief, he and Paul had been playing in musical ensembles since they were fifteen years old. There's no getting around the sadness Beatle fans felt at the waning of a show biz dream, but growth and change was inevitable.

Having ascended every possible entertainment plateau it was in certain ways scarcely surprising that Lennon with the encouragement of his wife Yoko Ono should turn his energies to avant-garde art events and various forms of social protest (e.g. their "bed-ins" for Peace). The films the husband and wife team made together—a camera ascending in the gondola of a balloon in Apotheosis, 331 Pairs of legs in Legs, a fly crawling up Yoko's stomach in Fly, all circa 1970-71—weren't likely to turn up at the local Bijou, but they weren't designed to.

For Paul, post-Beatles life took the form of revving up the machinery of pop music success all over again for his new group Wings created with his wife Linda and musician Denny Laine. The soft rock hit-making formula McCartney latched onto with this group—seen in action in the disappointingly ordinary looking rock concert film Rockshow, released in 1981—eluded George Harrison whose sporadic musical projects have yet to form a lasting public impression. Ringo Starr on the other hand, while continuing to record over the years, has established a career for himself as a comic actor.

While it's possible to question the wisdom of the different paths taken by the members of the group after their disbanding, one thing cannot be denied—each move, for better or worse, was taken on each Beatles' own initiative and inner conviction. This sort of self-determination wasn't possible when the group was together and had an image to look up to—an image that by the late sixties could

no longer really be called their own.

The cartoon feature *Yellow Submarine* (1968) is an important example of this kind of image functioning. On one level this sophisticated "family" entertainment is a triumph. Master animator George Duning and graphic designer Heinz Edelman took Beatle songs old and new and used them as a starting point for an incredible series of visual arabesques set to music. But on another level, *Yellow Submarine* is a step backwards. Its story—an expansion of the Beatles' kiddie pop hit tune of the same name—reduces the group to the level of classy playroom dolls, and transforms their former rebelliousness into open support of the status quo (i.e. saving the people of "Pepperland"—a "Merrie England"-style monarchy—from the "Blue Meanies").

Still, most viewers were more likely to sit back and let Duning and Edelman's designs wash over them than pay any attention to the "plot." "Eleanor Rigby" rendered as a series of eerie floating turn-of-the-century cutouts was the chief highlight of the film, with an appropriately "psychedelic" "Lucy In The Sky With Diamonds" not far behind.

Appearing on-screen at the end, The Beatles smiled and waved happily urging their fans to join in one last chorus of "All Together Now." It was their next to last "altogether." The final film *Let It Be* (1970), directed by Michael Lindsay-Hogg was a documentary of their recording sessions for the songs on the album of the same name, as well as a few of their "Abbey Road" album numbers.

Though musically compelling ("Across The Universe" and "Get Back" are among the Beatles' very best compositions) *Let It Be* documents a spiritually arid time. The strain of imminent parting is apparent everywhere. Only a sequence of an impromptu jam session on the roof of the recording studio shows any of the old fire.

With the passing of John Lennon, a new generation's interest in The Beatles phenomenon has come in to fill the gap of wistful longing felt by those fans who experienced the group "back when it all began." For some, The Beatles story was finished when Lennon declared in song that "the dream is over." For others it will never die mainly because, of all people, Ringo.

It's ironic that the least culturally "serious" member of the group should end up to be the one to continue to embody its spirit. But in whatever film he does a turn in—*Candy* (1968), *The Magic Christian* (1970), *Lisztomania* (1975)—Ringo carries something with him that's more than a wry smile and a raised eyebrow. It's something in his untrained non-actor's voice that has a way of cutting through whatever lines he's given to read (valid or nonsensical) that gives his presence in film's its *truth*.

In *Caveman* (1981) without benefit of lines, Ringo had his first chance since *Help* to demonstrate the kind of *physical* sophistication he's capable of creating. There's a wonderful, almost mythic moment in that film where Ringo and his band of misfit cave people make music round a campfire. It's fitting that a Beatle should be present at the birth of mankind's first musical sounds.

Of course, there is a good deal more of Beatles-on-film to be seen than the major releases covered in this chapter. While this other Beatles footage— primarily promotional shorts for Beatles singles—crops up fairly regularly at movie revival houses and Beatle memorabilia conventions, there's little question

that with John Lennon's passing this material (and more as yet unseen) will become more readily accessible. Hopefully Beatles film packages will be available in more suitable form than what's currently available—duplicate prints of dubious visual value.

The Beatles Come To Town (a.k.a. *Around The Beatles*) is a British television special from 1963. P.J. Proby and Cilla Black also appeared on this special, but these performers are cut from the version of the show exhibited theatrically. The music appears to be done "live" (though it's hard to tell), and the songs include "Twist and Shout," "Roll Over Beethoven," "I Wanna Be Your Man," and a hit medley of "Love Me Do," "Please Please Me" and "She Loves You."

In circulation as well are three concert films—*The Tokyo Concert* (1966), *The Washington Coliseum Concert* (1964), and *The Shea Stadium Concert* (1965). While the first two of these can only be recommended to the most fanatical of Beatle followers due to poor visual and sound quality, *The Shea Stadium Concert* is superb. Fifty-five minutes long, it was initially a television special. Though the prints we've seen of this film leave a lot to be desired, The Beatles shine through. They rip through eight songs without dropping a beat or messing up any of their delicate vocal harmonics. All this, mind you, is done in the face of 55,000 shrieking fans sounding like every fire engine in New York City going off at once.

Among the promotional shorts, *Hey Jude* (a videotape of a "live" TV satellite broadcast); *Revolution*, *Penny Lane* and *Strawberry Fields Forever* are the most notable. Among the post-Beatles there are *Instant Karma*, *Cold Turkey* and *Imagine* (John and Yoko), *Only You* (Ringo), *London Town*, *Silly Love Songs* and *Coming Up* (Paul).

The John and Yoko experimental films mentioned earlier in this chapter, were shown at avant-garde gatherings in the early seventies, but not—as of this writing—since then.

Subjects for further research:
How I Won The War, Sgt. Pepper's Lonely Hearts Club Band, Birth of The Beatles, Concert for Bangladesh, The Family Way, Go Go Big Beat, Go Go Mania, The Guru, Early Abstractions, That'll Be The Day, I Wanna Hold Your Hand.

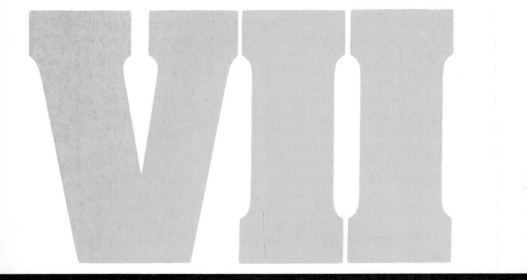

VII

SOUNDTRACK ROCK

I N THE 1950's ROCK was thought of exclusively as a passing fancy of the young. Unless a film's plot involved adolescents, there didn't seem to be any reason to use this "teen-age fad" for soundtrack scores. No one objected to hearing The Modern Jazz Quartet's cooler-than-cool sounds as accompaniment to the caper melodrama *Odds Against Tomorrow* (1959)—it was even thought to bring the film a "touch of class." That wouldn't have been the case had the film instead used the "low down" twangs of rock instrumentalists like Link Wray or Duane Eddy.

More damaging than the "gimmick" aspect was rock's reputation as an anarchic social force inextricably linked to violence. The not-so-subtle implication of *The Blackboard Jungle* that juvenile delinquency is being aided and abetted by the sound of "Rock Around The Clock" had left many with a lasting impression.

Rock's alignment with evil and sin could be found in other than leather jacket and switchblade contexts, as it was, for example, in the film *Baby Doll* (1956). Tennessee Williams' carnal comedy of manners (directed by Elia Kazan) used rocker Smiley Lewis's "Shame, Shame, Shame (on You Miss Roxy)" as a virtual clarion call to perdition. Denounced at the time of its release from the pulpit of St. Patrick's Cathedral by Francis Cardinal Spellman, today *Baby Doll* seems more First Tap Dance than Last Tango, though it's still not difficult to see what aroused the eminent Catholic prelate's ire.

While the adultery-skirting flirtation of Eli Wallach for Karl Malden's sexually frustrated child bride Carroll Baker, never gets further than the "heavy petting" stage, the desire to go "all the way" is foremost in all the principals' minds, and consequently in the viewers' as well. Baker's "Baby Doll" was like most teenagers in the sexually repressed fifties. Bodies were changing and nerve ends were awakening. Only sly lyrics and sultry rhythms like Smiley's offered any clue as to what was *really* going on.

While "where rock goes trouble follows" served for many years as Hollywood's primary attitude toward the musical phenomenon, European filmmakers tended to regard things more tolerantly. In *White Nights* (1957), a modern version of the Dostoyevsky short novel, director Luchino Visconti went so far as to insert a special rock and roll dance sequence in loving tribute to the vitality of contemporary youth. Others, however, took a less reverential view of the subject. In *La Dolce Vita* (1960), Federico Fellini found fun in ribbing Little Richard's classic "Ready Teddy," by having it performed by an overenthusiastic rocker in a Roman night spot who gyrates so wildly he throws himself off the stage. This parodistic approach also appears in *Bedazzled* (1967), Peter Cook and Dudley Moore's update of the Faust legend, directed by Stanley Donen. In a scene spoofing British TV's *Ready Steady Go*, Moore, as an Adam Faith-like balladeer, has all the "birds" swooning until Cook, a super-cool ultra-insolent popster, steals his thunder.

However, due to the Beatles, such mockery was less common by the mid-sixties. Rock, after all, had never taken itself so seriously as to exclude humor (e.g. *The Girl Can't Help It*), and the strides the music had taken into non-teenage social life was fast bringing the era of mainstream rock-resistance to a close.

Predictably the first few rocking steps taken in a direction away from strictly "kid" oriented subjects were timid ones. The Clive Donner-Woody Allen comedy *What's New Pussycat?* (1965) had a Burt Bachrach score, with several songs featuring the smooth ballad style of Dionne Warwick ("Here I Am") and the brassy pop crooning of Tom Jones (the title tune.) Best of all, Manfred Mann's "Little Red Book" popped up in the background to supply this sex farce a refreshing "British Invasion" rock flavor. Francis Ford Coppola's *You're A Big Boy Now* (1967) followed a similar line, using The Lovin' Spoonful to embroider that film's coming-of-age in New York story, with appropriately snappy strains even though that group's sound was closer to pop/romantic than hard-driving.

The watershed film of this period was *The Graduate* (1967) which took the integration of rock sounds with storytelling onto a new and more ambitious level. Director Mike Nichols needed a way to bring out the inner conflicts of his largely silent hero Benjamin (Dustin Hoffman), and who better than the inventors of the "Sound of Silence" themselves, Simon and Garfunkel. Cleverly mixing familiar Simon and Garfunkel hits like "Scarborough Fair" along with new numbers especially composed for the film ("Mrs. Robinson" etc.), *The Graduate* turned song into a form of interior monologue cum Greek chorus commentary.

The success of *The Graduate*—a film designed for the college crowd but which garnered mass appeal—signalled to alert film producers that pop songs could find favor on the largest possible scale when thoughtfully utilized in "straight" drama. However, the film most responsible for the impact rock music would eventually have on serious narratives came from the "underground" film scene.

Kenneth Anger's *Scorpio Rising* (1963), a thirty-one minute study of the homosexual leather and motorcycle set had a soundtrack consisting of eleven rock songs played in rapid-fire succession one right after the other. "My Boyfriend's Back" by The Angels, "I Will Follow Him" by Little Peggy March and "Hit The Road Jack" by Ray Charles are some of the numbers used in this audio-visual essay whose juxtaposition of naive lyrics with knowing imagery mixed "black" humor with "camp" (e.g. the camera caressing a Harley's gleaming chrome and its rider's leather and denim covered body as Bobby Vinton croons *She wore blue velvet . . .*).

Anger's sensibility was, needless to say, "too much" for Hollywood, but his methods—if properly adapted were just right for commercial films. In *Easy Rider* (1969) Anger's concept of music as dramatic superstructure was used on somewhat less volatile subject matter to highly lucrative results. Consisting of a series of very loosely strung-together scenes detailing the Kerouac-inspired travels of a pair of dope-dealing bikers (Peter Fonda and Dennis Hopper), *Easy Rider* took full advantage of rock music's ability to fill in gaps where narrative imagination flagged (or in this case, "nodded out"). Steppenwolf's "Born To Be Wild," The Byrds' "Wasn't Born To Follow" and Jimi Hendrix's "If Six Was Nine" are a few of the numbers that substitute for plot, dialogue and characterization in a film that puts two typical "misunderstood" hell-raisers of the fifties into the even more socially hostile atmosphere of the sixties.

Fonda and Hopper's deaths at the hands of two shotgun-wielding rednecks at the end of the film was a scene that sent chills down the collective spines of the so-called "counterculture." It seemed to crystalize the frustration and violence of the Viet Nam era. Rock in this film spoke through the gloom, giving voice to the feelings and ideas that both the characters and their champions in the audience couldn't possibly express.

Easy Rider's use of rock "up front" became fashionable for many sorts of projects over the years. Ironically the prototypes of this existential "road" movie—the motorcycle melodramas and hippies-on-the-loose exploitation programmers of the same period—featured far less in the way of rock music than their subject matter might suggest.

The Wild Angels (1966), Roger Corman's controversial celebration of the "Hell's Angels" motorcycle club's socially disruptive life style took chances on every level *except* the musical one. While Peter Fonda as "Heavenly Blues" (a rough sketch for his "Captain America" in *Easy Rider*) led his minions on a frenzied "acid"-inspired rampage, the throbbing insistent guitar chords of David Allan and The Arrows merely "dum-da-dummed" in the background. This heavy metal Muzak, the creation of soon-to-be Lt. Governor of California Mike Curb, set the style for most other chopper sagas like *The Devil's Angels, Hell's Angels On Wheels* (both 1967) and *Angels From Hell* (1968). Richard

Rush's *The Savage Seven* (1968) was an exception to this musical rule, using the truly rocking sounds of Iron Butterfly and Cream to accompany motorcycle madness provided by Robert Walker, Adam Roarke and a non-singing Duane Eddy.

Rush's giddy envisionment of the Haight-Ashbury scene, *Psych-Out* (1968) rocked to a softer beat, putting The Strawberry Alarm Clock behind the spacey struttings of Jack Nicholson and Susan Strassberg. This was also an exception, for most "acid"-excess cautionary tales like *Hallucination Generation* (1966), *Riot On Sunset Strip* (1967) and *Wild In The Streets* (1968) followed the cycle films' lead in *Curb*-ing their rock ambitions. The makers of these "sons" and "daughters" of *High School Confidential* probably thought that the wailings and writhings of the actors would be a sufficient audience lure. On that score they were correct, but on an esthetic level nothing could compare to an *appropriately* orchestrated "youth-must-have-its-flipout-er" like Roger Corman's *The Trip* (1967). Mike Bloomfield and The Electric Flag's music for this exploration (starring Peter Fonda) in "mind expansion" (closer to a Vincente Minnelli production number than an actual L.S.D. vision) provided definitive proof that rock can create textures as rich, varied and dramatically intricate as any conventional film score.

Unfortunately quality considerations weren't on many minds in the wake of the success of *Easy Rider*. As the sixties came to a close every major studio in Hollywood was knocking itself out in an attempt to come up with a project that would repeat that film's success. *The Strawberry Statement, R.P.M., The Revolutionary, The Magic Garden of Stanley Sweetheart* (all 1970 releases) and *Been Down So Long It Looks Like Up To Me* (1971) were among the many big budget items desperate to be "with it." Their failure was doubtless due to the public's sensing that these class "A" items weren't fundamentally much different from the cheaper "youthsploitation" B-films that had preceeded them. Like those films, these "counterculture" specials didn't feature much more than a few guitar strums in the way of rock music. However one film that did use an *Easy Rider* approach to scoring had no more success than the other "youth" flicks.

Zabriskie Point (1970) was the most grandly conceived and eagerly awaited of all the big time "revolutionary" epics. Its director, Michelangelo Antonioni, had risen from "art house" eminence to international blockbuster-maker with his enigmatic mystery-thriller *Blow-Up* (1966). A surprisingly on-target look at "swinging London," this story of a fashion photographer (David Hemmings) inadvertently uncovering a murder was highlighted by a scene of Who-inspired guitar destruction performed by The Yardbirds. M.G.M. was certain the Italian maestro could evoke American "consciousness III" on film with similar success.

On a visual level *Zabriskie Point* fulfilled its promise. Sharply photographed Panavision panoramas of Los Angeles' Pop Art ambiance (billboards, automobiles, and the movement of people in the streets mixed together to form a vast mural) captured the "look" of things in a way few films had done before or since. As a drama *Zabriskie Point* was disappointing.

The script that Antonioni and his collaborators (Tonino Guerra, Clare Peploe and Sam Shepard) had come up with was woefully thin—"revolutionary" boy on the run from a crime he may or may not have committed meets dippy hippie girl on her way to the desert for a spot of meditation. With the right performers this slim conceit might have just managed to get by. Unfortunately, Antonioni cast two inexperienced unknowns—Mark Frechette and Daria Halprin—who were physically right for their roles but totally unequipped to make their "Oh wow, far out" dialogue sound like anything more than unconscious parody.

Yet while Antonioni's story suggested that the filmmaker had only the most superficial knowledge of American youth circa the sixties, the musical sounds he used in the background were incredibly apt. The story and performers may have been noodle-limp, but Antonioni's stunning images leapt to attention when they were given the musical snap and crackle of The Grateful Dead's "Dark Star" or The Rolling Stones' "You've Got The Silver." Best of all were Pink Floyd's numbers: "Crumbling Land," "Heart Beat Pig Meat" (used over the film's credits), and "Come In Number 51 Your Time Is Up" (its bubbly electro-laser sound perfect for the film's finale of a house in the desert exploding in slow motion).

A much more truthful portrait of sixties youth—with an equally sensitive use of rock—was *Dusty and Sweets McGee* (1971.) A semi-documentary on the L.A. drug scene, it was a far cry from the "blissed-out" hedonism of *Easy Rider*. The mostly non-professional cast director Floyd Mutrux assembled for this gritty, thoroughly unglamorous view of heroin and amphetamine addiction —unlike Antonioni's performers—really *held* the screen. Golden "oldies" dominated the soundtrack—the only respite from the harsh reality on screen. Little Eva's "The Locomotion," Del Shannon's "Runaway" and, most poignantly, Van Morrison's "Into The Mystic" wove a path through the characters' bombed-out lives, underscoring the gaiety and high spirits they could no longer feel.

Compelling as it was, *Dusty and Sweets McGee* never found an audience. By this time moviegoers had become wary of anything the studios were offering with an aura of "hip" attached to it. But Hollywood's infatuation with "youth" had come to a close anyway, for 1971 saw the emergence of a new subgenre designed to flatter the sensibilities of another rock-oriented social group.

The "blacksploitation" cycle of the early seventies offered films that had about as much to do with the reality of black urban life as *Rock Pretty Baby* had to do with fifties teenagers. Still, just as with that group, America's blacks were glad to see *any* representation of their lives on screen, however fanciful. Moreover outside of visceral action thrills, these films featured up-tempo Rhythm and Blues on their soundtracks. The lowdown growl of Isaac Hayes' theme from *Shaft* and the high-flying "ooo" of Curtis Mayfield's score for *Superfly* (both 1971 releases), sounded the first notes of what promised at first to be a new sort of black musical explosion. Sadly, just as the films that followed proved to be dead ends—repetitive glorifications of super-sleuths (like *Shaft*) or super-pimps (like *Superfly*)—their soundtrack sounds had little to offer.

Marvin Gaye's music for *Trouble Man* (1972)—an otherwise unremarkable piece of detective nonsense starring Robert Hooks—is arguably the best of the "blacksploitation" scores, combining Gaye's tense cool phrasing with lush "R&B" orchestrations. As the on-screen parade of pushers, pimps and playboys became progressively more unreal, the music used to accompany their exploits became more simplified.

Quincy Jones' score for *Cool Breeze* (1972)—a black reworking of the classic caper melodrama *The Asphalt Jungle* (1950)—was typical of this musical non-style, utilizing endless repetitions of three and four note progressions in a manner closer to watered-down jazz than rock. Jones' work set the pace for black action films much as Mike Curb did for motorcycle adventures.

Still the Jones sound wasn't as bad as the "scores" slapped together for films like *Slaughter's Big Rip-Off, Black Caesar, Hell Up In Harlem* and *Cleopatra Jones* (all 1973 releases). James Brown, Edwin Starr and Millie Jackson contributed (respectively) title songs for these banal shoot-em-ups, with rudimentary orchestral doodlings serving to carry the rest of each picture.

Audiences quickly tired of watching Jim Brown, Fred Williamson, Richard Roundtree, Tamara Dobson and Pam Grier go through the same old paces. As quickly as it had come, the black film (and film music) phenomenon had vanished from American film screens.

In the meantime, George Lucas' *American Graffiti* had appeared to give the use of rock on film a new emphasis. When Floyd Mutrux used rock hits of the past for the soundtrack of *Dusty and Sweets McGee* it was more or less in the spirit of novelty. When Lucas did the same in *American Graffiti* it was to create another effect entirely. The social rites and rituals of teenagers had never been examined with the seriousness and sense of detail that was shown in this film. Rock music was the cornerstone of the characters' lives, and could be heard spilling out of car radios, jukeboxes, and record players in a non-stop flow. Heard through the film of memory Lucas' film created, the old songs acquired a new force.

As the hits of Fats Domino, Bill Haley, Chuck Berry and several dozen others rolled by, it was impossible for viewers who were young when these numbers first topped the charts, not to compare the lives of *American Graffiti*'s kids with their own. Cindy Williams and Ron Howard's on-again-off-again romance, Paul Le Mat's hot rod hot shot, MacKenzie Phillips' spunky "kid sister," and all the others formed a fresco of American youth so "typical" as to be "classic." At the same time, *American Graffiti* proved that the "gimmick" of rock and roll was something of enduring cultural value.

The golden "oldies" may have lost some of their original excitement and "novelty" in the intervening years, but they gained a sense of familiarity and warmth. After *American Graffiti* the sound of rock in the movies would no longer mean that the action would have to come to a halt, or that characters were about to be threatened by dangerous forces.

A rock "nostalgia" fad came in the wake of *American Graffiti* that threatened to reduce the classics of the fifties to the level of kiddie trivia (like the "Sha Na Na" television show). Nevertheless in the right hands, these songs could be used for other than "cute" effect.

Martin Scorsese's first feature *Who's That Knocking At My Door?* (1969)—made several years before the "oldies" boom took shape—used "I've Had It" by The Bellnotes to create a sense of encroaching ominousness for a scene where the camera prowled the streets of New York's "Little Italy." A highlight of this young-love-gone-wrong story is a scene where the hero (Harvey Keitel) explains to his girlfriend (Zina Bethune) what Percy Sledge's "When A Man Loves A Woman" means to him. All of the film's dark (and subtle) hints about the ruinous effects of a strait-laced Italian upbringing—especially in regard to the double standards of acceptable male and female behavior—are mirrored in the lyrics of this soul classic.

In *Mean Streets* (1973), Scorsese again grappled with the notion of rock's power to strike a personal chord. When Harvey Keitel, playing a small-time hood, enters his neighborhood hangout, swaying to the sound of The Rolling Stones' "Tell Me," it's as if the character's narcissism is suddenly altered and lessened through self-awareness. Keitel is moving through a familiar scene, going through motions he's made a million times before. As he floats specter-like through his small private world, the song seems to express all his longing for all the close-endedness of his life to magically open up.

Hal Ashby in his two films about the sixties, *Shampoo* (1975) and *Coming Home* (1977) created a similar sense of what might be called *anti*-nostalgia. In *Shampoo*, The Beach Boys' "Wouldn't It Be Nice?," with its simple boy-loves-girl lyrics, forms an ironic counterpoint to the far from simple bedroom antics of Beverly Hills hairdresser/lothario Warren Beatty and his bevy of willing maidens (Julie Christie, Goldie Hawn, and Lee Grant).

While *Shampoo* blew the whistle on the supposed innocence of the "love generation," *Coming Home* was an attempt to come to grips with that decade's most serious conflict—the Viet Nam war. Combining Lucas's non-stop soundtrack from *American Graffiti* with Scorsese's abstract approach to lyric content, Ashby created a unique interplay of image/sound.

The music used for this romantic melodrama about a Marine officer's wife (Jane Fonda) falling in love with a paraplegic Viet Nam veteran (Jon Voight) surrounds the drama to the point of overwhelming it. Playing on a separate track that's often pitched as loudly as the dialogue, The Beatles' "Hey Jude," Simon and Garfunkel's "Bookends" and Jimi Hendrix's "Manic Depression" (among others) are rarely cued to begin and end specific sequences.

This radical musical departure occasionally undercuts the dramatic effectiveness of certain of *Coming Home*'s scenes—especially the climax where wife, lover, and husband (Bruce Dern) confront one another as The Chambers' Brothers' "Time Has Come Today" plays *very* loudly *three* times in succession.

Most of the time though, Ashby doesn't let his penchant for musical diffuseness get in the way of making specific points. *You don't know what's goin' on/you've been away for much too long* warns The Rolling Stones' "Out of Time" played at the film's outset. We *had* been away from the recent past of the Viet Nam war, and from the vantage point of 1977 *were* hard-pressed to understand anything about the toll it had taken on American life.

By the mid-seventies, use of "oldies" in dramatic films was such a standard practice that it became a virtual audio-visual cliche. Original rock scores, on the other hand, were few and far between. Unless a production had a surefire supergroup or star, a rock score for anything less than an out-and-out musical could in some ways be a liability rather than an asset.

Mike Leander's score for *Privilege* (1967), Peter Watkins' harrowing envisionment of a rock star's rise to political power, had songs ("Free Me," "Onward Christian Soldiers") that worked beautifully in terms of the film's story, but weren't the stuff of which chartbuster hits are made.

Alan Price's score for Lindsay Anderson's *O Lucky Man!* (1973) suffered for similar reasons. An elaborate Bertolt Brecht-inspired epic of "England Today," *O Lucky Man!* charts the *Pilgrim's Progress*-style adventures of a "Young Man On The Move" (Malcolm McDowell.) The drama halts periodically to make way for musical commentary from Price and his band singing—Greek chorus style—in a studio setting placed totally outside of the story proper. Price's bluesy English music hall numbers ("Poor People," "Sell Sell," "My Home Town") keep many of Anderson's (and scriptwriter David Sherwin's) more pretentious touches in check, but when songs are so firmly attached to a story they can't be sold like a "Theme From Whatever" ditty.

Songs that were easily removable from the rest of the a score, proved to be the secret of the success of *Saturday Night Fever* (1977). Others had tried this tack in the past—*Here We Go Round The Mulberry Bush* (1967) with numbers by Traffic and Manfred Mann, and *The Magic Christian* (1970) with songs by Badfinger. But it wasn't until The Bee Gees, linked with the savvy salesmanship of The Robert Stigwood Organization, that the song soundtrack in tandem with dramatic action really hit multi-platinum paydirt.

Both the sales of the soundtrack album and the attendance figures for this tale of a hardware clerk (John Travolta) who waits all week to bust loose on Saturday night at a Brooklyn disco, are among the largest in their respective industries. While The Bee Gees are invariably thought of as the composers of *Saturday Night Fever*'s score, their choir-on-helium cooing (on such numbers as "How Deep Is Your Love," "Night Fever" and "More Than A Woman"), is only part of *Saturday Night Fever*'s sound. Trammps ("Disco Inferno"), Yvonne Elliman, and overall musical orchestrator David Shire, also make significant contributions to the film's success.

After *Saturday Night Fever* a number of films attempted a similar approach including *FM* (1978), a day in the life of a radio station featuring the sounds of The Eagles, Steely Dan and Reo Speedwagon; *Xanadu*, a musical fantasy with an Electric Light Orchestra score starring Olivia Newton-John as a Greek muse; and *Where The Buffalo Roam* (1980); a strained comedy starring Bill Murray as "gonzo" journalist Hunter S. Thompson with music by Neil Young. All of these projects generated record sales, but the lines outside the theatres showing the *films* were short ones.

Thank God It's Friday (1978), a slam bang disco-set comedy (featuring an appearance by Donna Summer singing "The Last Dance"), and *Times Square* (1980) a punk/"new wave" music drama about teenage runaways, were similar failures in spite of their efforts at copying *Saturday Night Fever* in dramatic style and music marketing strategy. Two other rock films, however, taking their cue from the bad track records of post-*Saturday Night Fever* film/album package deals, found success through embracing more traditional movie musical formulas.

Fame (1980) contained a fair number of disco-flavored tunes, complimenting the film's glossy Hollywoodized depiction of student life at New York's High School for the Performing Arts. The score, written mainly by Dean Pitchford, Leslie ("It's My Party") Gore and her brother Christopher, yielded songs that topped the charts for weeks on end ("Hot Lunch Jam," the ballad "Out Here On My Own" and the title tune.)

Jeff Barry's score for *The Idolmaker* (1980), a rock and roll show biz drama of the early sixties, was *supposed* to evoke the "Philly Sound" of that era's Frankie Avalon and Fabian—who rose to fame on film charts in slightly disguised form. But with one eye on record sales charts (a reflection of the understandable caution of the film's producers), Barry's orchestrations came out sounding pure 1980. ("Here Is My Love" was the film's big hit.)

As financially successful as these two rock dramas were, the use of rock here can't compare to a film like *Quadrophenia* (1979). Utilizing pre-existent music from the 1973 Who album of the same name, this British feature centered on a sixties era "mod" (Phil Daniels) whose sense of personal alienation was so strong as to eventually drive him into a state of psychotic frenzy.

Outside of a brief shot while singing on television, The Who don't appear in the film's action, but their presence through music is so strong it carries a force equal to that of Alan Price's on-screen work in *O Lucky Man!* Likewise, rock and roll in both that film and in *Quadrophenia*, wasn't merely tacked on as a sales gimmick.

In contrast to many of the other films in this chapter, *Quadrophenia*'s music and drama don't approach one another from oblique angles. The Who's songs aren't simply support, supplement or illustration of the story. Instead, they *are* the story—in a far more dynamic way than in *Easy Rider* or *The Graduate*. *Quadrophenia*'s music and lyrics perfectly embody the confusions and desires of the central character, "Jimmy."

As he slashes and claws his way through a jungle of tedious jobs, indifferent parents and uncomprehending friends, the rock refrains we hear aren't just catchy tunes, jangling about in his brain. Their lucid anguish evokes the very blood and marrow of his being.

When "Jimmy" and his friends spin "My Generation" on a record player in a party scene, it isn't done to flatteringly self-promote The Who, for *Quadrophenia* gives real expression to that song's unforgettably bitter lyric, *Hope I die before I get old.* Daniels as "Jimmy" is the very image of violence born of squalor and boredom. With his face contorted like an enraged squirrel, and his body spasmodically jerking to the stimulation of "5:15," "Love Reign Over Me" and other Who numbers, fueled by the pep pills he pops, he's a bundle of raw nerve ends scraping against one another.

Quadrophenia's innovative use of music in drama holds out the promise of rewarding new uses for rock on film. It need not be just an optional extra or sales gimmick, but rather the heart and soul of the film itself.

Subjects for further research:
Apocalypse Now, Beware of A Holy Whore, The American Friend, Radio On, The Bitter Tears of Petra Von Kant, Caged Heat, Midnight Cowboy, Fingers, The Secret Life of Plants, Looking for Mr. Goodbar, Sorcerer, Slap Shot.

VIII

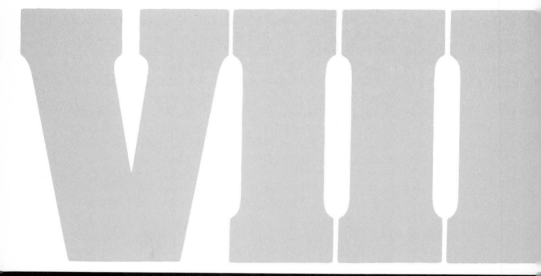

ROCKUMENTARY

CONSIDERING THE KIND of excitement a Little Richard or a Jerry Lee Lewis could generate in live performance, it's a wonder some enterprising fifties-era entrepreneur didn't just scrap the old rock musical plots altogether and concentrate instead on the music itself—say a film of one of Alan Freed's famed shows at the Brooklyn Paramount. However the time wasn't ripe for such forward thinking—nor in fact was rock music.

Back then, the available equipment was virtually unadaptable for a live concert situation, being far too complex and cumbersome. Moreover, the music of the day was geared to a quick-sell, three-minute long, 45-rpm format. A hypothetical "live" film from that era, consisting of such brief musical numbers would have been—in all its disjointedness—just as unsatisfactory as any plot-encumbered formula musical.

Only after *cinema verite* filmmakers like Jean Rouch and Richard Leacock broke new ground in experimenting with the first lightweight 16mm cameras and sound equipment (around 1960); and only after rock itself had become more musically expansive, could the free-swinging immediacy of the rock documentary become a reality.

By the mid-sixties, rock had thoroughly shattered the three-minute song time barrier, with acts like The Rolling Stones, Jimi Hendrix and The Who leading the way. The theatrical and highly personal definition of so many second generation rock acts like The Jefferson Airplane, The Grateful Dead and Big Brother and The Holding Company featuring Janis Joplin, cried out for capturing on the new film equipment.

For filmmakers these new rock spectacles provided an exciting challenge. Technical streamlining allowed cameramen to blend in unobtrusively with concert attendees. At their anonymous perches, camera operators had at their disposal perfected zoom lenses that could show performers either microscope-close or landscape-distant in a fraction of a second. Film stock had advanced to the point where once-needed mega-watt overkill was no longer mandatory for proper lighting.

Still with all the advantages and opportunities that were offered through these new approaches to rock on film, there were serious pitfalls inherent as well. No better illustration of these potential traps can be provided than that of the film that got the whole rock documentary ball rolling, *Monterey Pop* (1969).

Filmed by a number of cameramen (including Albert Maysles, Richard Leacock and Nick Proferes) overseen by director D.A. Pennebaker, this film is a record of the historic 1967 "Monterey (California) Pop and Jazz Festival"—the granddaddy of all rock fests—and as such is an indispensible document. The talent lineup is awesome—Big Brother and The Holding Company featuring Janis Joplin, The Jefferson Airplane, The Who, The Mammas and The Papas, Jimi Hendrix, Otis Redding, Eric Burdon and The Animals, and, in fact, just about everyone important in rock who didn't happen to be Elvis Presley, Bob Dylan, The Beatles or The Rolling Stones.

Yet the first time out of the gate with this new type of material, the film's makers often tripped and fell, for the sole record of the watershed musical event is frequently cluttered with unnecessary zooms, jerky pans and out-of-focus blurs. Perhaps Pennebaker and his associates only meant to lend the drug-related lyrics of certain of the performers' songs an appropriately "psychedelic" visualization. Or it could be that the filmmakers felt that these new-to-performing young talents couldn't hold a moviegoer's attention without the aid of visual lifts and spritzes. Whatever the actual intent, the result of Pennebaker and company's fuzzy, frenetic camerawork is an upstaging of the performers.

Otis Redding's unforgettably moving "Try A Little Tenderness," for example, is damaged in its transfer to the screen by Pennebaker's insistence on relying on camera angles that place the star in front of a glaring floodlight. The center of the scene then is *not* Redding, but rather the strobe effect created when the great soul singer bobs his head back and forth before this light. (This sequence is doubly distressing in light of the fact that the late Redding's work was captured on but a few scant pieces of film.)

Pennebaker's visual methods were put to better use in the film's opening sequence showing the arrival of the hippie "tribes" at the Monterey event (with Scott McKenzie's "If You're Going To San Francisco" playing in the background.) Freed from the responsibility of having to stay in one place and film a discreet event, Pennebaker's hop-skip-jump visual style works well.

As the list of concert movies lengthened on into the seventies, the temptation toward visual overkill grew even greater as rockumentary filmmakers turned to such devices as split screens and superimposition. In fact, alongside some later efforts, *Monterey Pop* appears as a model of visual poise and decorum.

The clumsily filmed *Celebration at Big Sur* (1971), for example, featured shots of Joni Mitchell singing "Woodstock" so optically altered as to make the singer virtually unrecognizable. *The Day The Music Died* (1977) created confusion by offering a collage of random rock clips with no game plan or guidance for the viewer. Likewise in *No Nukes* (1980), a film of an all-star anti-nuclear power rally, the camera is never in the right place at the right time, often missing the best moves of James Taylor, Carly Simon, Bruce Springsteen, Jackson Browne and other top performers.

Perhaps the makers of rock concert films from *Monterey Pop* on would have better served their material if they'd taken a good look at what qualifies as not only the *first* rock concert film, but also one of the best *ever* in the genre—*The T.A.M.I. Show* (1965).

This *"Teenage Music International"* awards presentation is a record of a 1964 gathering at the Santa Monica Civic Auditorium in California, which showcased both British acts (Gerry and the Pacemakers, Billy J. Kramer and the Dakotas, The Rolling Stones) and equally popular American performers (The Beach Boys, James Brown, The Supremes, Smokey Robinson and The Miracles, Marvin Gaye and Jan and Dean). *Filmed* in "Electronovision"— videotape transferred to film stock—there is a case to be made for taking exception to dubbing *The T.A.M.I. Show* a movie at all. It looks and acts just like a television special, replete with *moderne* simplistic decor, chiaroscuro lighting, and a troupe of go-go dancers wildly frugging away on and around background scaffolding *a la* TV's *Shindig*.

Still, possibly for reasons of its very primitiveness, *The T.A.M.I. Show* manages to get down on film an essential *something* that *Monterey Pop* couldn't. For example, the assurance and amusement in the eyes of Diana Ross in the face of her own *arrival* can be read easily because the camera isn't leaping all over the place. The evidence is obvious in *The T.A.M.I. Show* that black performers had finally taken the quantum leap from the last-gasp-of-vaudeville circuit they'd been confined to for so long.

In the early sixties rock music had mostly been an excuse for having a swell time, and this spirit comes across in *The T.A.M.I. Show*—especially in the great turns by James Brown and Smokey Robinson. With The Rolling Stones, it's apparent that the notion of rock as *mere* music (and live performance as just a show) is about to change drastically. The Stones at the time of *The T.A.M.I. Show* were making their first move on America, and their initial image was that of harmless ruffians—an answer to the "nice lads" aura emanating from The Beatles. In their sequence as Mick Jagger moves across the stage, his arm upraised as if to stroke the moving sea of several hundred (mostly female) fans that spread before him, there's an intimation of quasi-messianic power to come.

Nothing symbolizes this future flowering of rock power more than the Woodstock music festival, the event that served as the subject of the next major rockumentary after *Monterey Pop*—*Woodstock* (1970). By 1969 when the Woodstock event took place, rock and its practitioners had come to be so awesomely regarded that this gathering of musicians and their fans took on the significance of a religious pilgrimage or the founding of a new social order—a far cry from an earlier musical/cultural phenomenon like Benny Goodman merely blowing the lid off New York's Paramount Theatre.

As they had with the Monterey Festival, the trinity of Stones-Beatles-Dylan stayed away this time too (in spite of the fact that the event took place practically in the latter's upstate New York backyard), but scarcely anyone else of musical note begged off. The end result was like the Monterey occasion, only magnified fifty-fold, with stars like Joan Baez, Joe Cocker, Sly and the Family Stone, Crosby, Stills, Nash and Young, The Who and Jimi Hendrix among those on hand.

Filmmaker Michael Wadleigh and his crew were faced with the task of not only recording performers and whatever segment of the crowd that just might have been paying attention to the show at any given moment, but also training their cameras on the unprecedented *event* of what would become known as "The Woodstock Nation." We view a cast of hundreds of thousands as they toke, trip, flip-out, ball, blow bubbles, dance, roll in the mud and just generally *do* all the things that went along with being young, free and *hip* in the sixties.

Warner Brothers provided Wadleigh and his collaborators with all of the finest in the way of up-to-date editing and sound mixing equipment and, taking full advantage of it, the filmmakers produced what is surely the most elaborate display of split-screen imagery and stereophonic thrust ever put on the screen.

On an immediate level *Woodstock* was certainly more legible than its predecessor, *Monterey Pop*, but over the long haul of the three hours plus it takes to view it, Wadleigh's effects begin to wear the viewer down. Nevertheless the material was so strong—The Who's "Summertime Blues" and Jimi Hendrix's "Star Spangled Banner"—it made up for the film's visual excesses.

As musically enjoyable as it was, the Woodstock event was significant of certain less positive elements in the rock atmosphere. What had once only been a fifties era "guilty pleasure" had by 1970 become self-congratulatory and pretentious. Many compared Woodstock to a Nuremberg rally for teendom.

A short time later, however, this increasingly smug atmosphere would be brought down a peg or two via the notorious events at Altamont—a free San Francisco bay area Rolling Stones concert captured for the ages by Albert and David Maysles and Charlotte Zwerin in their *Gimme Shelter* (1970).

The actual event, according to The Stones, had begun innocently enough. The group wanted to climax their fabulously successful 1969 U.S. tour by staging a "Woodstock" of their own. It was to be for one day only (rather than Woodstock's weekend), and would feature such American supergroups as Santana, The Jefferson Airplane, and The Grateful Dead as musical guests of The Stones.

For security precautions, someone in The Stones' camp came up with the idea of deputizing members of the "Hell's Angels" motorcycle club as bodyguards. It was just a casual arrangement, and on paper it looked good. After all, this was the "flower power" generation, so how much actual security would The Stones require? Besides, it looked good for The Stones' bad boy image to have a flying wedge of the biggest *baddest* dudes around for protection.

Very quickly though, things began to go wrong, for at Altamont instead of the "peace" and "love" The Stones were expecting from a sea of blissed-out hippies, they were confronted with a mass of zoned-out bum-tripping hysterics. Mick Jagger had no sooner disembarked from the helicopter that brought him to the event than he was attacked by a man screaming "I hate you . . . I hate you." Meanwhile the "Angels", emissaries from a hostile, alienated subculture, stared at the wealthy, foppish Brits with a growing sense of confusion and resentment. Clearly the house of cards The Stones had erected at Altamont was set to tumble. The fall came when the "Angels"—who had been brawling with musicians and public alike—stabbed to death a black youth as he approached the stage carrying a gun.

Rockumentary films prior to *Gimme Shelter* couldn't claim to offer much in the way of food for thought. If you were drawn to a film's performers you went, if not you stayed away. *Gimme Shelter*—through this grotesque and tragic set of circumstances—became less a rock concert film than the *cinema verite* equivalent of Jacobean revenge tragedy.

The entire film came to be structured around this death, tinging everything else (including some great performance footage of a successful non-violent concert at New York's Madison Square Garden) with a sense of oncoming horror. It was in the words of Jean-Luc Godard "truth 24 times a second," but truth pushed to the extreme.

The problem was that such documentary truth could be made to lie. One shot of *Monterey Pop*, for example, shows Mama Cass Elliot mouthing "Oh Wow!," presumably in response to Janis Joplin's energetic rendering of "Ball and Chain." But the two singers are never shown together in the same frame, and one has to take it on faith that the two pieces of film (one of Joplin, the other of Elliot) are actually related in the way Pennebaker suggests. The possible "lie" in this *Monterey Pop* sequence was commented on by a number of film reviewers in a way that suggests the problems involved in getting at the "truth" of not only *Gimme Shelter*, but *Woodstock* as well.

The press presented Woodstock as "good" and Altamont as "bad." The editing in the case of the films made about them tended to reinforce these preconceived notions. The fact of the matter is that people died (albeit under less controversial circumstances) at Woodstock, and many present at Altamont (doubtless not too close to the stage) claim to have had a marvelous time there. Other factors enter into the picture as well.

"I don't wish to suggest that the 'Hell's Angels' should have been made the heroes," wrote critic Pauline Kael of *Gimme Shelter* in her book *Deeper Into Movies*, "but the fact of the matter is, they're made the patsies, while those who hired them are photographed all bland and sweet wondering how it all happened." There is, as Kael suggests, an apparently conscious attempt in *Gimme Shelter* to at least partially let The Stones off the hook through film editing techniques.

Cinematic slight-of-hand to one side, one thing that is apparent in *Gimme Shelter* is Mick Jagger's incredible power as a performer which, thanks to the Maysles clear direct treatment, comes across as effectively as if it had been witnessed in person. In the New York footage especially, all photographed from an on-stage vantage point, *Gimme Shelter* shows the wisdom of simplicity.

Even when the film gets fancy with a slow motion sequence of a scarf-

swathed Mick swirling around to the strains of "Love In Vain," it's done in a spirit that adds to, rather than detracts from the total effect. Neither the later Stones-produced *Ladies and Gentlemen, The Rolling Stones* (1974) nor Robert Frank's notorious peek at the group backstage, *Cocksucker Blues* (1976) come close to recording the Stones' star power as well as the Maysles film.

Unlike other types of show biz performers, mega-rock stars like Jagger aren't in the habit of dividing their public and private personae into nice neat packages; the potential textual interplay between film and viewer is much greater in a rockumentary than with other types of movie fare. Fans attend with highly pre-conceived notions of what they'll be seeing.

Watching Bob Dylan in *Don't Look Back* (1968) for example, as the folk-rock star dodges reporters queries about his "significance," confers with his manager Albert Grossman and plays his songs before hushed attentive crowds, makes one wonder where theatre ends and life begins. Dylan, in this clever D.A. Pennebaker rockumentary, is not *exactly* an actor, for we feel we *know* him

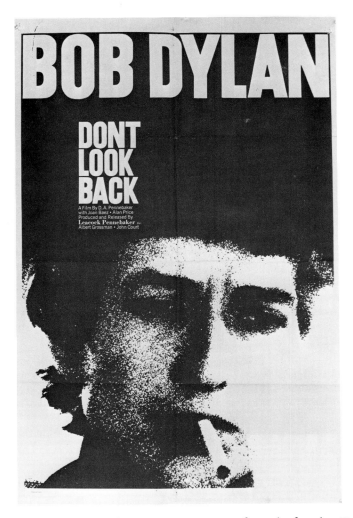

in some intimate way. Yet there's no getting away from the fact that Dylan is performing in this film both off stage and on.

Show biz savvy of a similar sort can be seen in *Lonely Boy* (1962), an early *cinema verite* short about Paul Anka, directed by Wolf Koenig and Roman Kroiter. This behind-the-scenes rock film documents fifties heartthrob, Anka, being groomed for his debut at New York's Copacabana. Although the film's poking and prying was, for the time, almost unprecedented, the singer is totally at ease before the camera. The Paul Anka on display here can already be seen becoming the glitzy Vegas-styled singer of a few years later. But whereas Anka seems accessible, the Dylan of *Don't Look Back* is totally closed off.

When Dylan tried, however, to inject his street-seer energy into a more intellectually demanding arena in *Renaldo and Clara* (1978) the results proved less satisfying. At 90 minutes *Don't Look Back* shrugged its shoulder, winked its eye and was gone. *Renaldo and Clara*, directed by Dylan, buttonholed viewers for a record (and boring) three hours and 52 minutes.

Running time wasn't the only evidence of directorial hubris in this project that was essentially a record of the singer's bi-centennial "Rolling Thunder Review." To the musical performance footage, Dylan also added loads of find-the-truth-and-reality-in-these-illusions fictional bits featuring himself his (then) wife Sara, Joan Baez, Allen Ginsburg, Ronee Blakely, Harry Dean Stanton, David Blue and a host of others. The result was an epic home movie that almost no one went to see. Audiences adept in the past at dealing with the baroque imagery of Dylan's songs just didn't have the patience to wade through a sea of would-be baroque images in this Bob Dylan's *Heaven's Gate*.

Pretensions of a similar but less extreme nature tested the loyalty of Neil Young's followers in two films he directed under the name "Bernard Shakey," *Journey Through The Past* (1973) and *Rust Never Sleeps* (1979), both of which mixed straight concert footage with fragmented fantasy bits.

Although none of the preceeding films are entirely without varying degrees of merit, their failures become most apparent when lined up alongside the no-nonsense straightforwardness of Martin Scorsese's *The Last Waltz* (1978). Essentially a filmed record of The Band's farewell 1978 performance at San Francisco's Winterland auditorium where the group shared the stage with Bob Dylan, Joni Mitchell, Muddy Waters, Van Morrison, Emmylou Harris, Neil Diamond and Neil Young, this impeccably-made feature also includes interviews with band members, and specially staged bits (featuring the Band, Harris and The Staple Singers) shot on a sound stage at M.G.M.

With the best in the way of 35mm hardware (nearly all rockumentary films are 16mm blown up to 35 for screening) Scorsese makes every moment count through meticulous planning of shots and camera moves in relation to the music. Scorsese is never so uncertain about what he's doing as to cut/cut/cut to create a false sense of movement.

The film's sole weak point is Robbie Robertson's endless harping about life "on the road." Still this shallow chatter doesn't get in the way of *The Last Waltz*'s music, the best of which is provided by The Band ("Stagefright") and Muddy Waters ("Mannish Boy"), or the Vincente Minnelli production number atmosphere of the M.G.M. soundstage scenes.

Divine Madness (1980) is an equally telling example of the still-untapped potential of 35mm rock concert movies. Though the film's star Bette Midler isn't *exactly* a rocker, to watch her in action as she runs the gamut from Broadway showstoppers to ballads with stops at punk and forties era swing in between, is to get a crash course not only in high-powered show biz, but rock and roll superstardom as well.

Director Michael Ritchie and his director of photography William Fraker know exactly how to structure their film around their star, conveying all that's *divine* in Midler's *madness*. As Franker's camera swoops across the stage midway through Midler's rendition of "Leader of The Pack," you can sense a film/performer interplay that's quite unique.

Even at their best however, conventional rockumentary films can only go so far in delving into the full impact of a rock performer. *The Kids Are Alright* (1979) and *Rude Boy* (1980) by moving away from the pure concert format reach into rock at a different and in some ways deeper level.

The Kids Are Alright, a compilation film of The Who, is made up not only of concert footage but promotional films and television appearances, all held (very loosely) together by Ringo Starr's on-screen narration. Contrasting different sorts of material filmed over a ten year period, director Jeff Stein offers Who fans a "greatest hits" package combined with an analytical breakdown of the evolution of the band's image over the years. Shots, for instance, of a young and uncertain Peter Townshend follow more recent ones of The Who leader assured and totally on top of things.

Rude Boy starring leading British punk rockers, The Clash, also breaks with, and further refines, the standard concert format by centering more than half of its attention on one of the band's real life fans—a dissolute London youth named Ray Gange. More than any other rock film yet made, *Rude Boy* tries to come to grips with the relationships of stars and fans.

The desperate circumstances of present day lower class British youth, mistrustful of "solutions" offered from both the left and right sides of the political spectrum, are laid bare in crisp, cooly-filmed tableaus. The Clash, with their sincere concern for "rude boys" like Gange, find themselves caught in the middle. With the very ability to articulate class problems through their music, they find themselves alienating the very people they wish to speak for—those like Gange who've been brought up to mistrust intellectual effort of any kind.

Rude Boy's directors, Jack Hazan and David Mingay, when focusing their cameras on The Clash's music, never stray from the stage. Consequently, we come to sense the raw energy flowing between performer and spectator—a back-and-forth participation endemic to rockers of the punk tradition.

For all the thoughtfulness that filmmakers like Scorsese, Ritchie, Stein, Hazan and Mingay have brought to rock concert films, there are still those fans who will go along with even the most rudimentary (and in some cases downright primitive) approaches to capturing their favorite rockers on film. Nearly every rock act of the last two decades has appeared in one sort of concert film or another, and film revival houses have in recent years found that there exists a healthy following for almost *all* rock and roll movies, regardless of quality.

In the wake of *Woodstock* and *Gimme Shelter*, dozens of rockumentaries began to be ground out, some focusing on a parade of performers, others on single stars. At the time of their initial release, for instance, neither *Let It Be* (1970), *The Song Remains The Same* (1976)—starring Led Zeppelin—or *The Grateful Dead Movie* (1977) were first run audience favorites. But all of these have prospered subsequently in specialty houses.

The continued popularity of Jimi Hendrix is largely a result of the fact that the singer-guitarist's appearances in *Experience* (1969), *Rainbow Bridge* (1971), *Jimi Plays Berkeley* (1971), and *Jimi Hendrix*, are in almost perpetual circulation on the revival circuit. Audiences respond to these and many other rockumentary films just as if they were at a real rock concert—applauding, smoking, and dancing in the aisles. It may not be the real, live Woodstock but it's still fun—the next best thing to having been there.

Subjects for further research:
Eat The Document, Janis, Let The Good Times Roll, The Big T.N.T. Show, Fillmore, Pink Floyd.

IX

ROCK
ACTING

ONE OF THE byproducts of Elvis Presley making his film debut in a downbeat western (*Love Me Tender*) was the shattering of Hollywood's previously held notion that rock and rollers were only of use for all-singing-all-dancing motion pictures. So successful was Elvis in this featured role, that the same studio that produced *Love Me Tender*, Twentieth-Century-Fox, soon turned to the *acting* services of teen heartthrob, Tommy Sands, for the 1958 drama, *Sing, Boy, Sing* (whose storyline, ironically, drew upon the life of Elvis).

Although not a blockbuster like the Presley film, the Sands project was successful enough to convince the movie industry that some of rock's magic could rub off onto more "serious" productions the same way it had with the jukebox musicals of the 1950's.

Today when a Bowie, Jagger or Midler do dramatic parts, the occasion in no way carries "dancing bear" overtones. Going "straight" is only thought of as a natural progression in a rocker's career, but for a few years after Sands and Presley moved on to acting, rocking thespians continued to be thought of as a novelty. In 1968 singer Roy Orbison starring in a low budget Sam Katzman western, *The Fastest Guitar Alive* caused double takes; today, no one would bat an eyelash.

Unlike Elvis, most early rocker-turned-actors had short-lived dramatic careers. As actors, both Orbison and Sands are long gone. Other rock performers also found their days as "straight" players outnumbered. Fabian, who starred in *Hound Dog Man* (1959), came and went very quickly as an actor—although the Philly rocker still crops up from time-to-time today on TV and in low budget action films. Bob Dylan was one of the stars of the ill-fated 1973 Sam Peckinpah western, *Pat Garrett and Billy the Kid*; and Dennis Wilson and James Taylor, both bit the dust as actors in one fell swoop in the highly-touted, but quickly-forgotten 1971 "road" movie, *Two Lane Blacktop*.

One other rock performer who, as an actor, came and went quickly is Ricky Nelson. He had begun in show business appearing on tv's *Ozzie and Harriet* in the early 1950's, and through that show, in 1957, Nelson became a "teenage idol" (the title of one of his hit recordings.) Because of Elvis' success in *Love Me Tender*, it isn't surprising, then, that the young singer was cast in a featured part in the 1959 Howard Hawks western classic, *Rio Bravo*. What was a surprise was how well Nelson held his own against a seasoned professional cast which included John Wayne, Dean Martin and Walter Brennan. His low-key, un-actory manner (learned from all those years on TV) proved a perfect complement to Hawks' loose, semi-improvised style of direction. Since then, however, Nelson has only made a few, scattered film appearances—even though his reviews for *Rio Bravo* were excellent.

Two early rock favorites who turned to acting and stuck with it were Bobby Darin and British star, Adam Faith.

There was nothing exceptional about singer Bobby Darin's screen debut in a frothy 1961 comedy, *Come September*. However, later that year in *Too Late Blues*, directed by John Cassavetes, Darin turned in an incredible performance as a tortured, young jazz musician that earned him strong critical acclaim. His later acting work in *Pressure Point* (1962) and *Captain Newman, M.D.* (1964), in both of which Darin played psychotics, secured his reputation as an actor, and he continued to work regularly as one until his death in 1974. At the time of his passing he was thought of by the public more as an actor than as the singer who'd popularized "Splish Splash" and "Queen of the Hop" in the late 1950's.

Adam Faith became popular as a singer in England at around the same time Darin first hit big. Then he switched to acting in 1960 with *Never Let Go*, a bleak melodrama in which he played a Teddy Boy accomplice to gangster, Peter Sellers. Although, since then, Faith has continued on as a singer, he has also shown great skill at projecting a restrained style of acting (much like Ricky Nelson's in *Rio Bravo*.) His performances as an emotionally unsettled rock supergroup manager in *Stardust* (1975) and in *McVicar* (1980) as a prison-hardened sidekick to Roger Daltry have solidified his standing as one of Britain's finer young actors.

As actors both Faith and Darin left their rock images almost entirely behind when they turned up in dramas. Mick Jagger and David Bowie, on the other hand, not only brought their images with them when they turned to drama, they expanded upon them—respectively in *Performance* (1970) and *The Man Who Fell to Earth* (1976).

Jagger has always been one of rock's more interesting paradoxes ever since The Rolling Stones first hit the musical scene in 1963. On stage he has always come off a dervish-like dynamo burning up enough energy to light up a small town. Ironically, though, the picture we have of Jagger offstage is fairly much the opposite of his performing self. In "real life" Jagger suggests a rather quiet, reserved intellectual type.

Nicholas Roeg and Donald Cammell's *Performance*, splits the difference between these two disparate Jagger "selves." In this unusual suspense melodrama Jagger plays "Turner," a sexually ambiguous rock star of the sixties (half-James Cagney, half-Marlene Dietrich) now retired to the Howard Hughes-like seclusion of his London mansion with *two* girlfriends—"Lucy" (the alarmingly androgynous Michele Breton) and "Pherber" (the voluptuous yet "butch" Anita Pallenberg.)

Into this ordered disorder of smoke, feathers and psychedelia stumbles a young hoodlum on the run, "Chas" (James Fox)—a sleek Teddy Boy embodying all the outlaw thrills "Turner" has sung about in the past. However it is the rock star rather than the criminal who has the upper hand in this collision of art and life.

"Chas" may be a societal menace, but paradoxically he still possesses more in the way of "traditional moral values" than "Turner," the ambisexual pop idol. "Turner's" little world with its drugs and free love shocks, confuses and disarms "Chas," who underneath his tough pose is actually a prim, middle-class sort of fellow.

Through it all, the Jack Nitzsche-arranged music, sung off-screen by Randy Newman, Merry Clayton and others, and on-screen by Jagger, further pumps life into a story already overflowing with "atmosphere." Mick's *performance* (in every sense of the word) of his and Keith Richard's "Memo From Turner," in a production number dream sequence hallucinated by "Chas," is the point in the film where the gangster and pop worlds finally mesh as one.

Fox is a fine actor and has no difficulty in conveying all of the complex moods of "Chas." But he's still no match for Jagger who takes total control of *Performance* every time he appears on screen. You could say that because he's an actual rock star Jagger has an acting advantage in this role, i.e. he's just "being himself." But the character of "Turner," though proceeding from Jagger's rock personality, is in most ways quite unJagger-like. For from the moment he first broke into the limelight Jagger has never shown any hint of ever wanting to call things quits and retire "Turner"-fashion; and while Jagger's off-stage self is reserved, it suggests none of the woozy trance-like delirium, occasionally rising to bursts of violent energy, of the "Turner" character.

The Man Who Fell to Earth shows off David Bowie in similar high style. Although this film has no musical numbers like *Performance*'s climactic "Memo From Turner," director Nicholas Roeg shows even more sensitivity to the nuances of rock music myth than he did in his earlier collaboration with Donald Cammell.

Just as *Performance* was made to order for Jagger, this adaptation (by Paul Mayersberg) of Walter Tevis' science-fiction novel of the same name proved ideal for the "thin white duke" of techno-rock. Bowie's music had always involved sci-fi imagery, especially in the albums *Ziggy Stardust and the Spiders From Mars, Diamond Dogs* and *The Man Who Sold the World*. His spectacular stage shows with their many costume and lighting changes went even further in playing up this "other worldly" aspect. He was, then, a "natural" for the part of Thomas Jerome Newton, visitor from some distant water-starved planet looking for help from a moisture-rich earth.

Roeg's elliptical methods for disclosing plot information—vague visual hints which slip across the screen—perfectly complement Bowie's theatrics in a style remindful of the singer's lyrics.

Like "Turner" in *Performance*, "Newton" is a passive androgyne, but the violence which surrounds him isn't his direct doing. By purposely keeping "Chas" in his home, "Turner" provokes *Performance*'s shoot-em-up finale. Newton, on the other hand, is quite unaware of the conniving business interests that lead to his downfall.

Creating an electronics empire on Earth so as to eventually be able to ship water back to his planet, "Newton" runs afoul of unscrupulous competitors who will stop at nothing to keep his all too successful ideas off the market. On a personal level, this interstellar stranger finds himself in an equally strange land. He forms a romantic attachment with an uneducated but enormously sensitive hotel chambermaid (Candy Clark) who is willing to accept him even after she discovers the truth of his origins. But with his mission a failure, "Newton" can no longer trust humankind, and he spurns her support only to collapse into alcoholic self-pity at the film's conclusion.

That these two films meshing rock myth and drama stand almost entirely alone isn't only because sympathetic sensibilities like Roeg's are difficult to come by—rock stars on the mythic level of Jagger and Bowie are in short supply. The sad truth of the matter is that with the deaths of Janis Joplin, Jimi Hendrix and Jim Morrison in 1968, the three most larger-than-life rock person-alities of the sixties were gone, and no one since then (with the exception of cer-tain punk rockers whose appeal is defiantly *anti*-star) has come forward with anything close to their charismatic power.

Two films from the late seventies, *A Star is Born* (1976) and *The Rose* (1979), were Hollywood's way of responding to the rock world's triple loss. *The Rose* took the events of Janis Joplin's storm-tossed life, threw them up in the air, and when they came down again cast Bette Midler as a too-much-too-soon-too-everything sixties mega-rocker. As "Rose" Midler ran the gamut of drugging and drinking that reached a climax of dying on stage, a human sacri-fice was given to the cause of rock and roll.

While this film was primarily about the life and hard times of Janis Joplin (in spite of its makers' denials), *A Star is Born* picked over and rummaged through the lives and myths of a host of sixties rock luminaries. As a rocker heading for a fast fade, Kris Kristofferson's "John Howard Norman" dresses like Morrison, sings like Joe Cocker, and lives in the baronial splendor of Rod Stewart. As his lady love, Barbra Streisand's "Esther Hoffman" comes off sug-gesting a composite of several singer/songwriters of the Joni Mitchell/Laura Nyro "school." In this way, the meaning is telegraphed that "Hoffman's" musical wares (unlike those of "crass" rock minstrels of the fifties) are not schlock but *art*. It's a measure of the "truth" offered up in this bleak portrait of the rock music business, that in contrast to the first and second film versions of *A Star is Born* (1937 and 1954), the lead female character does not change her name when she begins her show business career—here Streisand starts as "Esther Hoffman" and stays that way.

Both *A Star is Born* and *The Rose* work hard at trying to establish credentials as "mature," "grown-up" works. They are films about adults, not kids (even if their subject matter *is* rock and roll), and both of them attempt to deal realistically with the problems of drugs, alcohol and sexual excess. In the end, however, these projects come off as little more than rockified soap operas, for the very reason of trying too hard to portray the rock world as Serious and Respectable.

One seventies rock-*gotterdamerung did* manage, however, to convincingly show the perils of stardom.

Stardust (1975) was a sequel to an earlier and more modestly scaled rock drama, *That'll Be The Day* (1973). In the first film rock only played a marginal part in the action. The filmmaker's main goal was to take a nostalgic look at British industrial small town life in the late fifties. Starring David Essex, Keith Moon and Ringo Starr, *That'll Be The Day* concluded with Essex, as "Jim MacLaine," chucking it all, leaving wife and family behind to become a rock musician. When we rejoin him in *Stardust*, he has become the leader of "The Stray Cats" (whose other members are played by Keith Moon, Dave Edmunds, Paul Nicolas and Karl Howman.) In rapid order the group turns into an international musical phenomenon *a la* The Beatles, and Essex breaks away from the outfit to become an even bigger solo smash.

Mixing aspects of the artistic and personal lives of, (aside from The Beatles), David Bowie and Bob Dylan, *Stardust* presents a sardonic view of the paranoia and disillusionment that comes from living in the rock and roll fast lane. It's easy to merely wag a finger at the *results* of rock life excess as did *A Star is Born* and *The Rose*, but unlike those films, *Stardust* displays real knowledge of its source material that makes its message all the more convincing.

Stardust paints a picture of true *self*-destructiveness. If you go around treating people like gods, the film says, they'll eventually come to believe their deification. Essex as "Jim MacLaine" is cast adrift in a fantasy world brought on by trying to live up to his own publicity. The Midler and Streisand sagas, on the other hand, portrayed their heroines as totally at the mercy of external forces over which they had no control.

Not all backstage rock dramas present such a fatalistic picture of rock stardom however. *One-Trick Pony* and *The Idolmaker* (both 1980 releases), get their lumps in at the bitch-goddess success, but neither syringes nor "Southern Comfort" wait at the end of these rock rainbows.

In *One-Trick Pony* (directed by Robert M. Young from a script by Paul Simon, who also starred) the central character "Jonah," is a sixties folk-rocker (not at all unlike Simon) who finds it hard to adjust to the rock demands of the seventies. Though Simon-the-writer's view of his protagonist's situation is needlessly over-solemn, the film (which also features appearances by Sam and Dave, The B-52's and The Lovin' Spoonful) does manage to spotlight some of the more workaday aspects of a pop star's "glamorous" life (e.g. the boredom of travel, indifferent audiences). Likewise while the film's broadsides against a

The Fabulous Fabian In His First Motion Picture
...With That "Blue Denim" Girl!

20. Century-Fox presents

JERRY WALD'S PRODUCTION OF

HOUND-DOG MAN

COLOR by DE LUXE
CINEMASCOPE

STARRING FABIAN · CAROL LYNLEY
STUART WHITMAN · ARTHUR O'CONNELL
AND INTRODUCING DODIE STEVENS

DIRECTED BY DON SIEGEL · FRED GIPSON and WINSTON MILLER SCREENPLAY BY

disco-mad record industry are hardly daring, its emphasis on family problems of a more middle-class sort than usually associated with rock music makes for an off-beat change of pace.

The Idolmaker charts the rise and fall of an early sixties pop promoter, loosely based on Frankie Avalon and Fabian discoverer Bob Marucci (who served as technical advisor on the film). Directed by Taylor Hackford from a script by Edward Di Lorenzo, this musical drama contains as much in the way of exciting backstage action as it does in on-stage performances. As played by Ray Sharkey, manager "Vinnie Vacarri" is a rock Pygmalion with more energy and drive than either of his teen heartthrob Galateas, "Cesare" and "Tommy Dee" (Peter Gallagher and Paul Land). The film is a gleeful celebration of unabashed commercialism and savvy showmanship, totally avoiding both the "downer" overtones of The Rose and the sobersided outlook of One-Trick Pony.

Sharkey's "Vinnie" knows that "the look" is more important than actual talent when it comes to making it big in show biz, and as we watch him mold each corny gesture of "Tommy" and "Cesare" into a style, we can't help but admire his efforts as some cockeyed form of genuine artistic achievement. Over and above this, The Idolmaker captures a sense of rock spectacle that most musicals miss. In the film's best scene, when Gallagher's Fabian-styled "Cesare" faces a mob of pubescent girls who've been whipped into a sexual frenzy through "Vinnie's" promotional blitz, it almost parodies the histrionic-filled finale of The Rose. In The Idolmaker, showmanship is all that really matters; and all we have to do is sit back, relax and enjoy. Thanks to Hackford's sharp direction and Di Lorenzo's good-natured script, we can do just that. With The Idolmaker, Hollywood's view of rock and roll comes close to matching the excitement of the real thing without excess "morality play" baggage.

All of the rock dramas discussed up until now have been either fictionalized amalgams or a clef exposes of real life performers. In The Buddy Holly Story (1978) however, Hollywood for the first time took the life of a rock star and gave it the full scale glamour treatment; at times the film comes perilously close to feeling like The Glenn Miller Story.

Yet even with the massive liberties taken with the late rockabilly singer's life (especially in regard to the film's heavily idealized view of Holly's love life), The Buddy Holly Story emerges as one of the better rock dramas of recent years—thanks largely to Gary Busey's performance. Busey's musical work (he sang and played all his numbers) had a thoughtfulness and charm that made up for the film's script deficiencies, and his performance (which won him an Academy Award nomination) had a solidity and strength that held the whole film together.

As much as any rock drama discussed in this book, The Buddy Holly Story underscores Hollywood's shifting sentiments toward rock on film. It's a long way from the inanity of a Go Johnny Go and the neo-thug atmosphere of High School Confidential to the spirit of veneration this film lavishes on a rock legend like Buddy Holly.

Subjects For Further research:
Payday, Sparkle, Nashville, Lisztomania, Union City, Just A Gigolo, Carny, Shining Star.

X

ROCK FEVER
AND BEYOND

B Y THE LATE 1960's rock on film was an accepted fact, but it wasn't until 1977 with *Saturday Night Fever,* that rock movies had a *My Fair Lady*—that is, a box office blockbuster of absolutely epic proportions. Next to this Robert Stigwood production, even the profits from the extremely lucrative Elvis and Beatles debut films look meager.

Based on a *New West Magazine* article about a Brooklyn discotheque, *Saturday Night Fever* couldn't have come along at a better time. In larger U.S. cities, Latins, blacks and homosexuals had taken to the dance floor in aggressive high style; and "cafe society," always on the lookout for a new thrill, had followed suit. Tales of the "beautiful people" bumping-and-grinding their cares away began appearing in mass circulation magazines and television shows, spreading the news of disco far and wide. To those living in the "boondocks," however, this new-style light fantastic tripping seemed a dream out of reach. What the "new journalism" styled article by Nik Cohn suggested to the Robert Stigwood Organization, *Saturday Night Fever*'s producers, was a way to recast the disco *demi-monde* into a more acceptable "mass audience appeal" form.

Detailing the lives of young people frequenting the "2001 Odyssey" disco, the Cohn article painted a picture of violence and down-and-out despair relieved only by drugs and the fleeting sense of glory provided by a Saturday night's worth of disco-ing. Norman Wexler's script cleaned up some of the seamier aspects of the original article, and John Badham's directions gave the whole show a lush dreamy patina, resulting in a film that offered both realism *and* glamour.

However it was the combination of the film's two other important elements—John Travolta's performance in the leading role and The Bee Gees' music, that put *Saturday Night Fever* over the top.

Travolta (a familiar figure with teenagers from his appearances on *Welcome Back Kotter*) made such an impact in the film he became the subject of much discussion comparing his "star quality" to Dietrich, Gary Cooper and many others. But while Travolta *is* impressive, his success wouldn't have been possible without the musical context supplied for him by The Bee Gees. (When Travolta turned up without the group's music in *Moment By Moment* and *Urban Cowboy*, response to the actor was nowhere near as enthusiastic).

Producer Stigwood had been managing The Bee Gees for a number of years prior to *Saturday Night Fever*, so their inclusion in the film's overall "package" was hardly coincidental. But these musical brothers, so popular in the mid-sixties, had by the mid-seventies found public response to their songs on the wane.

Thanks to disco, however, in the period just prior to *Saturday Night Fever*, they were beginning to make a comeback. They'd had a hit single, "Nights On Broadway;" and its sound of falsetto coos over a lush throbbing beat, would set the pace for the music used later in *Saturday Night Fever*. The Bee Gees' sound meshed perfectly with the character Travolta played, "Tony Manero"—paint store clerk by day, disco king by night. You could go so far as to say that The Bee Gees' music was the real star of the film. But an in-person appearance by the group wasn't necessary. When Travolta danced he literally *became* The Bee Gees and their music.

A disco-curious America couldn't have asked for more, for here was all the glitz and glamour of "the scene" but without its sense of upper-class social intimidation.

While the film's box office bullseye was the upshot of many months of carefully planned media strategy on the part of RSO, certain factors necessary for the film's unprecedented success had been evolving for some time. The public had been much hungrier for trends and *sounds* than for specific stars for several years prior to disco's emergence. The *phenomenon* of Woodstock, for example, was more a source of interest than the actual music made there; and the dominance of musical trends in addition to disco (and at the expense of mega-stars in general) since the mid-seventies (i.e. punk, reggae, country and western) is further evidence of this new attitude of pop/rock and its audience.

Though *Saturday Night Fever did* punch all the right buttons in satisfying the disco needs of the largest possible public (it wasn't just a hit with kids), many of the similarly-styled projects following in its wake failed to cash in on that movie's hit film/soundtrack formula.

The stakes were so high that casting around for just the right combination of elements became progressively more complicated. For example, Hollywood turned to rock-oriented Broadway musicals like *The Wiz* (1978) and *Hair* (1979) to remake into "feverish" movie/recording events. But neither the Diana Ross version of *The Wizard of Oz* nor Milos Forman's adaptation of the long-running "tribal love-rock musical" set public temperatures rising.

Can't Stop the Music (1980), though it did have an original screenplay also failed, for disco novelty recording act, The Village People, did not have the *movie* future predicted by the film's makers.

Influential director, Robert Altman *(MASH, Nashville)* met a similar rock Waterloo with *A Perfect Couple* (1979), featuring Keepin' em off the Streets, a group he'd nurtured. This mix of a Woody Allen-styled romantic mismatch (Paul Dooley and Marta Heflin) with the backstage struggles of an up and coming rock band proved unattractive to audiences, especially since "Streets" hadn't any prior public exposure.

Even Robert Stigwood lost his magic touch with *Sgt. Pepper's Lonely Hearts Club Band* (1978), an elaborate visualization of The Beatles classic concept album with a cast that included The Bee Gees, Earth, Wind and Fire, Peter Frampton, Alice Cooper and Billy Preston. In spite of a huge publicity build-up almost no one went to see this rock vaudeville show.

While it is true that bad judgement, miscalculation and just plain old-fashioned ineptitude all played a part in the failure of these projects, there's still the show business crapshoot factor to consider. Otherwise how else to explain winners like *Grease* (1978) and *The Blues Brothers* (1979).

Grease was supposed to evoke the doo-wop era of leather jackets and poodle skirts, but this Robert Stigwood/Allan Carr co-production based on the Broadway musical of the same name ended up looking more eighties disco than fifties malt shoppe. *The Blues Brothers*, based on John Belushi and Dan Ackroyd's sunglassed white hipster routine on *Saturday Night Live*, was supposed to be a tribute to the black rhythm and blues tradition, but its grotesque comic trappings totally swamped the guest star performances of such noted r & b greats as Aretha Franklin, James Brown and Ray Charles.

Neither of these films were any better than "Sgt. Pepper," but where the high powered marketing strategy for that film failed, the ones used for *Grease* and *The Blues Brothers* somehow connected.

While those heavily ballyhooed spectaculars were off making their megabucks, one historically accurate and musically sincere evocation of rock's past got lost in the shuffle. Directed by Floyd Mutrux, *American Hot Wax* (1978) took on all the cliches of early jukebox musicals (e.g. *Shake, Rattle and Rock*) and reworked them through humor, but it never descended to the elbow-in-the-ribs level of *Grease*.

Purportedly depicting a week in the life of legendary rock promoter/deejay Alan Freed, *American Hot Wax* is climaxed by a re-creation of one of Freed's famed Brooklyn Paramount shows featuring "live" performances by Chuck Berry, Jerry Lee Lewis and Screamin' Jay Hawkins, among others. Mixing nostalgia with an updated understanding of rock and roll's energy, the film forcefully demonstrates why rock's power to effect its listeners' lives has lasted so long. In one early scene which details the excitement surrounding a rock recording session, Mutrux's camera quickly cuts between the performers in the studio and their friends and fans on the other side of the glass partition. You can hardly tell them apart, for the barrier between audience and performer has been shattered by the energy of rock and roll.

Throughout the 1970's, while recording and filmmaking interests were searching for trends in music to capture the public's fancy, a sub-cultural phenomenon had sprung up bringing with it a trend all its own. *The Rocky Horror Picture Show* (1975) had come along to inspire a cult whose enthusiasm and devotion continues to this day.

Movie cults, of course, are nothing new. Just prior to "Rocky Horror's" arrival, two "non-conformist" lifestyle tales, *King of Hearts* (1967) and *Harold and Maude* (1971), with music by Cat Stevens, had found followings on the college film circuit. Years earlier, *Beat the Devil* and *All About Eve* showings were accompanied by audiences shouting out favorite lines.

But *The Rocky Horror Picture Show* and *its* cult was a different matter. Audiences didn't just go to it to cheer their favorite moments and repeat the dialogue by heart; instead they went so far as to interpolate *new* dialogue and to *act out* scenes with an elaborate array of props and costumes brought along to screenings.

As a hit stage production, *The Rocky Horror Show* began in London in 1973. Shortly afterwards it opened on Broadway and was a resounding flop. But record/film producer, Lou Adler (who had bought the film rights) didn't let the New York disaster stop him from going on to make the movie version. With "Picture" added to its title, the film opened in 1975 and at first seemed destined for the same fate as the New York stage production.

But when it surfaced on the midnight movie circuit, the totally unexpected happened—*The Rocky Horrow Picture Show* became an enormous hit. (The first showing was at New York's Waverly Theatre, but it has since gone on to play weekly at some 200 sites nationwide.)

"Rocky Horror's" theatrical origins account, in part, for the audience/movie screen interface, for when the rock musical with music and lyrics by Richard O'Brien, was transferred to film, the actors in the screen version (somewhat like in a play) directed their gestures toward a movie camera. The upshot of all this highly stylized "acting up" with its stagey pauses was that *Rocky Horror* seemed to cry out for some sort of reaction on the part of the audience. And it got it!

Combining bi-sexual chic with a send-up of Hammer horror films, *The Rocky Horror Picture Show* is made up of an almost constant barrage of loving rock parody. As mad scientist, "Dr. Frank N. Furter," Tim Curry, in high heels, a corset and mascara, runs through almost every rock gesture, stance and pose imaginable. Curry's energy and enthusiasm are so infectuous it's no wonder so many got totally caught up in his performance. It's as if he were saying, "You too can be a rock star." And all across the U.S., every Friday and Saturday night, many thousands of (mostly) teenagers take him up on his implied promise. It's all "outrageous" and yet essentially harmless.

In the years following *Rocky Horror* a new rock music movement emerged to take up "Dr. Frank N. Furter's" cry of "Don't dream it, be it!"—punk rock.

Punk first took hold in an economically depressed British lower middle-class. Groups like The Sex Pistols and The Clash sported a defiance that seemed to harken back to the roots of rock and roll. But whereas Little Richard and Jerry Lee Lewis merely tweaked at propriety and social conventions, these new groups (which also included such colorfully named bands as The Electric Chairs, The Stranglers and Siouxsie and The Banshees) were out to indict the entire culture. The Clash produced (and continue to produce) songs in the best tradition of British social comment. But with the majority of other punk bands, The Sex Pistols' dead-ended attention-getting nihilism was the rule. Convulsive, unfocussed rage is a good opening gambit, but when you can't follow it up with new ideas burn-out is the end result.

Nevertheless this kamikaze style of performing and living has captured the imagination of a sizeable portion of British and U.S. youth.

The Sex Pistols were together as a band for a little more than a year-and-a-half, but their legend lives on thanks largely to the films made about them. *The Great Rock and Roll Swindle* (1980) was to have been The Pistols' *A Hard Day's Night*, but halfway through its production the group began to come apart at the seams. Originally it was conceived as a musical spoof called *Who Killed Bambi?*, to be directed by softcore sex king, Russ Meyer. Instead, the film turned into a documentary parody (directed by Julian Temple) about the rise and fall of the band. Rather than The Pistols' leader Johnny Rotten, Malcolm McLaren, the group's manager, is the center of this haphazardly constructed (but often very funny) lecture/demonstration on how to create a rock and roll sensation.

Claiming that The Sex Pistols were a fraud from the very beginning, McLaren explains in the film how he created "cash from chaos" by pandering to the media's desire for sensationalism. The Pistols' infamous U.K. television interview where they scandalized the nation by using four letter words on the air is the centerpiece of *The Great Rock and Roll Swindle*, and this is juxtaposed with concert and club appearances, interviews with punk fans, animated cartoons and a spy adventure sub-plot.

D.O.A. (1980), a documentary of the U.S. tour that spelled The Pistols' demise as a working unit, is even more of a mixed bag. Lech Kowalski, the director, combines Pistols film with scenes of other punk bands (X-Ray Spex, Sham '69) and fans talking about the meaning of it all. Disorganized and occasionally incoherent, this film nevertheless manages to convey a sense of the atmosphere surrounding The Sex Pistols during their seven-city '78 U.S. tour.

THE DECLINE . . . of western civilization (1980), a similar mixture of concert and interview footage, is just as informative as *D.O.A.*, though better assembled, largely because director Penelope Spheeris confined her study to Los Angeles bands (The Germs, Black Flag, "X" and others) and fans.

Even more home-made and rawer-looking are the super-8 dramatic films springing out of the punk movement. Deliberately unfocussed and grainy, these rough-hewn assemblages attempt to reflect, visually, the anarchy of the music they're involved with.

Rome '78 (1978), a spoof of Hollywood spectaculars featuring Lydia Lunch of Teenage Jesus and The Jerks, and *Underground U.S.A.* (1980), a Warhol-inspired reworking of *Sunset Boulevard* (with new music by The Lounge Lizards) are two of the best of these low-budget wonders. More about the "scene" than the music itself, these films offer an insider's view of punk. If you know the codes and lore, in all likelihood you'll get caught up in the action;

otherwise, you can find yourself lost at sea—just like at a showing of *The Rocky Horror Picture Show* attended by the uninitiated.

However, such willful primitivism isn't the only possible route to take in carrying on the spirit of rock rendition, as shown by *Rock and Roll High School* (1979). This "New World Pictures" production takes the teen rock/sock hop movies of the fifties (the kind that used to star Sandra Dee, John Saxon and Sal Mineo) to their ultimate logical conclusion, i.e. burning down the high school (in this instance "Vince Lombardi High.")

Back in the fifties, rock and roll films about teenagers almost invariably ended on a rosy note. What was going on underneath, though, was a sociological sell-out. Still, those sunny smiles from the teens and nods of approval from authority figures (parents, principals, teachers, police) just before fade-out time didn't really fool anyone. All the moral posturings had to be endured for the trade-off of some choice turns from Jerry Lee Lewis or Eddie Cochran.

In *Rock and Roll High School* (directed by Allan Arkush), this fifties tradition is turned inside out, for at one and the same time, this low-budget effort manages to operate as: 1. a devastating satire of jukebox musicals; 2. a sociopolitical statement (the part where they burn down the high school . . . yeaa!); 3. an in and out of itself moderately engaging story where—thanks to talented performers like P.J. Soles, Paul Bartel and Mary Woronov—you *care* about the characters; and most importantly 4. a vehicle for the presentation of several first-rate musical sequences featuring premiere New York punk rockers, The Ramones.

Rock and Roll High School proves that after all these years, with the multitudes of musical stars and trends that come and go, it's still possible to make a rock and roll film in the same spirit of unpretentious fun as *The Girl Can't Help It*. It's the fan's reward for a quarter of a century of sitting in the dark, patiently waiting for the *good parts* of these hundreds of films—the parts where it's all just good old rock and roll.

Subjects for further research:
The Harder They Come, Breaking Glass, Cha Cha, The Kids Are United, The Blank Generation, The Punk Rock Movie.

XI

MOST OF THE FILMS dealt with in this book's two main sections are productions containing heavy doses of rock and roll music, distributed (in most instances) on an international basis, and generally available for viewing on television or in movie theatres. In addition to these films however, there is a sub-category of rock or rock-related film deserving of passing mention. Some of these more marginal items presently exist only in the hands of private collectors, while others were national or regional releases not intended for distribution outside their area or country of origin.

Many American made films, for example, are hard to come by even in the states. *Hawaiian Boy* (1959) with Carl Perkins and *The Legend of Bo Diddley* (1966), a featurette displaying the unique talents of the great rock/blues guitarist are two such hard-to-get-ahold-of items. Among the rock films that never made it out of the southern U.S. drive-in circuit (like *Rock Baby Rock It*, mentioned in our rock film guide) is *Bootleggers* (1974), with music by Dorsey Burnette, and an especially arcane little item called *Blast-Off Girls* (1966) a *very* low budget sci-fi spoof set to a rock and roll backbeat. In the same financial league is *Pelvis* (1975) a barely/rarely shown send-up of (vaguely) Elvis. Also put together for fast play-off of a different kind were two compilation films from the late fifties: *Rock and Roll Review*, featuring The Crew Cuts, and *Harlem Rock and Roll* with The Clovers and Joe Turner.

Among the nations having their own strictly not-for-export rock films is Israel with its series of *American Graffiti*-like features called *Lemon Popsicle* (#1, #2, #3, etc.) And Italian audiences couldn't get enough of *Rock and Roll* (1979), a feature very similar in tone to *Saturday Night Fever* (only Italian-style).

But of all countries with an active regional rock cinema, the foremost is Great Britain (especially in the late fifties and early sixties) where Elvis-inspired rockers Cliff Richard and Tommy Steele had long-running movie careers. Steele's credits include: *Kill Me Tomorrow* (1957), *The Duke Wore Jeans* (1958), *Tommy The Toreador* (1959) and *It's All Happening* (1963). Later he abandoned rock entirely for mainstream musical comedy and starred in the U.S. produced musicals *Finian's Rainbow* (1968) and *Half A Sixpence* (1969). Richard's films include: *Serious Charge* (1959), *The Young Ones* (1961), *Summer Holiday* (1963), *Rhythm 'n Greens* and *Wonderful Life* (both 1964) and *Finders Keepers* and *Two A Penny* (both 1967).

Billy Fury who went on to later star in the successful *That'll Be The Day*, had earlier hits with *Play It Cool* (1962) also featuring the popular Helen Shapiro, and *I've Got A Horse* (1965). Like Richards' and Steele's films these Fury features were similar in tone to such lightweight American pop productions as *Rock Pretty Baby*. British rocker Adam Faith's features on the other hand were most often downbeat dramas like *Mix Me A Person* (1961) and *Never Let Go* (1963).

Other British productions geared toward the local market include *The Golden Disc*, starring Terry Dene and Nancy Whiskey; *Rock You Sinners*, featuring Tony Crombie, Don Lang and Art Baxter (both produced in 1957); *Climb Up The Wall* (1960) with Craig Douglas and Russ Conway; *What A Crazy World* (1963) with Joe Brown and Freddie and The Dreamers; *It's All Over Town* (1964) with The Springfields and The Hollies; *Just for You* (also 1964) featuring the Applejacks and Al Saxon and The Orchids; and *Disk-O-Tek Holiday* (1966), a filmed vaudeville which presented such U.S. acts as The Chiffons and Freddie Cannon as well as British groups like The Merseybeats, The Vagrants and The Warriors.

Even after the rock and roll world was given a new lease on life by the "British Invasion," England continued on with productions designed primarily for home consumption. Some of these more recent films include *Pop Down* (1968) with Zoot Money and Brian Auger; *Rope Ladder To The Moon* (1969) with Jack Bruce and John Mayall; *Glastonbury Fayre* (1973) featuring Terry Reid and Fairport Convention; and the latter group also appeared in a 33 minute documentary, *Fairport Convention and Matthew's Southern Comfort* (1970). *Rory Gallagher—Irish Tour '74* and *Side By Side* with Mud and The Rubettes are two 1975 productions that played primarily local engagements in Britain, as did *Slits Pictures* (a long-ish promo film featuring the all-girl group The Slits) and another punk rock oriented production *Crash 'n Burn*. Both of these films were 1979 releases.

Like the English, the French have turned out a number of films that have bypassed foreign distribution, among them: *Cinema Pas Mort Monsieur Godard* (1978) a ninety minute documentary featuring clips of Patti Smith and The Doors, and several features starring France's answer to Cliff Richard—Johnny Hallyday—such as *D'Ou Viens-Tu Johnny* (1963). Similarly, a Canadian-made film with music by Ron Lane and Ron Wood, *Mahoney's Last Stand*, hasn't been shown much outside of Canada.

Besides the other soundtrack scores by rockers mentioned elsewhere in this book, it should be noted that B.B. King provided background music for Russ Meyer's court room drama *The Seven Minutes* (1971), Country Joe McDonald did the score for the Swedish-produced film of Henry Miller's *Quiet Days In Clichy* (1969), and that the music of Pink Floyd was used for the surfing documentary *Crystal Voyage* (1974).

As we've also mentioned elsewhere, the music used for most blacksploitation films has only a tenuous connection to rock and roll (i.e. a chunk-a-funk beat, glissando strings and some occasional souful wailings by one soul star or another). Some additional scores falling into this category include: *Black Samson* (1975) with music by Allen Toussaint; *Cleopatra Jones* (1973) with its Millie Small and Joe Simon vocals; and *Together Brothers* (1974) scored by Barry White.

With music much more in a rock vein (but still tending to come under the heading of twilight/obscure/regional/gone with the wind, etc.) are such items as: *Somewhere Between Heaven and Woolworths*, with The Easybeats; *Harry and Ringo's Night Out* (1974), a short with Harry Nilsson and Ringo Starr; *The Lone Ranger* (1968), a twenty minute film with music by Pete Townshend; *Stunt Rock* (1978) with an appearance by the Swedish group Sorcery; *The Music Machine* (1979) a British *Saturday Night Fever* variant; and *Supershow* (1970), a concert film heavy on non-rock, but with appearances by Colliseum, Led Zeppelin, Eric Clapton and Jack Bruce.

Strictly for the fringe list are items like *2000 Years Later* (1969) with Monte Rock III; a Mickey Dolenz appearance in a beyond the pale comedy called *Keep Off, Keep Off* (1975) and a straight (i.e. non rock) Joey Dee musical, *Two Tickets To Paris* (1962).

As for rock stars in dramatic parts, in addition to the others mentioned elsewhere, a tip of the hat to Lulu for her fine performance in *To Sir With Love* (1967)—where she also sang the title song. The Band's Levon Helm was also a standout as country and western star Loretta Lynn's father in *Coal Miner's Daughter* (1980). Another country-music tinged project was *Honeysuckle Rose* (1980) with Willie Nelson in the lead. (He was also the center of the 1977 documentary, *Willie Nelson's Fourth of July Picnic*, which also featured Leon Russell, Waylon Jennings and Doug Kershaw.)

Though television productions are outside the parameters of our research, we feel attention should be paid if *Deadman's Curve* (1978) a biodrama of singers Jan and Dean starring Richard Hatch and Bruce Davison, or *The Heroes of Rock and Roll* (1980) a compilation film produced by Malcolm Leo and Andrew Solt narrated by Jeff Bridges, should pop up on your tv screen. Likewise the British series *Rock Follies* (1975), Howard Stein's wonderful show biz satire starring Julie Covington and the one and only Rula ("I've been showing some friends round London!") Lenska with songs by Roxy Music's Andrew Mackay is must-see "televiewing" (as is its sequel, *Rock Follies '77*).

Moving outward toward more elusive films once again, there was a Becker and Fagin (Steely Dan) score for a barely released 1971 film featuring Richard Pryor called *You Gotta Walk It Like You Talk It (or You Lose That Beat)*. Even more esoteric is *Under My Thumb* (1969), a *silent* (we repeat, *silent*) film of The Rolling Stones' Hyde Park Concert. At least Brenda Lee could be heard in her one motion picture appearance, *Two Little Bears* (1961), which also featured Soupy Sales.

Other odds and ends: *Be Glad For The Song Has No Ending* (1969), starring the arty folk-rock ensemble The Incredible String Band; German actor director Ulli Lommell's *The Blank Generation* (1980)—not to be confused with Amos Poe's film of the same name—starring Richard Hell, Carole Bouquet and Andy Warhol; *5 + 1* (1968) featuring the unlikely combination of the Stones Hyde Park concert footage and a clip of Johnny Hallyday; and *Winter A Go Go* (1965) with Joey Lyman and The Reflections and the ever-popular Nooney Rickett Four!

Finally—last but not least—let us not forget that Neil Sedaka made an even *worse* movie than *Decoy For Terror* called *Sting of Death* . . . . a film so obscure it *might* not even be in the hands of private collectors.

THE FILMS

FOR SYMBOLS

TITLE (Year)

M—Musical or comedy
D—Drama
R—Rockumentary/Documentary
Color—Black/White

- Screenplay
- Director
- Producer
- Studio
- Time
- Stars
- Featuring
- Soundtrack

Abbreviations for Studios

AIP	American International Pictures
COL	Columbia
DCA	Director's Corporation of America
MGM	Metro Goldwyn Mayer
PAR	Paramount
UA	United Artists
UI	Universal International
WB	Warner Brothers

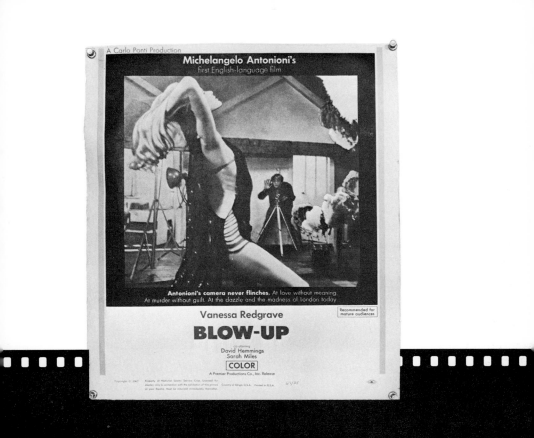

ABBA The Movie (1977)

    R—Color
- Lasse Hallstrom
- Lasse Hallstrom
- Stig Anderson, Reg Grundy
- WB
- 95m.
- ABBA

    Visual record of ABBA's 1977 Australian tour, with fictional subplot of reporter trying to secure an interview with the Swedish stars. Even though ABBA is often billed as "the most popular group in the world," this film has had only limited distribution in the U.S. Included are some of their marshmallow-rock classics such as "Dancing Queen," "The Name of The Game" and "S.O.S."

AC/DC: Let There Be Rock (1980)

    R—Color
- Eric Dionysius, Eric Mistler
- High Speed Films
- 94m.

✪ AC/DC

Filmed coverage of Australian band AC/DC's '78 appearances in Belgium and Paris intercut with quasi-fictional interludes.

ALABAMA (1969)

    D—Color / B/W
- Wim Wenders
- Wim Wenders
- Wim Wenders
- Hochschule (Germany)
- 25m.
- Paul Lys, Werner Schroeter, Muriel Schrat

According to writer-director Wenders, "It's a story and it's *not* a story . . . The subject is death. You could say that much about the story: it deals with death. In the end the camera is dying . . . you see the camera dying which means a very very slow fadeout." *Whatever*, this moody fragmented narrative of people wandering around Berlin is about, there's a lot of music on its soundtrack: the title number by jazzman John Coltrane, the Stones' "2000 Light Years From Home," and two versions of "All Along The Watchtower," one by Bob Dylan (the original) and another by Jimi Hendrix. "You might say," Wenders continues, "that the film is about the difference between 'All Along The Watchtower' when Bob Dylan sings it from the way Jimi Hendrix sings it."

ALICE IN THE CITIES (1974)

    D—B/W
- Wim Wenders
- Wim Wenders
- Joachim von Mengershausen
- New Yorker Films
- 110m.
- Rudiger Vogler, Yella Rottlander, Lisa Kreuzer
- Chuck Berry

A German journalist gets saddled with a precocious youngster on a trip from New York to Holland. Writer-director Wenders has shown sensitivity to the "found poetry" of rock songs in all of his films. In the opening of this charming "road" movie, the hero is discovered singing "Under The Boardwalk"—while sitting under the boardwalk at Coney Island. Near the end, Chuck Berry can be seen singing "Memphis Tennessee" at a concert in Holland that the characters attend.

ALICE'S RESTAURANT (1969)

    D—Color
- Venable Herndon
- B/O the song "Alice's Restaurant Massacre" by Arlo Guthrie
- Arthur Penn
- Joe Manduke, Hillard Elkins
- UA
- 110m.
- Arlo Guthrie, Pat Quinn
- Jeff Outlaw, Pete Seeger
- UA

A hippie commune and restaurant serves as a haven for draft evader, Guthrie, in this episodic sixties serio-comedy. Arlo's famed talking blues, "Alice's Restaurant Massacre" is better when heard on record, than *seen* in this dramatic reenactment. Film features use of a Joni Mitchell composition, "Song to Aging Children," in a touching scene which takes place in a graveyard.

ALL THIS AND WORLD WAR II (1976)

R—Color / B/W
- ■ Susan Winslow
- ▦ Sandy Lieberson
- ☎ TCF
- ● 88m.
- ○ TCF

Beatles' "significance" pushed to the breaking point in this bizarre documentary that juxtaposes their songs—sung by a number of rock stars—with World War II newsreel footage. Helen Reddy sings "Fool On The Hill" while Hitler relaxes at Bertchtesgaden. Rod Stewart husks "Get Back" while Nazi troops goose step. Others heard include The Bee Gees ("She Came in Through The Bathroom Window"), Tina Turner ("Come Together"), Leo Sayer ("I Am The Walrus"), Bryan Ferry ("She's Leaving Home"), Frankie Valli ("A Day in The Life"), and Elton John ("Lucy in The Sky With Diamonds").

ALMOST SUMMER (1978)

D—Color
- ➤ Judith Berg, Sandra Berg, Martin Davidson and Marc Reid Rubel
- ■ Martin Davidson
- ▦ Rob Cohen
- ☎ UI
- ● 89m.
- ○ Bruno Kirby, Lee Purcell, John Frederich, Didi Conn, Tim Matheson
- ➔ Fresh
- ○ MCA

Brian Wilson of the Beach Boys co-penned the title tune and one other, ("It's O.K.") for this film which starts as a light satire about high school elections, but quickly turns (for the worse) into a "serious" study of youthful values. Other soundtrack sounds include "Cruisin' " and "Sad Sad Summer," written and sung by Mike Love; and "We Are The Future" sung by High Inergy. Fresh appear at a dance scene singing "Summertime" and "She Was A Lady." Music by Charles Lloyd and Ron Altbach.

AMERICAN FRIEND, THE (1977)

D—Color
- ➤ Wim Wenders
- ▮ *Ripley's Game* by Patricia Highsmith
- ■ Wim Wenders
- ▦ Pierre Cottrell
- ☎ New Yorker Films
- ● 123m.
- ○ Dennis Hopper, Bruno Ganz
- ➔ Nicholas Ray, Samuel Fuller

The character played by Hopper promises Ganz he'll bring the Beatles back to Hamburg if Ganz will aid him in some shady dealings. Ganz is seen soulfully singing along to The Kinks' "Too Much on My Mind" in one scene (other Kinks sounds are heard in the background at other points) in this sleekly mounted modern *film noir.*

AMERICAN GIGOLO (1980)

D—Color
- Paul Schrader
- Paul Schrader
- Jerry Bruckheimer, Freddie Fields
- PAR
- 117m.
- Richard Gere, Lauren Hutton
- Casablanca

A high class call boy (Gere) is framed for a murder rap, but the wife (Hutton) of a prominent senator, sacrificing her own good name, saves him at the last minute. Rock, for the first time, appears as an artifact on film of "the good life." Gere cruises SoCal freeways as Blondie's "Call Me" blasts forth from a Mercedes car radio. Smokey Robinson's "The Love I Saw in You Was Just a Mirage" is also heard, as well as are several other songs written for the film by its musical director, Georgio Moroder.

AMERICAN GRAFFITI (1973)

D—Color
- George Lucas, Willard Huyck and Gloria Katz
- George Lucas
- Francis Ford Coppola and Gary Kurtz
- UI
- 110m.
- Ron Howard, Richard Dreyfuss, Cindy Williams, Harrison Ford, Suzanne Somers, MacKenzie Phillips, Paul LeMat, Candy Clark, Charles Martin Smith and Wolfman Jack
- MCA

Twenty-four hours in the lives of a group of California small town teenagers in the film that (though set in the sixties) almost singlehandedly invented fifties rock and roll nostalgia. If George Stevens had directed a beach party movie, it might have looked something like this. Rock fills the air from beginning to end in this semi-classic that helped bring youth flicks to a new respectable plateau. Among the sounds spun by dee-jay Wolfman Jack are such inarguable classics as "Why Do Fools Fall in Love?" by Frankie Lymon and the Teenagers, "Little Darlin'" by The Diamonds, Fats Domino's "Ain't That A Shame," and Chuck Berry's "Johnny B. Goode." Other well-known numbers heard include "Green Onions," "The Stroll," "Teen Angel," "Get A Job," "To The Aisle," "All Summer Long," "Since I Don't Have You" and "Do You Wanna Dance?" Note: When the film was re-released in 1979 certain sequences, originally cut due to the insistence of Universal's top brass, were put back in by director Lucas; so great was his clout after the success of *Star Wars.*

AMERICAN HOT WAX (1978)

M—Color
- John Kaye
- Floyd Mutrux

Art Linson
PAR
91m.
Tim McIntire, Laraine Newman
Chuck Berry, Jerry Lee Lewis, Screamin' Jay Hawkins
A & M

Robert Altman-esque week in the life of pioneer rock dee-jay, Alan Freed. Cheerful, if somewhat over-reverential, overview of rock's beginnings recycles the shared plotline of all those 50's musicals about irate town fathers and mothers trying to shut down rock and roll. The myth of Freed (and rock) endlessly reflects back and forth in an infinite hall of mirrors to extremely satisfying results! Sparked by Jerry Lee Lewis thrashing out "Whole Lotta Shakin' Goin' On" and "Great Balls of Fire;" Chuck Berry duck-walking and wailing his way through "Reelin' and Rockin'" and Screamin' Jay Hawkins howling out "I Put a Spell On You,"—all in a specially staged live concert sequence. Atmospheric soundtrack music by Jackie Wilson, Buddy Holly, The Drifters, The Moonglows, The Cadillacs, The Turbans, The Spaniels, The Elegants and The Zodiacs.

AMERICAN POP (1981)

M—Color
Ronni Kern
Ralph Bakshi
Martin Ransohoff, Ralph Bakshi
COL
MCA

Animation used to tell the story of four generations of an American family and the music they (and by extension the entire nation) were involved with. Though the musical eras portrayed run all the way from vaudeville to new wave, the film concentrates heavily on contemporary sounds. Some of those used in conjunction with Bakshi's none-too-impressive rotoscope animation techniques include: Pat Benatar's "Hell is For Children," Fabian's "Turn Me Loose," The Doors' "People Are Strange" and Big Brother's "Summertime." The final blowout production number is done to Bob Seger's "Night Moves"—the dubious implication being that this song represents the alpha and omega of American Pop to date. (An okay song, but music of the spheres it's not!)

AMERICATHON (1979)

M—Color
Neil Israel, Monica Johnson, Michael Mislove
an idea by Neil Israel, Peter Bergman, Philip Proctor
Neil Israel
Joe Roth
UA
85m.
Harvey Korman, John Ritter
Elvis Costello, Eddie Money, Meatloaf
COL

The time is the near future (1998); the U.S. is broke and the President (Ritter) hosts a national telethon to keep the country from going under. Feeble satire based on an idea by two members, (Proctor and Bergman) of the Firesign Theatre. Eddie Money sings "Get a Move On" and "Open Up Your Heart;" Elvis Costello does ("I Don't Want To Go To) Chelsea" and "Crawlin' to New York." The Beach Boys and Nick Lowe heard on soundtrack.

ANGEL, ANGEL DOWN WE GO (see CULT OF THE DAMNED)

APOCALYPSE NOW (1979)

D—Color

- Francis Ford Coppola, John Milius
- the novel *Heart of Darkness* by Joseph Conrad
- Francis Ford Coppola
- Francis Ford Coppola
- UA
- 139m.
- Marlon Brando, Martin Sheen
- Elektra

Vietnam acid-napalm phantasmagoria of Conrad's *Heart of Darkness* to the strains of a remixed version of The Doors' "The End" (effectively used at the film's beginning) and The Stones' "Satisfaction" at an appropriately nervous lull in the bloody proceedings. Other music by Francis and Carmine Coppola and Hendrix sound-alike, Randy Hansen.

ARMY OF LOVERS (1979)

R—Color

- Rosa Von Praunheim
- Rosa Von Praunheim
- Rosa Von Praunheim
- Trikont-Verlag
- 107m.
- Rosa Von Praunheim, Fred Halstead
- Grace Jones

Quirky, extremely personal diary-style documentary of German Gay rights activist Von Praunheim's sojourn in the U.S. Tom Robinson and his band sing "Glad To Be Gay" on the soundtrack. Grace Jones is seen writhing her way through "I Need A Man" at a rally and is sharply criticized for doing so by a Lesbian feminist.

BABY DOLL (1956)

D—B/W

- Tennessee Williams
- Elia Kazan
- Elia Kazan
- WB
- 116m.
- Karl Malden, Carroll Baker, Eli Wallach
- Columbia

The rivalry between two cotton plantation owners is exacerbated when one of them (Wallach) seduces the child bride (Baker) of the other, played by Malden. Linking a prestigious product (script by Tennessee Williams, direction by Elia Kazan) with rock and roll was radical for its time (1956), but how better to convey the unbridled lust of Baker's "Baby Doll" than through the lowdown strains of Smiley Lewis' "Shame, Shame, Shame (on you Miss Roxy)" ever-spinning on her Victrola? Non-rock score by Kenyon Hopkins.

BABY SNAKES (1979)

R—Color
- Frank Zappa
- Frank Zappa
- Intercontinental Absurdities
- 166m.
- Frank Zappa, Bruce Bickford, Adrian Belew, Tommy Mars, Ed Mann, Peter Wolf

Concert footage, live action and claymation combine in what has been described as either a whole lof of fun or a megalomaniacal exercise in cinematic self-indulgence. The truth lies somewhere between these two positions. Complete versions, or portions of fifteen Zapa compositions are featured.

BAD (1977)

D—Color
- Pat Hackett and George Abagnalo
- Jed Johnson
- Andy Warhol and Fred Hughes
- New World
- 94m.
- Carroll Baker, Perry King, Susan Tyrrell, Stefania Cassini, Geraldine and Maria Smith, Brigid Polk

Electrolosist (Baker) living in the suburbs earns more money through her side trade—manager of an all-girl "hit" squad. When a male (King) joins her ranks, trouble brews. Music by Mike Bloomfield for this Andy Warhol produced would-be bad taste epic in the John (Pink Flamingos) Waters mold. Close but no cigar. Baker and King are just too. . .well, charming.

BAD TIMING: A SENSUAL OBSESSION (1980)

D—Color
- Yale Udoff
- Nicolas Roeg
- Jeremy Thomas
- World-Northal
- 123m.
- Art Garfunkel, Theresa Russell

Professor of psychoanalysis (Garfunkel) becomes involved with a married woman of easy virtue (Russell). Director Roeg, successful at transforming such musical personalities as Mick Jagger and David Bowie into screen icons, fails to do the same, here, with Art Garfunkel in this confused tale of love gone wrong. "Who Are You," by The Who, featured prominently on the soundtrack—as well as songs by Billie Holiday, Zoot Money and Tom Waits ("Invitation to the Blues"). Score by Richard Hartley.

BALLAD IN BLUE (see BLUES FOR LOVERS)

BANJOMAN (1975)

D—Color

- ◼ Richard G. Abramson, Michael C. Varhol
- ⊞ Richard G. Abramson, Michael C. Varhol, Robert French
- ☰ Blue Pacific
- ● 105m.
- ✪ Earl Scruggs, Ramblin' Jack Elliot, Joan Baez, Tracy Nelson and Mother Earth, David Bromberg, The Nitty Gritty Dirt Band, The Byrds
- ◑ Sire

Film of concert tribute to famed country music man, Earl Scruggs. Most of the music is in the C&W vein, but performances by The Byrds on "Mr. Tambourine Man" and "Roll Over Beethoven," and Baez singing "The Night They Drove Old Dixie Down" and "You Ain't Goin' Nowhere" should be of interest to rock listeners.

BE MY GUEST (1965)

- M–B/W
- ☰ Lyn Fairhurst
- ◼ Lance Comfort
- ⊞ Lance Comfort
- ℤ Rank
- ● 73m.
- ✪ David Hemmings, Avril Angers
- ⊐ Jerry Lee Lewis, The Nashville Teens, The Zephyrs, Kenny and The Wranglers, Niteshades

A family inherits a seaside hotel and has trouble filling it up until their son's (Hemmings) rock group begins packing 'em in. This feature was one of several British films from the mid-sixties which offered the added inducement of a guest appearance by Jerry Lee Lewis. Songs: the title tune and "Somebody Help Me."

BEACH BALL (1965)

- M–Color
- ☰ David Malcolm
- ◼ Lennie Weinrib
- ⊞ Bart Patton
- ℤ PAR
- ● 107m.
- ✪ Edd Byrnes, Chris Noel
- ⊐ The Supremes, The Righteous Brothers, The Four Seasons, The Hondells, The Walker Brothers

A music store owner wants his unpaid-for musical instruments back, but "The Wigglers" stall him until the crucial battle-of-the-bands concert. Dispirited lip-sync performances of the title tune and "Surfer Boy" (The Supremes); "Baby What You Want Me To Do?" (Righteous Bros.); "Dawn" (Four Seasons) and several other songs in this cinematic equivalent of red tide. A twice-xeroxed, videotaped ersatz *Beach Party*.

BEACH BLANKET BINGO (1965)

- M–Color
- ☰ William Asher, Leo Townsend
- ◼ William Asher
- ⊞ James H. Nicholson, Samuel Z. Arkoff

- ⚡ AIP
- ● 98m.
- ○ Frankie Avalon, Annette Funicello, Buster Keaton, Paul Lynde, Harvey Lembeck
- ➡ The Hondells
- ○ American-International

More of the same amiable nonsense, fourth in the AIP "beach" series. This time, "Dee Dee" (Funicello) is distraught when "Frankie" falls for another girl, "Sugar Kane," played by TV's *The Big Valley*'s Linda Evans. The usual musical hired hands in these frolics, Dick Dale and The Del Tones, replaced here by The Hondells; and the "Dee Dee"/"Frankie" solos and duets ("I Think," "These Are the Good Times," etc.) are as uninspired as ever.

BEACH PARTY (1963)

- M—Color
- ≈ Lou Rusoff
- ◼ William Asher
- ▦ James H. Nicholson, Lou Rusoff
- ⚡ AIP
- ● 101m.
- ○ Frankie Avalon, Annette Funicello
- ➡ Dick Dale and The Del Tones
- ○ American-International

"Frankie's" (Avalon) plans for a moonlight beach tryst with "Dee Dee" (Funicello) get side-tracked when she invites the whole gang along. So *he* retaliates by faking an affair with a beach vamp, played by Eva Six. Biker "Eric Von Zipper" (Harvey Lembeck) pops up to wreak havoc every so often, and all the while a sympathetic anthropologist (Bob Cummings) hovers around the edges of the activity taking notes on teen tribalism—in this true slice of pop art Americana. Don't blink or you'll miss Beach Boy Brian Wilson standing around in the background as an extra in this, the first of AIP's fabulously successful "beach" series. The nearly non-stop farcical fun only pauses long enough for an occasional sappy solo or duet by Funicello and/or Avalon, but the music revs up again when Dick Dale and The Del Tones turn on their tangy surfin' beat. Songs by Roger Christian and Gary Usher include: "Surfin' and Swingin'" and "Treat Him Nicely."

BEAT GIRL (*see* WILD FOR KICKS)

BEATLES ON FILM. In addition to the major productions mentioned elsewhere in this book, there are numerous other official and semi-official films featuring The Beatles in circulation. Information concerning the making of many of these productions is scanty, for most of them are transfers to film from TV footage, newsreels and promo films. Distribution of most of these is understandably somewhat sporadic, but if you come across a theatre advertising a "five-hour Beatle film fest," or if you attend a Beatles collectors convention you will surely see one or more of the films listed herein. *Around The Beatles* is a 1964 TV special featuring JPG&R, Cilla Black, Sounds Incorporated, Murray the K and P.J. Proby. Generally when this black-and-white kinescope is shown it is minus all but The Beatles, with the running time hovering around the forty-minute mark. Good live performances of most of the early hits, plus (in the complete version) some clowning around by the boys. *What's Happening* is a thirty-minute Maysles Brothers docu of the fab four touching down in the U.S., for the first time, in 1964, including Airport footage, the press conference, the ride to Manhattan with Murray the K. and much more of The Beatles arriving at and departing stops along the way on their first stateside junket. *The Beatles on David Frost* consists of a 1968

BBC interview and a performance of "Hey Jude." *The Man Behind The Beatles* is a short featuring an interview with John Lennon on the set of *How I Won the War*. *The Beatles From Liverpool to Ed Sullivan* includes a bit of Cavern Club footage (singing "Twist and Shout" and "Some Other Guy") and all of their second Ed Sullivan Show appearance (Feb. 16, 1964). They sing "She Loves You," "Please, Please Me" and "I Wanna Hold Your Hand." This film's running time is nine-and-a-half minutes. *The Beatles at the Cavern Club* uses the same clip from Liverpool as used in *From Liverpool to Ed Sullivan*. Another variant is *The Beatles on Ed Sullivan #2*. This is the same footage as in "From Liverpool" minus the Cavern Club clip. In a major vein is *Beatles Tokyo Concert*, a videotape-to-film transfer of their 7/2/66 appearance in Japan. This thirty-minute color production finds the foursome singing: "Rock and Roll Music," "She's a Woman," "Day Tripper," "I Feel Fine," "Yesterday," "I'm Down," "If I Needed Someone," "Baby's in Black," "I Wanna Be Your Man," "Nowhere Man" and "Paperback Writer." *The Beatles Washington Coliseum Concert* was originally part of a closed circuit theatrical presentation broadcast in movie houses on March 14-15, 1964. This is the quartet's first American concert, which took place in D.C. on Feb. 11th of the same year. Technical quality of this half-hour black-and-white presentation is shaky, but the fervor displayed in the performance of the songs compensates for all the grain and audio static. They perform: "Roll Over Beethoven," "From Me to You," "I Saw Her Standing There," "This Boy," "I Wanna Be Your Man," "Please, Please Me," "All My Loving," "Till There Was You," "She Loves You" and "I Wanna Hold Your Hand." From a 1963 concert, *The Beatles Come to Town* is an extremely well-photographed Pathe newsreel of a performance in Manchester, England. Color cameras capture the foursome doing "She Loves You" and "Twist and Shout." Later this seven minute clip was incorporated into the feature *Go Go Mania*. (See separate listing.) The most frequently shown of all the more obscure films is *The Beatles at Shea Stadium*, taken from a 1966 television broadcast of their August, 1965 appearance in New York City before a crowd of 60,000. The Beatles are in top form, and the technical quality is excellent. (Most of the prints we've seen, though, have been badly botched.) Among the many promo films and musical shorts are: *Penny Lane, Hey Jude,* (and *Hey Jude-Rehearsal*), *Revolution, Strawberry Fields Forever, Good Day Sunshine, The Ballad of John and Yoko, The Plastic Ono Band* (John and Yoko at Madison Square Garden singing "Come Together") and *Mrs. Lennon* (with John singing the title tune while walking with Yoko in a forest). Other promo ventures by single members of the group include: *Cold Turkey* and *Instant Karma* (John), *Maybe I'm Amazed* and *My Love* (Paul) and Ringo's *Sentimental Journey*. A film entitled *Montreal Bed-In* features John and Yoko singing "Give Peace a Chance" in their hotel bed as part of their efforts to end the Viet Nam war. Around 1970 the twosome also began making a series of experimental films of varying lengths whose titles include: *Rape* (80 min.), *The Fly* (45 min.), *Apotheosis* (30 min.) and *Legs* (30 min.).

BEATLEMANIA (1981)

■   R–Color
■   Joseph Manduke
▦   Edie and Ely Landau, Steve Leber and David Krebs
✪   American Cinema
●   95m.
✪   Mitch Weissman, Tom Teely, David Leon, Ralph Castelli

Film of long-running stage show featuring four young musicians dressed-up to look like the Beatles singing the songs the Fab Four made famous in as-near-to-identical sound-style as possible, occasionally interrupted by slides and film clips of 60's era events. Not our cup of tea, but for some people, imitations like this are the next best thing to actually *being there*. Songs include "Twist and Shout," "She Loves You," "Strawberry Fields Forever," "A Day In The Life," "Helter Skelter," "With A Little Help From My Friends," "Penny Lane," "Revolution," "Let It Be," "The Long and Winding Road" and other Beatles hits.

BECAUSE THEY'RE YOUNG (1960)

M–B/W
- 🎬 James Gunn
- 📖 *Harrison High* by John Ferris
- 🎥 Robert Peterson
- 💲 Jerry Bresler
- 🎞 COL
- ● 102m.
- ✪ Dick Clark, Michael Callan, Tuesday Weld
- ➡ Duane Eddy and The Rebels, James Darren

Blackboard Jungle-style high school melodrama (with Clark in the Glenn Ford role) contains musical appearances by Eddy playing one of his twangy specialties, "Shazam," and Darren singing the title song.

BEDAZZLED (1967)

M–Color
- 🎬 Peter Cook
- 🎥 Stanley Donen
- 💲 Stanley Donen
- 🎞 TCF
- ● 107m.
- ✪ Peter Cook, Dudley Moore

This comic update of the "Faust" legend contains one of the few film instances of successful rock parody, in a TV studio sequence that spoofs Britain's *Ready, Steady, Go*. Cook and Moore sing contrasting versions—emotional and emotion*less*—of the title song. Otherwise non-rock score by Moore.

BETWEEN THE LINES (1977)

D–Color B/W
- 🎬 Fred Barron
- 🎥 Joan Micklin Silver
- 💲 Raphael D. Silver
- 🎞 Midwest Films
- ● 101m.
- ✪ John Heard, Jeff Goldblum
- ➡ Southside Johnny and The Asbury Jukes

Story of an underground newspaper in Boston about to be taken over by big business has songs and an appearance ("We're Havin' a Party") by Southside Johnny. Other songs by the group include: "I Don't Want To Go Home" and "Love Is On Our Side." Other music in the film includes: "You To Me Are Everything" (Eric Mercury) and "Heat Treatment" (Graham Parker).

BEWARE OF A HOLY WHORE (1970)

D–Color
- 🎬 Rainer Werner Fassbinder
- 🎥 Rainer Werner Fassbinder
- 💲 Rainer Werner Fassbinder
- 🎞 New Yorker Films

103m.

Lou Castel, Hanna Schygulla, Eddie Constantine, Werner Schroeter, Magdalena Montezuma, Rainer Werner Fassbinder

At a Spanish hotel a film's cast and crew wander about aimlessly while waiting for the star (Constantine) and director (Castel) to arrive and bring some order to the proceedings. They show up but things don't get any better. The jukebox in the hotel lobby is almost a cast member in this autobiographical film about filmmaking—Fassbinder's *8½*. A quarter here will get you Ray Charles, Elvis Presley, Leonard Cohen ("Suzanne" and "Bird On A Wire" are spun several times), Spooky Tooth and even Donizetti. Scene of principals wrecked on "Cuba Libres" stumbling about and collapsing is fittingly choreographed to Charles' "Let's Go Get Stoned."

BEYOND THE VALLEY OF THE DOLLS (1970)

D—Color
Roger Ebert, Russ Meyer
Russ Meyer
Russ Meyer
TCF
109m.
Erica Gavin, Edy Williams, Charles Napier, John La Zar, Michael Blodgett, Dolly Reed, Cynthia Myers, Marcia McBroom
The Strawberry Alarm Clock
TCF

An all-girl rock encounter the slings and arrows of fame and fortune in "nudie" king Russ Meyer's outrageous send-up of the Hollywood music scene. Meyer and scriptwriter Roger Ebert pile on enough characters and sub-plots to induce hyperventilation in the viewer. Best to just lay back, roll with it and enjoy. Music by Stu Phillips and Bill Loose. "A Girl From The City" and "I'm Comin' Home" and sung by The Strawberry Alarm Clock (who appear in one of *BVD*'s many party scenes.) The Sandpipers sing the title song.

BIG BEAT, THE (1957)

M—Color
David P. Harmon
Will Cowan
Will Cowan
UI
82m.
William Campbell, Gogi Grant
Fats Domino, The Del Vikings, The Diamonds

When father's back is turned, his visionary son (Campbell) resuscitates dad's moldy old record label by producing rock and roll, then enterprisingly selling the results at supermarket checkstands. Strictly plain wrap. At least it's in color, but the rock quotient is way too low, with only Fats Domino ("The Big Beat," "I'm Walkin'"), The Diamonds ("Little Darlin'") and The Del Vikings ("Come Go With Me") on hand to offset the consciousness-one musical efforts of The Four Aces, The Mills Brothers and a bevy of other strictly pop acts.

BIG TIME (1977)

D—Color

- ◼ Andrew Georgias
- 🎬 Smokey Robinson
- ⚡ World Wide Films
- ● 91m.
- ✪ Jayne Kennedy, Christopher Joy
- ◗ Tamla

Smokey Robinson produced this little comedy caper of a small time hood (Joy) who finally makes the big time. Robinson also wrote the score and sings the title tune, "Hip Trip," "So Nice To Be With You" and "If We're Gonna Act Like Lovers" on the soundtrack.

BIG TNT SHOW, THE (1966)

ROCK 'N ROLL · TRADITIONAL BLUES · COUNTRY WESTERN and FOLK ROCK

The BIG TNT SHOW — FROM AMERICAN INTERNATIONAL

- R–B/W
- ◼ Larry Peerce
- 🎬 Phil Spector
- ⚡ AIP
- ● 93m.
- ✪ The Byrds, Joan Baez, The Lovin' Spoonful, Ike and Tina Turner, Ray Charles, Donovan, Petula Clark, The Ronettes, Bo Diddley

This concert film arrived hard on the heels of, and is similar to, the very successful *TAMI Show*. Just like that film, *TNT* was filmed with the "Electronovision" process, and before it was released was slated to be called *The TAMI Show II*. Two music personalities of note not listed in the official credits appear in *TNT*, for at one point producer Spector can be seen accompanying (of all people!) Joan Baez, on the piano; and at another, when Pet Clark reaches out to touch the hand of an adoring fan it turns out to be none other than a young (pre-Seeds) Sky Saxon—again, of all people! Filmed in 1965 at Los Angeles' Moulin Rouge night club, while *TNT* lacks the impressive talent lineup of *TAMI*, it is still recommended viewing. Performances of note: The Ronettes singing "Be My Baby;" Charles doing "Georgia On My Mind;" The Byrds with "Tambourine Man;" Clark's "Downtown" and a manic Bo Diddley's "Hey, Bo Diddley."

BIG WEDNESDAY (1978)

- D–Color
- ✑ John Milius and Dennis Aaberg
- ◼ John Milius
- ◼ Alex Rose and Tamara Asseyev
- ⚡ WB
- ● 119m.
- ✪ Jan-Michael Vincent, William Katt, Gary Busey, Patti D'Arbanville, Lee Purcell

Episodes in the lives of three California surfers, following them through the 60's, touching on the Vietnam war and its aftermath. A very moving and sensitive look at southern California youth that never found its audience—in spite of some spectacular surfing footage. Background sounds at the many lively parties in the film include "The Locomotion" by Little Eva, "He's A Rebel" by The Crystals, "Sherry" by The Four Seasons, and "Do You Want To Dance" by Bobby Freeman. Other non-rock music by Basil Poledouris.

BIKINI BEACH (1964)

- M–Color
- ✑ William Asher, Leo Townsend, Robert Dillon

- ■ William Asher
- 🎬 James Nicholson, Samuel Z. Arkoff
- ☪ AIP
- ● 100m.
- ✪ Frankie Avalon, Annette Funicello
- ⇒ Little Stevie Wonder, The Pyramids, The Exciters

Two Frankie Avalons for the price of one are offered in this lightly entertaining entry in the "Beach Party" series. The singer-actor appears as both the regular "Frankie" character *and* a Beatle-wigged Britisher called "Potato Bug." Keenan Wynn appears as a real estate speculator who wants to take over the surf crowd's playground in a sub-plot. This musical is primarily devoted to kidding the American teenager's infatuation with things English. Little Stevie Wonder lets loose with "Fingertips" in the finale.

BIRD ON A WIRE (1972)

- R—Color
- ☎ Tony Palmer
- ■ Tony Palmer
- 🎬 Martin Machat, Ron Kass
- ☪ EMI
- ● 92m.
- ✪ Leonard Cohen

You might call it Leonard Cohen's *Don't Look Back*. The gravel-voiced songsmith moodily strolls through the byways of various European venues and is seen in concert performing "Sisters of Mercy," "Marianne," "Suzanne," "That's No Way To Say Goodbye," "One of Us Can't Be Wrong" and the title tune.

BIRTH OF THE BEATLES (1979)

- D—Color
- ☎ John Kurland, Jacob Erskendar
- ■ Richard Marquand
- 🎬 Tony Bishop
- ☪ Dick Clark Productions
- ● 104m.
- ✪ Stephen Mackenna, Rod Culvertson, John Altman
- ⇒ Rain

Biopic about the formation of The Beatles, on up through their early successes. Even though the fab four unsuccessfully sued to try and stop this film from being made, the final result isn't all that bad. Dick Clark's production company were the makers of this nicely photographed dramatization of events leading up to the Liverpudlian shot heard 'round the world. Originally made for U.S. TV, *BOTB* also made European theatrical rounds. Most of the early Beatles hits ("I Wanna Hold Your Hand," "She Loves You," "Can't Buy Me Love" and more) are performed, with the precise off-screen approximation of the sound of the group laid down by a group called Rain. Musical direction: Carl Davis.

BITTER TEARS OF PETRA VON KANT, THE (1972)

- D—Color
- ☎ Rainer Werner Fassbinder

- ■ his play of the same name
- ■ Rainer Werner Fassbinder
- 🎬 Rainer Werner Fassbinder
- 🎞 New Yorker Films
- ● 124m.
- ✪ Margit Carstensen, Hanna Schygulla, Irm Hermann

A wealthy fashion designer degrades herself for the love of a sadistic young woman. Recordings of The Platters' "Smoke Gets in Your Eyes" and "The Great Pretender" are played for ironic effect in this high-pitched *tour-de-force* (all shot on a single set). Bertolt Brecht meets Coco Chanel, so to speak. The Walker Brothers (singing "In My Room") and excerpts from the operas of Giuseppe Verdi are also used.

BLACK AND BLUE (1980)

- R–Color
- ■ Jay Dubin
- 🎬 George Harrison
- 🎞 Daltyn Filmworks
- ● 87m.
- ✪ Black Sabbath, Blue Oyster Cult

Concert film of 1980 East Coast U.S. performances by these two heavy metal organizations, *Black* Sabbath and *Blue* Oyster Cult. Songs include: "Iron Man," "Heaven and Hell," "Paranoid" and "Die Young" (Black) and (Blue) "Born to Be Wild," "Cities on Flame With Rock and Roll" and "The Marshall Plan."

BLACKBOARD JUNGLE, THE (1955)

- D–B/W
- ⬛ Richard Brooks
- ■ the novel by Evan Hunter
- ■ Richard Brooks
- 🎬 Pandro S. Berman
- 🎞 MGM
- ● 101m.
- ✪ Glenn Ford, Vic Morrow, Sidney Poitier

Ford portrays a school teacher "Dadier" who's unprepared for the caged animals he meets up with at his new assignment at a blighted New York City school. The high school toughs taunt him (they call him "Daddy-O"), and rape and pillage left and right in this grim portrait of the failure of the American educational system. If it weren't for this film, you might not be reading this book right now. The bold (for 1955) and successful use of Bill Haley's recording of "Rock Around The Clock" on the soundtrack made *Blackboard Jungle* the *official* first-ever rock and roll movie. *Apres Haley, le deluge*!

BLANK GENERATION, THE (1976)

- R–B/W
- ■ Amos Poe, Ivan Kral
- 🎬 Amos Poe, Ivan Kral
- 🎞 Poe Visions, Inc.
- ● 55m.

☼ Patti Smith, Television, The Ramones, Blondie, Talking Heads, Miamis, The Shirts, The Marbles, Wayne County, Tuff Darts (with Robert Gordon), The Dolls, Harry Toledo, The Heartbreakers

The cream of New York new wave/punk filmed "live" at CBGB's when the scene was just beginning. The *look* of this blown-up-from-super-8, and largely sound-unsynced docu, is as raw and rough-edged as the music itself. Patti sings "Gloria;" The Ramones do "Shock Treatment" and "1-2-3-4, Let's Go;" Blondie performs "He Left Me;" Talking Heads are viewed singing "Psycho Killer"—and much, much more.

BLINDMAN (1971)

D—Color
- Tony Anthony, Piero Anchisi and Vincenzo Cerami
- Ferdinando Baldi
- Tony Anthony and Saul Swimmer
- TCF
- 105m.
- Tony Anthony, Ringo Starr

Ringo plays a badman named "Candy" in his only serious non-singing dramatic role to date. He rapes, pillages and comes to a suitably bad end in this rather tepid spaghetti western (about a blind "man with no name") that waffles on the edge of parody.

BLISS OF MRS. BLOSSOM, THE (1968)

C—Color
- Alec Coppel and Denis Norden
- the play of the same name by Alec Coppel
- Joseph McGrath
- Josef Shaftel
- PAR
- 93m.
- Shirley MacLaine, Richard Attenborough, James Booth
- The New Vaudeville Band
- DOT

The wife of successful brassiere manufacturer (known to the trade as "the Orpheus of the undieworld") finds a way to make her already happy marriage happier by keeping a lover in the attic. The New Vaudeville Band sings "I Think I'm Beginning To Fall in Love" in a party sequence in this charming British comedy of manners. Other non-rock music by Riz Ortolani.

BLOW-UP (1966)

D—Color
- Michelangelo Antonioni, Tonino Guerra
- a short story by Julio Cortazar
- Michelangelo Antonioni
- Carlo Ponti
- MGM
- 110m.
- David Hemmings, Vanessa Redgrave
- The Yardbirds

○ MGM

A photographer (Hemmings) finds that he has inadvertently photographed a murder scene, and the haunting and often cryptic aftermath of his discovery is the basis for the action of this major Antonioni film. The Yardbirds, singing "Stroll On," imitate The Who's art-damage act in the most famous scene in this definitive portrait of 60's "swinging London." Jazz score by Herbie Hancock.

BLUE COLLAR (1978)

	D—Color
✍	Paul Schrader, Leonard Schrader
▣	Paul Schrader
▦	Don Guest
✇	UI
●	114m.
✪	Richard Pryor, Harvey Keitel, Yaphet Koto
○	MCA

A robbery of union funds, and the disastrous consequences following the heist, form the storyline of this moody, downbeat effort. This drama of disaffected assembly-line workers has an original score by Jack Nitzsche. Ry Cooder (credited with "special musical arrangements") is featured playing the bluesy sounds crafted for the film and, in addition, recordings by Howlin' Wolf, Ike and Tina Turner and Lynyrd Skynyrd are heard. "Hard Workin' Man," written by Nitzsche, Cooder and Paul Schrader, and sung by Captain Beefheart over the credits, is a musical highlight.

BLUE HAWAII (1961)

	M—Color
✍	Hal Kanter
▣	Norman Taurog
▦	Hal Wallis
✇	PAR
●	100m.
✪	Elvis Presley, Joan Blackman, Angela Lansbury, Jenny Maxwell
○	RCA

Elvis in a musical drama/comedy about a poor little rich boy who yearns for a simple life, without the influence of his domineering mother. Playing the part of the son of a wealthy pineapple plantation owner, Elvis spends most of his screen time horizontal and supine in a film marking the beginning of a thirteen-year cinematic decline from which he never fully recovered. The tepid songs, which form a large part of the problem here, include: "The Hawaiian Wedding Song," "Ku-U-I-Po," "Beach Boy Blues" and "Ito Eats." Elvis #8.

BLUE SUEDE SHOES (1979)

	R—Color
▣	Curtis Clark
▦	Penny Clark
✇	World Northal
●	85m.
✪	Bill Haley, Ray Campi, Freddie "Fingers" Lee

Tommy Steele, Cliff Richard, Billy Fury, Gene Vincent, Eddie Cochran

Filmed record of the first Rock and Roll Weekend at England's Great Yarmouth Holiday Camp. Leather clad unreconstructed rockers and their pony-tailed girlfriends look on at the music making of simpler and more fun-filled kind of rock by Ray Campi and Matchbox, and Freddie "Fingers" Lee. Also included is coverage of a 1978 London concert by Bill Haley and His Comets as they zip through enthusiastically received replays of "Rock Around the Clock" and "Shake, Rattle and Roll." Some vintage clips of Gene Vincent, Eddie Cochran and several other first-wave rockers are also thrown in for good measure.

BLUES BROTHERS, THE (1980)

M—Color
- Dan Ackroyd, John Landis
- John Landis
- Robert K. Weiss
- UI
- 120m.
- John Belushi, Dan Ackroyd
- Aretha Franklin, Ray Charles, James Brown, John Lee Hooker, Booker T. Jones, Steve Cropper, Cab Calloway.
- Atlantic

"Jake" (Belushi) and "Elwood" (Ackroyd), the Blues Brothers, are sprung from the pokey, and waste no time getting back into musical action. The only question is, does the music scene want them back? $30,000,000 worth of car chases and wrecked property are sunk into the oldest plot in the movie musical business—raising money for an orphanage by putting on a show. Belushi and Ackroyd's besuited and sunglassed "hipsters" weren't terribly funny on *Saturday Night Live* (or at least a little went a long way), and they are even less so here. Aretha Franklin's roof-raising version of "Think" *almost* singlehandedly manages to turn this bloated sub-Abbott and Costello programmer around, but the racist tendencies of this backhanded tribute to rhythm and blues undoes the well-intentioned work of Aretha, Ray Charles ("Shake a Tail Feather"), James Brown ("The Old Landmark") and Cab Calloway ("Minnie the Moocher"). Booker T. and Steve Cropper also appear as supporting musicians, but Sam and Dave, on whom the Blues Brothers' act is based, are conspicuous by their absence. The excellent musical direction is by Ira Newborn.

BLUES FOR LOVERS (*orig.* BALLAD IN BLUE) (1966)

D—B/W
- Burton Wohl
- Paul Henried
- Herman Blaser
- TCF
- 89m.
- Ray Charles, Thom Bell
- The Raelets

Charles plays himself in this British drama about a blind child who is lent encouragement by The Genius. Charles sings "I Got a Woman" and "What'd I Say."

BOB MARLEY AND THE WAILERS *LIVE!* (1978)

    R–Color
- ▪ Keith Macmillan
- ▦ Scott Millaney
- ✆ Blue Mountain Films
- ● 78m.
- ✪ Bob Marley and The Wailers

    Concert film sponsored by Marley's record label, Island, captures the singer/musician and his band in performance at a 1977 London concert. Although somewhat wearing on the eyes, *Wailers LIVE* probably represents the best extant footage of the late reggae mega-star, Marley. Songs include: "Trenchtown Rock," "I Shot The Sheriff," "Lively Up Yourself," "Running Away," "No More Trouble," "Exodus" and "The Heathen."

    BOONE, PAT. Someone, somewhere could conceivably take issue with the exclusion of films starring fifties "cover record" specialist, Boone. Our department of mollification, then, takes note of three (decidedly non-rock) movies made by Boone while he was still at the top of record sales charts with his inauthentic versions of Fats Domino and Little Richard originals—*April Love*, *Bernardine* (both 1957) and *Mardi Gras* (1958).

BORN TO BOOGIE (1972)

    R–Color
- ≡ Ringo Starr, Marc Bolan
- ▪ Ringo Starr
- ▦ Ringo Starr
- ✆ Apple Films
- ● 67m.
- ✪ Marc Bolan, T-Rex, Ringo Starr

    Documentary about T-Rex also includes concert footage and staged sequences, i.e. a mad tea party take-off. Ringo's directorial work here remindful of touches he used in *Magical Mystery Tour*. A musical highlight is Mark and the band's working over their hit, "Bang A Gong." Other songs include: "Children of the Revolution," "Cosmic Dancer" and "Tutti Frutti."

BREAKING GLASS (1980)

    D–Color
- ≡ Brian Gibson
- ▪ Brian Gibson
- ▦ Davina Belling, Clive Parsons
- ✆ PAR
- ● 104m.
- ✪ Hazel O'Connor, Phil Daniels
- ✪ A&M

    Birth-of-a-band saga about a group, "Breaking Glass" (led by O'Connor as "Kate"), whose purist punk intentions become subverted by commercial exploitation. "Kate" becomes a trendy new wave superstar, while the rest of the band, looking on in disgust and pity, falls by the way-side. Neo-punk panache pretty much fails to salvage this U.K. film of the ages-old story of a rock band's climb up the show-biz ladder. (As if we didn't already know by now how lonely life at the top can often prove.) This film, with music and lyrics by O'Connor, was widely shown in England, but failed to get off the ground in the U.S. Version shown in U.S. eliminates British finale which finds a burned-out "Kate" locked up in an asylum. Songs include: "Writing on the Wall," "Monsters in Disguise," "Come Into the Air" and "Big Brother."

BREWSTER McCLOUD (1970)

M—Color
- Doran William Cannon
- Robert Altman
- Lou Adler
- MGM
- 101m.
- Bud Cort, Sally Kellerman
- MGM

Robert Altman's lunatic fantasy about a teenage Icarus, a kind of *Peter Pan* meets *Phantom of The Opera*, has a score by Papa John Phillips, which is sung by Phillips and Merry Clayton. Musical highlight: Merry's rendering of "Lift Every Voice and Sing" (the black national anthem). Note: Film marks debut of actress Shelley Duval.

BROKEN ENGLISH: THREE SONGS BY MARIANNE FAITHFULL (1979)

M—Color / B/W
- Derek Jarman
- Derek Jarman
- Guy Ford
- Mainline (England)
- 13m.
- Marianne Faithfull
- Island

Faithfull (one of a handful of rock stars to ever re-emerge after professional eclipse, ie. make a comeback) in Scopitone-like visualizations of three songs from her 1979 return to recording, the *Broken English* album. Director Jarman (*Sebastiane, Jubilee, The Tempest*) is up to his usual florid tricks in this bit of abbreviated visual razzmatazz. Marianne, walking through Picadilly circus at night sings "The Ballad of Lucy Jordan" as giant orange flames suddenly shoot up in the background. Also seen and heard are "Witches' Song" and the title tune.

BUDDY HOLLY STORY, THE (1978)

D—Color
- Robert Gitler
- *Buddy Holly: His Life and Music* by Alan Sawyer
- Steve Rash
- Freddy Bauer
- COL
- 113m.
- Gary Busey, Don Stroud
- Epic

Film of the life of early rock great, Buddy Holly. This throwback to the era of Universal Picture's musical biopics of the fifties (i.e. *The Glenn Miller Story*, etc.) takes massive liberties in retelling the life of rockabilly king, Holly (Richie Valens and The Big Bopper are portrayed, but nowhere in sight is Holly mentor, Norman Petty)—but Gary Busey (doing all his own singing) scores on the dramatic level in an Oscar-nominated performance. Music includes nearly all the Holly hits including: "That'll Be The Day," "Peggy Sue," "Rave On," "Maybe Baby" and "It's So Easy." Musical director: Joe Renzetti.

BUNNY LAKE IS MISSING (1965)

	D–B/W
📷	John and Penelope Mortimer
■	the novel by Evelyn Piper
▦	Otto Preminger
🎞	Otto Preminger
✇	COL
●	107m.
✪	Lawrence Olivier, Carol Lynley
⇥	The Zombies
◗	RCA

A young American woman (Lynley) tells police that her daughter has been kidnapped, but an inspector (Olivier) assigned to the case begins to suspect she is imagining things. A surprise twist/climax, though, proves him wrong. The British Zombies are more prominent in the trailer for this film, singing "Come On Time," than in the film proper (where they're only glimpsed on TV). In the coming attractions the group holds center stage with sequences never appearing in the final film. Other music by Paul Glass.

BYE BYE BIRDIE (1963)

	M–Color
📷	Irving Brecher
B/O	the stage musical by Charles Strauss and Lee Adams
■	George Sidney
🎞	Fred Kohlmar
✇	COL
●	112m.
✪	Dick Van Dyke, Ann-Margret, Bobby Rydell
◗	RCA

When Elvis-like rocker pays a visit before his induction into the army, havoc is raised in a small town, by both its oldsters and (especially) youngsters. Presley-mania was already past its peak (and The Beatles were waiting in the wings) when Hollywood turned out this version of the hit Broadway musical. The film was a launching vehicle for Ann-Margret, whose diminutive milquetoast boyfriend is played by Philly rocker, Bobby Rydell. Jessie Pearson bumps and grinds like Al Capp's "Stupifyin' Jones" in the Presley-esque part of "Conrad Birdie."

CAGED HEAT (1974)

	D–Color
📷	Jonathan Demme
■	Jonathan Demme
🎞	Samuel Gelfman
✇	New World

- 83m.
- Erica Gavin, Barbara Steele

A woman convicted for robbery is sent to a bizarre prison run by a wheelchair-ridden warden, where illegal brain surgery experiments are conducted. The looniest of New Worlds' womens' prison epics, (Barbara Steele as the warden gets to parody Liza Minnelli in a dream sequence) *Caged Heat*'s story is so fragmented as to be almost incomprehensible. But oh that *mise en scene*! Brilliant synthesizer and violin score by John Cale outdoes even Jack Nietzsche's music for *Performance* in its acid-paranoia intensity.

CANDY (1968)

D—Color
- Buck Henry
- the novel of the same name by Terry Southern and Mason Hoffenberg
- Christian Marquand
- Robert Haggiag
- Cinerama Releasing
- 124m.
- Ewa Aulin, Marlon Brando, Richard Burton, Ringo Starr, Walter Matthau, Elsa Martinelli, John Huston
- Anita Pallenberg
- ABC

Candide-like innocent adventures take Candy from one unwitting seduction to another in another in her search for higher spiritual truth. Steppenwolf and The Byrds (who had a moderate-sized hit with soundtrack song, "Child of The Universe") provide the background score for Marquand's clumsy and styleless film of Terry Southern's and Mason Hoffenberg's very funny novel. Even Ringo—as a horny Mexican gardner—gets lost in this noisy shuffle. The international cast all speak English, but the sound mixing and recording is so far off you'd swear the whole thing was dubbed from the Italian.

CAN'T STOP THE MUSIC (1980)

M—Color
- Bronte Woodard, Allan Carr
- Nancy Walker
- Allan Carr
- AFD
- 122m.
- The Village People, Valerie Perrine
- The Ritchie Family
- Casablanca

Cop, construction worker, serviceman, leather guy and Indian meet up with struggling songwriter. Together they invent . . . disco. The Village People, closet gaydom's answer to The Mouseketeers, star in the extravaganza that brought their careers to a screeching halt. Drew flies stateside; but a big hit in Australia, we hear. "YMCA," "Liberation" (from what, is never exactly made clear), "Do The Shake," "Sound of the City" and other K-Y Klassics included here are crafted by the Svengali of these leather 'n rhinestone Trilbys, Jacques Morali. Also on view, The Ritchie Family singing "Give Me a Break." Our sentiments exactly for *CSTM* is not *even* camp.

CAR WASH (1976)

- M—Color
- Joel Schumaker
- Michael Schultz
- Art Linson, Gary Stromberg
- UI
- 97m.
- Richard Pryor, Garrett Morris
- The Pointer Sisters
- MCA

Unpretentious semi-musical about a day in the life of a car wash was a big hit with both black and white audiences. While stylistically influenced by Robert Altman's *Nashville*, because of its numerous parallel story lines, it is still closer in spirit to the Bowery Boys—especially in the instance of Pryor's "Daddy Rich" character. A musical highlight is the title tune choreographed to the washing of a car. Norman Whitfield's soundtrack score is performed by the group Rose Royce.

CARNIVAL ROCK (1957)

- D—B/W
- Leo Lieberman
- Roger Corman
- Roger Corman
- Howco
- 75m.
- Susan Cabot, Dick Miller
- The Platters, The Blockbusters, The Shadows, David Houston, Bob Luman

Early Corman effort about the lower depths of show business, and of a carnival clown (David J. Stewart) and his unrequited love for hipster Cabot. Tears are allayed from time to time by the appearances of several rock and country acts.

CARNY (1980)

- D—Color
- Thomas Baum
- Robert Kaylor
- Robbie Robertson
- UA
- 105m.
- Robbie Robertson, Gary Busey, Jodie Foster
- WB

A young runaway (Foster) causes dissension between carny workers, Robertson and Busey, but eventually she proves herself a worthy member of the troup. The Band's Robertson is impressive in his dramatic debut in this darkly-tinged drama of life on the carnival midway. He also produced the film and wrote (along with Alex North) much of *Carny*'s score whose songs include: "Garden of Earthly Delights," "Freak's Lament" and "Pagan Knight." Film also includes a version of Fats Domino's and Dave Bartholomew's "The Fat Man."

CARRY IT ON (1970)

R—B/W
- James Coyne, Robert Jones, Christopher Knight
- James Coyne, Robert Jones, Christopher Knight
- Maron Films
- 95m.
- Joan Baez, David Harris
- Vanguard

Documentary about singer Baez and her husband, Harris, who was jailed for draft evasion. Material from various concert dates of Baez's, plus biographical footage of her life combine for a feature-length movie/anti-Vietnam war tract.

CATALINA CAPER (1967)

M—Color
- Clyde Ware
- Lee Sholem
- Bond Blackman, Jack Bartlett
- Crown-International
- 84m.
- Tommy Kirk, Del Moore, Peter Duryea, Lyle Wagoner
- Little Richard, The Cascades, Carol Connors

Vacationing teens become involved in amiable crook Moore's plan to swindle an even shadier con-man. Lots of business about the old switcheroo of a phony and real Chinese scroll. Late entry beach feature has appearances by: Little Richard ("Scuba Party"), ex-Teddy Bear Carol Connors ("Book of Love") and The Cascades ("There's a New World Opening For Me"). Mary Wells is heard singing "Never Steal Anything Wet"—the original title of this lightweight quickie.

CATCH MY SOUL (1974)

M—Color
- Jack Good
- Good's stage musical of the same name, adapted from Shakespeare's *Othello*
- Patrick McGoohan
- Richard Rosenbloom, Jack Good
- TCF
- 95m.
- Richie Havens, Bonnie and Delaney, Tony Joe White
- Metromedia

Flaccid update of Shakespeare's *Othello*, featuring Havens in the title role and White as Cassio. The setting is a hippie commune in the Southwest U.S., with the strained attempts to parallel the original source material sometimes reaching ludicrous heights. Music written mostly by White, with some songs contributed by Bonnie and Delaney and others.

CAVEMAN (1980)

M—Color
- Rudy De Luca and Carl Gottlieb
- Carl Gottlieb

■ Lawrence Turman and David Foster
ℭ UA
● 91m.
✪ Ringo Starr, Barbara Bach, Dennis Quaid, John Matuszak

Misfit caveman Atouk (Ringo) leaves the tribe of the bullying Tonga (Matuszak) and sets up his own prehistoric society. Ringo and his friends' discovery of music through an impromptu stone age jam session is a highlight of this wonderful "Alley Oop"-like comedy. Music by Lalo Schifrin.

CELEBRATION AT BIG SUR (1971)

R–Color
■ Baird Bryant, Joanna Demetrakis
■ Carl Gottlieb
ℭ TCF
● 82m.
✪ Joan Baez, Crosby, Stills, Nash and Young, John Sebastian, Joni Mitchell, The Flying Burrito Brothers, Mimi Farina, The Edwin Hawkins Singers

Woodstock-style coverage of the intimate and scaled--down 1969 Big Sur Folk Festival. Musical highlights include: Joni Mitchell singing "Woodstock," CSN&Y doing "Sea of Madness" and "Get Together," a duet on "Mobile Line" by Sebastian and Stills, Sebastian performing his "Red Eye Express" and a finale by all on "Oh Happy Day."

CHA CHA (1979)

R–Color
▬ Herbert Curiel
■ Herbert Curiel
■ Herbert Curiel
ℭ Concorde Films
● 90m.
✪ Herman Brood and His Wild Romance
⤴ Nina Hagen, Lene Lovich, Les Chappell

Bank robber (Brood) tries to go "straight" by becoming a rock and roll star. Loosely-filmed drama takes place in and around Amsterdam's punk/new wave scene. Music by Brood, and dramatic appearances by Chappell and Lovich.

CHANGE OF HABIT (1969)

M–Color
▬ James Lee, S.S. Schweitzer, Eric Bercovici
■ Michael Moore
■ Joe Connelly
ℭ UI
● 93m.
✪ Elvis Presley, Mary Tyler Moore

Elvis portrays a doctor at a poor folks' clinic, where his aides include sister Mary and two other of the cutest "new nuns" you ever did see. (Change of HABIT, get it?) This is Elvis' next-to-last story film before turning to concert films to shore up his sagging movie career. Ostensibly this is a straight drama but Presley still manages to sing "Rubberneckin'," and toward the climax he also gets a chance to lay down his scalpel long enough to take part in a citified evangelistic hoe-down, singing "Let's Pray Together." ELVIS #30.

CHAPPAQUA (1966)

	D—Color/B/W
☰	Conrad Rooks
◼	Conrad Rooks
▦	Conrad Rooks
☮	COL
●	82m.
✪	Conrad Rooks, Jean-Louis Barrault, William Burroughs
⊐	The Fugs, Allen Ginsberg, Ravi Shankar, Ornette Coleman

A young man struggles to overcome his heroin addiction at an exclusive clinic in France. Rooks—heir to a large cosmetics fortune—wrote, produced, directed and starred in this elaborate autobiographical therapeutic home movie, beautifully photographed by Robert Frank. Barrault, Burroughs (seen at one point on ice skates!), The Fugs, Ginsberg, Shankar and Coleman are some of the notables flitting in and out of Rooks' fevered celluloid hallucinations in this the *Gone With The Wind* of "rich hippie" movies. Note: Ornette Coleman wrote an original score for this film, but it was never used.

CHARLIE IS MY DARLING (1965)

	R—Color
◼	Peter Whitehead
▦	Andrew Loog Oldham
☮	Lorrimer
●	50m.
✪	The Rolling Stones

Documentary of The Rolling Stones' 1965 two-day tour of Ireland. Interviews with fans and the Stones themselves take up much of the film's running time, with only a brief amount of footage used for "live" performance, with versions of "This Could Be the Last Time" and "It's Alright." The band is also viewed backstage, jamming on an old music hall ditty, "Maybe It's Because I'm a Londoner." While the group incessantly gets in and out of limos, and on and off stage, their actions are accompanied on the soundtrack by sounds from many of their recordings, including: "Get Off of My Cloud," "Heart of Stone," "Satisfaction" and "Goin' Home." Additionally there is a score based on Stones' songs by Mike Leander.

CHARRO (1969)

	D—Color
☰	Charles Marquis Warren
◼	Charles Marquis Warren
▦	Charles Marquis Warren
☮	National General
●	98m.
✪	Elvis Presley, Ina Balin

Elvis gives his chops a rest and warbles only one song (the title tune) in a routine western about a reformed outlaw (Presley) framed for the robbery of a Mexican national treasure. ELVIS #29.

CHASTITY (1969)

- D—Color
- Sonny Bono
- Alessio de Paola
- Sonny Bono
- AIP
- 98m.
- Cher, Barbara Loden
- Atco

Cher, as a runaway, brushes up against prostitution and has a near miss with lesbianism in this torpid road movie. Hubby Sonny wrote script, produced and also penned score. Cher sings "Band of Thieves."

CHELSEA GIRLS, THE (1966)

- D— Color / B/W
- Ronald Tavel/partial
- Andy Warhol
- Andy Warhol
- Filmmaker's Co-op
- 210m.
- Ondine, Brigid Polk, Mary Woronov, Nico, Eric Emerson

Nico doesn't sing here, but instrumental noodling by The Velvet Underground (playing just out of camera range) is heard toward the conclusion of Warhol's mostly improvised epic of sixties New York bohemia.

CHRISTIANE F. (1981)

- D—Color
- Herman Weigel
- Ulrich Edel
- Bennd Eichinger and Hans Weth
- New World
- Natja Brunkhorst, Thomas Haustein
- David Bowie
- RCA German

A teenager (Brunkhorst) drifts into a life of heroin addiction. David Bowie wrote the score, and makes a brief on-screen appearance in a rock club scene in this German film about the near-epidemic of youthful drug addiction in major German cities. Songs performed by Bowie and the Bewley Brothers include the classics "Station To Station" and "Heroes."

CISCO PIKE (1972)

- D—Color
- Bill L. Norton
- Bill L. Norton
- Gerald Ayres
- COL
- 94m.
- Kris Kristofferson, Gene Hackman

Crooked cop blackmails a down-on-his-luck rocker, Pike (Kristofferson), into dealing drugs. The cop (Hackman) is killed toward the film's climax, but not before Pike's life is irreversably shattered. Five songs written and sung by Kristofferson, mostly off-screen, are used for atmospheric purposes. Music by Sonny Terry and the Sir Douglas Quintet is also heard in Kristofferson's dramatic debut.

CLAMBAKE (1967)

	M—Color
☷	Arthur Browne, Jr
▥	Arthur H. Nadel
▦	Arnold Laven, Arthur Gardner, Jules Levy
⚡	UA
●	98m.
✪	Elvis Presley, Will Hutchins, Shelley Fabares
◔	RCA

Prince-and-pauper story of rich boy, Elvis, trading places with po' boy, Hutchins. (Who really gets more screen time here than the probably otherwise indisposed star.) Presley stands in front of an endless succession of rear screen racing and water skiing footage and sings one LP's worth of ditties—one of which, by the way is NOT "Do the Clam." (Nope! *That's* from *Girl Happy*.) But he does sing, among others, the title tune, "Singing Tree" and "How Can You Lose What You Never Had?" ELVIS #25.

CLAUDINE (1974)

	D—Color
☷	Tina Pine, Lester Pine
▥	John Berry
▦	Hannah Weinstein
⚡	TCF
●	92m.
✪	Diahann Carroll, James Earl Jones
◔	Buddah

Slice of life in Harlem comedy-drama about a divorcee (Carroll) with a house full of kids and an empty bank account. When she falls in love with Jones, things get all the more complicated, for his life, isn't exactly a bed of roses either. Curtis Mayfield songs performed on soundtrack by Gladys Knight and The Pips include: "Mr. Welfare Man," "To Be Invisible," "On and On," "The Makings of You" and "Hold On."

C'MON LET'S LIVE A LITTLE (1967)

	M—Color
☷	June Starr
▥	David Butler
▦	June Starr, John Hertelandy
⚡	PAR
●	85m.
✪	Jackie DeShannon, Bobby Vee
◔	Liberty

Jukebox musical goes topical with a free speech on campus sub-plot dropped into the more standard boy-girl malt shoppe goings on. As nearly the last gasp of the teen rock musicals, it packs a pretty feeble punch. Songs include: "Baker Man," "For Granted" by DeShannon, who also sings a duet with Vee, "Back Talk."

COCKSUCKER BLUES (CS Blues) (1976)

R—Color / B/W
- Robert Frank, Daniel Seymour
- Marshall Chess
- 95m.
- The Rolling Stones
- Stevie Wonder, Dick Cavett

Suppressed backstage docu of The Rolling Stones' '72 American tour was commissioned by "the Stones" who, ironically, were the ones to nix its showing after they saw the finished product. Were they trying to spare the morals of America's youth, or only their image? By today's standards it's pretty tame stuff—a little sexual foreplay, a TV set thrown out a window, some drug use. And tedium! Miles of it, in this 16mm "expose" by eminent American photographer, Robert Frank. For *CS Blues* (the film's alternate title) dwells primarily on the behind-the-scenes life of the great British band, wherein a mostly somnambulistic cast of characters passes in parade, including Stevie Wonder, Andy Warhol, Truman Capote, Terry Southern and Lee Radziwill. The brighter side of things can be viewed in the *straight* concert movie, *Ladies And Gentlemen: The Rolling Stones*, filmed at the same time. On-stage and rehearsal versions (complete and in part) of numerous Stones songs are featured including, "Satisfaction," "Jumpin' Jack Flash," "Honky Tonk Women" and "Street Fightin' Man." Note: Finally, in '79 The Stones relented and allowed for future showing of *CS Blues*—but only under the most stipulatory and complicated conditions.

COLD TURKEY (1971)

M—Color
- Norman Lear
- Norman Lear
- Norman Lear, Bud Yorkin
- UA
- 102m.
- Dick Van Dyke, Pippa Scott

Effective comedy of tobacco interests wagering 25 million dollars that all the smokers in a small city won't be able to give up cigarettes for one month. Score for this Capra-meets-Sturges satire by Randy Newman. No soundtrack album available, but one song from Newman's *Sail Away*, "He Gives Us All His Love," is used over opening and closing credits.

COLLEGE CONFIDENTIAL (1960)

D—B/W
- Irving Shulman
- Albert Zugsmith
- Albert Zugsmith
- UI
- 91m.
- Steve Allen, Mamie Van Doren, Rocky Marciano, Walter Winchell
- Conway Twitty

An egghead sociology prof (Allen) ignites nationwide controversy when he administers a campus sex survey. Singer Conway Twitty, in a dramatic part, portrays a student who gets all the answers WRONG on the questionnaire—but Mamie Van Doren scores a hundred in this oh-how-the-mighty-have-fallen delight, featuring appearances by the great Herbert Marshall, champ Marciano and Walter Winchell.

COLLISEUM AND JUICY LUCY (1970)

R—Color
- Tony Palmer, Paul Williams
- 33m.
- Colliseum, Juicy Lucy

Clumsy videotape-to-film transfer of concert performances by the two featured outfits.

COME BACK CHARLESTON BLUE (1972)

D—Color
- Bontche Schweig
- the novel *The Heat's On*, by Chester Himes
- Mark Warren
- Samuel Goldwyn, Jr.
- WB
- 100m.
- Godfrey Cambridge, Raymond St. Jacques
- Atco

A followup to *Cotton Comes To Harlem*. Detectives, Coffin Ed Johnson (St. Jacques) and Gravedigger Jones (Cambridge), bust up a gang smuggling drugs in Thanksgiving turkeys. Donny Hathaway and Quincy Jones did the music for this wacked-out comedy sequel. Title tune sung by Hathaway and Valerie Simpson.

COMING HOME (1978)

D—Color
- Waldo Salt, Robert C. Jones, Nancy Dowd
- Hal Ashby
- Bruce Gilbert
- UA
- 128m.
- Jane Fonda, Jon Voight, Bruce Dern

Fonda portrays a woman who—while her soldier-husband is in Vietnam—falls in love with a returned paraplegic veteran, Voight. Eventually Fonda's husband (Dern) comes home, and the ensuing fireworks provide a shattering climax to this popular film. Many complained over the hammered-home, overamplified recordings by Simon and Garfunkel, The Chambers Brothers, Dylan, Hendrix and other evocative sixties sounds. This ham-fisted tactic *did*, however, result in a period feel for this erotic soaper/anti-'Nam tract. The ultimate use of rock as surround—right up there with *American Graffiti*. The soundtrack features such songs emblematic-of-an-era as "Hey Jude," "Strawberry Fields," "Just Like A Woman," "Time Has Come Today," "Sympathy For The Devil," "Manic Depression" and "Bookends"—and on, and on . . .

COMMITTEE, THE (1968)

D–B/W
- Max Steuer, Peter Sykes
- the short story by Max Steuer
- Peter Sykes
- Max Steuer
- Planet Films
- 58m.
- Paul Jones, Tom Kempinski
- The Crazy World of Arthur Brown

Kafkaesque fantasy of crime and punishment features the cryptic storyline of a hitchhiker (*Privilege*'s Paul Jones) being driven to a mansion occupied by a rather sinister "committee." Score by Pink Floyd, and an appearance by Arthur Brown singing "Nightmare."

CONCERT FOR BANGLADESH (1972)

R–Color
- Saul Swimmer
- Saul Swimmer
- George Harrison, Allen Klein
- TCF
- 99m.
- George Harrison, Bob Dylan, Eric Clapton, Ravi Shankar, Ringo Starr, Leon Russell, Klaus Voorman, Badfinger, Billy Preston
- Apple

Film of one of the major media events of 1971, a benefit concert at New York's Madison Square Garden (planned by Harrison) for the starving nation of Bangladesh. Highlights include Harrison's "Bangladesh" and Dylan's singing of "Blowin' In The Wind." Also seen and heard: "Something" (Harrison), "It Don't Come Easy" (Starr), "Just Like a Woman" (Dylan). Recording supervision by Phil Spector.

COOL ONES, THE (1967)

- M—Color
- Joyce Geller
- Gene Nelson
- William Conrad
- WB
- 96m.
- Debbie Watson, Gil Peterson
- Glen Campbell, The Leaves, The Bantams, T.J. and The Foundations

Pop star (Peterson) whose career is on the skids gets involved in a publicity romance with a teen star (Watson) only to, predictably, actually fall in love with her by the film's finale. Musical appearances by several pop and rock acts (Campbell, The Leaves, etc.) in a TV show sequence. Lee Hazelwood wrote most of the songs and acted as the film's musical supervisor. A character part essayed by sixties off-key singing phenomenon, Mrs. Miller; and choreography by Toni Basil.

COOLEY HIGH (1975)

- D—Color
- Eric Monte
- Michael Schultz
- Steve Kranz
- AIP
- 101m.
- Lawrence Hilton-Jacobs, Garrett Morris, Glynn Turman
- Motown

Adventures of four friends at a black high school in the early sixties centers on the coming of age of a young man, played by Turman. A score by Freddie Perrin and a compilation of blue chip Motown oldies (Temptations, Supremes, Smokey Robinson, Four Tops, Stevie Wonder and others) provide the musical atmosphere as *Car Wash* meets *American Graffiti*.

COSMIC RAY (1961)

- M—B/W
- Bruce Conner
- Bruce Conner
- Bruce Conner
- Filmmakers Co-op
- 4m.

Classic experimental short uses Ray Charles' "What'd I Say" as aural accompaniment to constantly shifting collage of female nude, cartoons, and newsreels of atomic bomb explosions.

CRACKING UP (1977)

- M—Color
- Ace Trucking Co., Credibility Gap, Proctor and Bergman, The Graduates, Neil Israel and "Kansas City" Bob McClurg
- Rowby Goren and Chuck Staley
- C.D. Taylor and Rick Murray
- ITC
- 69m.

✪	Ace Trucking Co., Credibility Gap, Procter and Bergman, The Graduates, Neil Israel, Harry Shearer
➦	The Tubes

Improvisational comedy groups let loose with a mixed-bag of jibes at commercial tele-vision, occasionally interrupted by The Tubes wailing out "White Punks On Dope," "What Do You Want From Life" and "Proud To Be An American."

CREAM'S FAREWELL CONCERT (1968)

	R—Color
☰	Tony Palmer
▣	Tony Palmer
▦	Robert Stigwood
●	90m.
✪	Cream

Just what you'd think this film is, from its straightforward title—a record of the group's very last concert ever, performed in 1968 at London's Royal Albert Hall. Musical highlights: "Spoonful," "Politician," "I'm So Glad" and lots of others of the best-selling songs by this early proto-supergroup (Jack Bruce, Eric Clapton and Ginger Baker). Note: 52m. and 40m. versions of this film, a.k.a. *Cream's Last Concert*, also are in circulation.

CRUISIN' (1977)

	R—Color B/W
▣	Curtis Clark, Tim van Rellim
▦	Curtis Clark, Tim van Rellim
⊄	CIC
●	30m.

Documentary of British teens making like American ones of the 50's and 60's. Greatly influenced (to put it mildly) by *American Graffiti*, this English tribute to U.S. car culture is high-lighted by soundtrack rock and roll. Songs include "I Get Around" by the Beach Boys, "Good Golly Miss Molly" by Little Richard, "Three Window Coupe" by The Rip Cords, and "Joy Ride" by Randy and the Rainbows.

CRUISING (1980)

	D—Color
☰	William Friedkin
▮	the novel by Gerald Walker
▣	William Friedkin
▦	Jerry Weintraub
⊄	UA
●	106m.
✪	Al Pacino, Karen Allen
◑	A&M

A New York city detective (Pacino) goes undercover in the city's homosexual world in order to try and crack a series of unsolved murders. An original score by Jack Nitzsche, and a daring and mostly first-rate (by-and-large punk) collage of sounds from The Cripples, Willie De Ville, The Germs, Rough Trade, John Hiatt, Mutiny, Madelyn Von Ritz, Egberto Gismonti, Barre

Phillips, Ralph Towner and Tom Brown incessantly flood the soundtrack to provide atmosphere for this controversial (purported) slice of gay life.

CUCKOO PATROL (1965)

M–B/W
- Lew Schwarz
- Duncan Wood
- Maurice J. Wilson
- Grand National
- 76m.
- Freddie and The Dreamers, Kenneth Connor

Knockabout British farce of a scout club that gets involved with apprehending thieves during an outing. The British Film Institute bulletin called this film, "a plotless and incredibly unfunny farce with the further embarrassment of grown men (Freddie and group) impersonating boy scouts." C'mon BFI, lighten up!

CULT OF THE DAMNED (orig, ANGEL ANGEL DOWN WE GO) (1970)

D–Color
- Robert Thom
- Robert Thom
- Jerome F. Katzman
- AIP
- 103m.
- Jennifer Jones, Jordan Christopher, Holly Near

Christopher (from the group The Wild Ones) portrays Jim Morrison-like demi-god rocker who, *Teorama*-fashion, services everyone in sight in this high camp concoction. Songs by Barry Mann and Cynthia Weil.

DADDY-O (1959)

D–B/W
- David Moessinger
- Lou Place
- Elmer C. Rhoden, Jr.
- AIP
- 74m.
- Dick Contino, Sandra Giles

Contino plays the part of an ersatz rock singer, who when not engaged in belting out such ditties as "Rock Candy Baby," is otherwise disposed busting up a teen-aged drug ring. A skeleton in *Star Wars'* composer John William's closet, for if the wonderfully gawdawful *Daddy-O* isn't the worst film ever made, still is oh so deliciously disreputable. The silly songs Contino sings go, unintentionally, beyond rock parody; and the unforgettable Giles shows great promise, alas unrealized (where *are* you, Sandra Giles?), of becoming one of the all-time great good-bad teen vamps.

DANCE CRAZE (1980)

R—Color
- Joe Massot
- Joe Massot
- Playpont Films
- 89m.
- Bad Manners, The Boysnatchers, The English Beat, Madness, The Selector, The Specials
- Chrysalis

Ska music is not quite reggae, and just this side of rock and roll—somewhere in between, actually; and this performance film is the first feature to be devoted exclusively to 1980's practitioners of this Jamaican-inspired hybrid sound. Most of the bands are young, British AND racially integrated, and the music they make here is as infectious as it is offbeat. The visual quality of this ska "TAMI Show," however, leaves much to be desired. The Specials do "Concrete Jungle," "Man at C and A," and "Nite Club;" The Selector skanks out on "Three Minute Hero" and "Missing Words" and The English Beat reprise their hit, "Mirror in the Bathroom."

DARIN, BOBBY. Quite a few rock stars have proved more than capable at straight dramatic playing, i.e. Diana Ross, Mick Jagger, Adam Faith, Roger Daltry and Robbie Robertson, to name a few. But Darin in his dramatic roles was consistently an actor of exceptional skill; especially in *Too Late Blues* (1962), *Pressure Point* (1962), *Captain Newman M.D.* (1963) and *Happy Ending* (1969). Ironically Darin's musical work in movies was almost nil—there was some incidental music he did for the totally forgettable *The Lively Set* (1964), and beyond that only some title songs sung over the credits of some equally inauspicious productions.

DATELINE DIAMONDS (1965)

D—B/W
- Tudor Gates
- Jeremy Summers
- Harry Benn
- Rank
- 70m.
- William Lucas, Kenneth Cope
- The Small Faces, The Chantelles, Kiki Dee, Mark Richardson, Kenny Everett

A pirate rock radio ship features prominently in this British programmer about diamond smuggling. On-screen musical appearances by "the Faces," Kiki Dee and others.

DAVID BOWIE (1975)

R—Color
- D.A. Pennebaker
- David Bowie

Elaborate concert presentations form the major part of this unreleased Bowie feature.

DAWN OF THE DEAD (1979)

D—Color
- George Romero
- George Romero

- Richard Rubenstein
- United Film Distr.
- 120m.
- David Emge, Ken Foree
- Varese/Sarabande

The dead rise up once again in this sequel to the classic, *Night Of The Living Dead*. Italian techno-rock score by Goblin and Dario Argento.

DAY THE MUSIC DIED, THE (1977)

R—Color
- Bert Tenzer
- Bert Tenzer
- Bert Tenzer
- Atlantic Releasing
- 97m.
- Jimi Hendrix, Mountain, Van Morrison, Steppenwolf, Dr. John
- Murray the K

Rockumentary culled from an earlier movie entitled *Free*. In 1973 director Tenzer put together a concert film of the 1970 Randall's Island music festival. Four years later some of the footage from that film cropped up in this other Tenzer venture. Retained from the earlier release are performances by Hendrix, Mountain, Morrison, Steppenwolf and Dr. John. Added for this occasion is some on-screen narration by "fifth Beatle," Murray the K, as well as snippets of performances and newsreels of The Beatles, Marvin Gaye, The Doors, The Temptations, Phil Ochs, Otis Redding, Gary Lewis and The Playboys, Little Anthony, Dionne Warwick, Jan and Dean, Herman's Hermits, The Ronettes, Johnny Rivers, Rhinoceros and Elephant's Memory.

DECLINE . . . of western civilization, THE (1980)

R—Color
- Penelope Spheeris
- Gordon Brown, Jeff Prettyman
- Spheeris Films
- 105m.
- "X", Alice Bag Band, Black Flag, Catholic Discipline, Circle Jerks, Fear, Germs
- Slash

What do "X" do in their spare time? What kind of pets did the late Darby Crash keep? Do punk rockers put their pants on one leg at a time, just as you and I, or are they *lowered* into them? All these questions, and more, are answered in this excellent made-for-mass-(well, almost)-consumption collection of interviews and performances with/by some of L.A.'s premier punk bands. Music: "White Minority," "Depression," "Revenge" (Black Flag); "Manimal" (Germs/Darby Crash); "Underground Babylon" (Catholic Discipline); "Beyond and Back," "Johnny Hit and Run Paulene," "We're Desperate" (X), and much more by "Bags," "Jerks" and Fear.

DECOY FOR TERROR (*alt. title* PLAYGIRL KILLER) (1970)

D—Color
- Erich Santamaria
- William Kerwin
- Neil Sedaka

Spectacularly awful Canadian-made thriller about a deranged painter (Kerwin) whose particular eccentricity is murdering his models after capturing them on canvas. Neil Sedaka's participation in this clunker took place just prior to his impressive seventies comeback from sixties teen idol oblivion. He sings two songs: "If You Don't Wanna, You Don't Hafta" and (shudders!) "Do the Waterbug;" and for his appearance in this skid row special, Neil was nominated for a Medved Brothers Golden Turkey Award in the category of worst film performance by a popular singer.

DEEP END (1971)

	D—Color
📽	Jerzy Skolimowski, Jerzy Gruza, Boleslaw Sulik
🎬	Jerzy Skolimowski
🎞	Lutz Hengst
ⓩ	PAR
●	88m.
✪	Jane Asher, John Moulder-Brown

Modern day down-and-out-in-London story of young, ill-fated lovers (Asher and Moulder-Brown) has music by Cat Stevens and Can.

DEVO FILMS. Made for this highly theatrical techno-bubble-gum group by filmmaker Chuck Statler, these clever Richard Lester inspired shorts have been shown both at Devo concerts, as visual accompaniment, and in theaters as films in their own right: *De-Evolution Band/Secret Agent Man/Jocko Homo* (1976) C-15m; *Satisfaction* (1978) C-4m; *Come Back Jonee* (1978) C-4m.; *Freedom of Choice* (1980) C-3m.; *Girl U Want* (1980) C-2m.

DIARY OF A MAD HOUSEWIFE (1970)

	D—Color
📽	Eleanor Perry
📖	a novel by Sue Kaufman
🎬	Frank Perry
🎞	Frank Perry
ⓩ	UI
●	95m.
✪	Carrie Snodgress, Richard Benjamin, Frank Langella
➔	Alice Cooper

A Manhattan housewife (Snodgress), terrorized by the demands of her social-climbing husband (Benjamin), finds herself drifting into an affair with a narcissistic actor (Langella) that proves to be equally unsatisfying. Alice Cooper and his band appear at a party scene playing quietly in the background then destroying their instruments like The Yardbirds did in *Blow-Up* (Which in turn was an imitation of The Who).

DISK JOCKEY JAMBOREE (see JAMBOREE)

DIVINE MADNESS (1980)

	R—Color / B/W
📽	Jerry Blatt, Bette Midler, Bruce Vilanch
🎬	Michael Ritchie

■ Michael Ritchie
■ WB
● 94m.
● Bette Midler
➲ The Harlettes
● Atlantic

Elaborately staged docu of Midler's 1979 concerts in Pasadena, Ca. Bette has gone way beyond being just another capable clown princess, and it shows in this appealing film. While the divine Miss M. may not be everyone's idea of a rock singer, her excellent concert film can teach a thing or two to all rockers with a yen for the leap to the big screen. Songs include: "Paradise," "Boggie Woogie Bugle Boy," "Big Noise From Winnetka" and "Shiver Me Timbers."

D.O.A. (1980)

R—Color
■ Lech Kowalski
■ Lech Kowalski
■ High Times Films
● 90m.
● The Sex Pistols, Iggy Pop, The Clash, The Dead Boys, Stiv Bators, Rich Kids, X-Ray Specs, Generation X, Sham '69, Augustus Palo, Terry and The Idiots

Extensive coverage of The Sex Pistols' seven-city U.S. tour, combines with film of other groups and interviews for an overview of the international punk scene, circa '78. Some critics heaped scorn on this music documentary when it opened. We feel, however, that the film's messiness and scattergun approach tends to complement its subject matter, punk rock music. With mechanical regularity *D.O.A.* shifts away from The Sex Pistols to interview fans, and zeros in on the music of groups that followed in the wake of The Pistols, like The Clash and The Dead Boys. Also seen are several poignant segments featuring Terry and The Idiots—a motley London band inspired by The Sex Pistols who are shown playing in a pub, and throwing in the towel, after literally being spat upon exactly ONCE. Most fascinating, however, is what one might call "The Sid and Nancy Show"—an extremely intimate and intense film of terminally wasted "Pistol," Sid Vicious, and his nearly as far gone girlfriend, Nancy Spungen, being interviewed in a hotel room. Writers used to trot out adjectives like "harrowing" for this sort of Sid/Nancy thing, and it seems to fit most aptly here. (Spungen and Vicious died shortly thereafter.) The Sex Pistols are seen on their whistle-stop tour doing "Anarchy in the U.K.," "God Save the Queen," "Pretty Vacant" and several others. Iggy Pop, although listed in the cast, is only *heard* singing "Nightclubbing," X-Ray Specs (Spex) sing "Oh Bondage, Up Yours" on screen.

DON'T KNOCK THE ROCK (1956)

M—B/W
■ Robert E. Kent
■ Fred F. Sears
■ Sam Katzman
■ COL
● 84m.
● Bill Haley and His Comets, Alan Freed, Alan Dale
➲ Little Richard, Dave Apple and The Applejacks

A riot breaks out at a rock and roll dance, and although the music played there by Bill Haley wasn't *really* to blame, town elders place a ban on "the new sound"—until dee-jay, Alan

Freed, convinces all concerned that rock is but "a harmless outlet for today's youth." Who says that sequels are never up to the originals? For this film is even more inspired than the movie that started it all, *Rock Around The Clock*. It tackles head-on such controversial and burning issues of the day as "suggestive dancing," heavy petting, payola and teen-age curfews. Haley and his Comets are on hand again from "Clock" (doing the title tune, "Calling All Comets," "Rip It Up" and others); but the *real* rock and roll here is courtesy of Little Richard, on display with "Tutti Frutti" and "Long Tall Sally."

DON'T KNOCK THE TWIST (1962)

M—B/W
- James B. Gordon
- Oscar Rudolph
- Sam Katzman
- COL
- 86m.
- Chubby Checker, Mari Blanchard
- Gene Chandler, The Carroll Brothers, Linda Scott, The Dovells, Vic Dana, Dee Dee Sharp
- Parkway

Twist king with a philanthropic bent, Checker, helps to stage a telethon for underprivileged kids, thus elevating *mere* dance craze to a whole new plateau of social respectability. Checker works out on "Slow Twistin'" (with Dee Dee Sharp), "The Fly" and several others; The Dovells do "The Bristol Stomp" and Chandler assumes his pose as "The Duke of Earl." This is the follow-up to producer Katzman's earlier (1961), successful Checker entry, *Twist Around The Clock*.

DON'T LOOK BACK (1967)

R—B/W
- D.A. Pennebaker
- Albert Grossman, Don Court
- Leacock-Pennebaker
- 95m.
- Bob Dylan, Joan Baez, Albert Grossman, Bob Neuwirth, Tito Burns, Derrol Adams
- Donovan, Alan Price, Allen Ginsberg

Dylan's cryptic responses to reporters' questions caused almost as much comment as his singing when this *cinema verite* documentary of his 1965 British tour was first released. Alternately playful and sullen, Dylan takes to the camera like an acting pro. Others appearing in the star's general vicinity—especially Price, Baez and Grossman—quickly become performing partners in a series of theme and variation improvisations on the meaning of personality and the role of the artist in the world. Songs include: "Death of Hattie Carroll;" "The Times They Are A-Changin'" and "Subterranean Homesick Blues" (with Dylan, standing in an alleyway, holding up cue cards with lyric lines written on them as Ginsberg cavorts in the background.)

DON'T MAKE WAVES (1967)

C—Color
- Ira Wallach and George Kirgo
- *Muscle Beach* by Ira Wallach
- Alexander MacKendrick
- John Calley, Martin Ransohoff

♉ MGM
● 97m.
♻ Tony Curtis, Claudia Cardinale, Sharon Tate, David Draper, Mort Sahl, Edgar Bergen
♻ MGM

A con-man (Curtis) has an on-again-off-again romance with an Italian businesswoman (Cardinale) amid the blissed-out splendor of Southern California. Some gentle—perhaps too gentle—kidding of L.A. lifestyles in this pleasant comedy, the last (to date) work of British veteran MacKendrick (*The Man in The White Suit*, *The Sweet Smell of Success*.) Title song by Chris Hillman and Jim McGuinn, sung by The Byrds.

DOORS (THE), and especially its lead singer, the late Jim Morrison, in recent times have become, next to The Beatles, the most widely written about and highly venerated of all sixties rock groups. A major, best-selling bio of Morrison, *No One Gets Out of Here Alive* by Jerry Hopkins and Danny Sugarman, has appeared, and surely a film version of that book will eventually come to pass. Because of renewed interest in The Doors many of their old Elektra label albums are reappearing on lp sales charts, and much has been written in periodicals lately about the fables and fortunes of Lizard King Morrison and the other three members of the outfit, Robby Krieger, John Densmore and Ray Manzarek. While much in the way of performance on film by these four exists, little of it is available to the general public. The most widely shown Morrison film memento is a 40-minute Doors-produced documentary called *Feast of Friends* (1969). Staged bits and concert footage form the core of this ambitious effort which The Doors (and especially Morrison who'd been a film student at one time) hoped would establish their group as something more than a recording and performing outfit. This work contains much good "live" Doors and some fascinating Morrison-induced crowd hysteria. There is also a 2:25 sec. color promo film made for Elektra Records, *Break on Through*, and also for that label the group made another promo item, *The Unknown Soldier*, which was frequently shown at the band's concerts, There's also *The Doors Are Open* (1968), described by Hopkins and Sugarman in their book as "black and white live footage intercut with political events of 1968." Finally, there is a free-form narrative work *HiWay* (1969) directed by Morrison, with the assistance of Frank Lisciandro and Paul Ferrara—much of which takes place in the desert. Doubtless the upsurge of interest in The Doors will help these films become more easily accessible.

DOOR-TO-DOOR MANIAC (*orig.* FIVE MINUTES TO LIVE) (1966)

    D—B/W
✍ Cay Forester
🎬 Bill Karn
▦ James Ellsworth
♉ AIP
● 80m.
♻ Johnny Cash, Ron Howard

Turgid "thriller" of a gang who holds a bank president's wife for ransom. This is one project Cash would probably just as soon forget. Ron Howard, too, for that matter. Not to mention Vic Tayback and Pamela Mason, who also appear. Cash plays a psychotic, guitar-playing thug whose big number in the film is a song entitled "I've Come To Kill."

DOUBLE TROUBLE (1967)

    M—Color
✍ Jo Heims and Marc Brandel

- ◼ Norman Taurog
- ▦ Judd Bernard and Irwin Winkler
- ✇ MGM
- ◉ 92m.
- ✪ Elvis Presley, John Williams, Norman Rossington, Chips Rafferty, Annette Day, Yvonne Romain
- ◐ RCA

A singer (Presley) saves an heiress (Day) from a series of mysterious threats on her life. Threats can't stop Elvis from warbling the likes of "Long-legged Girl," "Could I Fall in Love," "Blue River" and the title tune in this standard operational Presley musical. Elvis #24.

DOUBLE TROUBLE (*see* SWINGIN' ALONG)

DRILLER KILLER (1979)

- D—Color
- ⭆ Nicholas St. John
- ◼ Abel Ferrara
- ▦ Rochelle Wiesberg
- ✇ Rochelle Films
- ◉ 90m.
- ✪ Carolyn Marz, Jimmy Laine
- ⮑ Tony Coca Cola and The Roosters

Noise from a punk rock band living downstairs distracts an artist from his work. But does he do what any law-abiding citizen would do—say, call the police? No! Instead, he drills "Texas Chainsaw" fashion, everyone in sight to death—*except* the punk rockers. Or maybe he killed them after all (in an unfilmed sequel), for the band in question, "The Roosters," haven't been heard from since this film was unleashed, urr, released.

DUSTY AND SWEETS McGEE (1971)

- D—Color
- ⭆ Floyd Mutrux
- ◼ Floyd Mutrux
- ▦ Floyd Mutrux
- ✇ WB
- ◉ 95m.
- ✪ Billy Gray
- ◐ WB

Semi-fictionalized documentary of the L.A. drug scene centering around the title characters, their love for each other shattered by mutual addiction to heroin. Straight to the camera monologues by others in their set are used in counterpoint to the couple's "story." (Billy Gray, "Bud" in TV's *Father Knows Best*, makes an appearance as a drug dealer.) Use of rock especially sensitive in a scene where Dusty and Sweets sit around sadly shooting up to the strains of Van Morrison's "Into the Mystic." Also heard are Del Shannon ("Runaway"), The Monotones, The Marcels, Little Eva and Harry Nilsson.

DYNAMITE CHICKEN (1971)

	M—Color
▰	Ernest Pintoff
▰	Ernest Pintoff
▦	Ernest Pintoff
☡	VPS
●	76m.
✪	Richard Pryor, Paul Krasner
⊒	Jimi Hendrix, John Lennon, Leonard Cohen, Sha-Na-Na, Cat Mother and the All Night Newsboys, Lenny Bruce, Joan Baez, Yoko Ono, The Velvet Underground, The Muddy Waters Blues Band

Most of the musicians in this mixed media collage appear in snips and snatches from old footage, mixed in with new satiric material featuring Pryor and the Ace Trucking Company.

EARLY ABSTRACTIONS (1965)

	R—Color
▰	Harry Smith
▦	Harry Smith
☡	Filmmaker's Co-op
●	97m.

Ten short animated films made in the 1940's and 50's by Smith. In 1965 he got the inspired idea of stringing these works together (they run 6 to 20 minutes) and using side one of *Meet The Beatles* for a soundtrack. The results are sensational—colors and shapes dancing wildly to a Beatles beat.

EARLY CLUE TO A NEW DIRECTION, AN (1966)

	D—B/W
▰	Andrew Meyer
▰	Andrew Meyer
▦	Andrew Meyer
☡	Filmmakers Co-op
●	28m.
✪	Joy Bang, Prescott Townsend, Rene Ricard
⊒	The Unidentified Flying Objects

An engaging dialogue between an old bohemian (Townsend) and a young teenybopper (Bang) is the centerpiece of this charming short narrative. The Obejcts, an all-woman Boston-based ensemble, provide the soundtrack score and can be seen belting out "I'm A Woman" in a coffee house scene. The film's title comes from a line in *A Hard Day's Night* (a snatch of whose soundtrack can be heard at the opening of this film).

EASY COME EASY GO (1967)

	M—Color
▰	Allen Weiss and Anthony Lawrence
▰	John Rich
▦	Hal Wallis
☡	PAR
●	97m.

⊐ Elvis Presley, Dodie Marshall, Pat Preist, Elsa Lanchester
◑ RCA

    A soon-to-be-released-from-service Navy frogman discovers sunken treasure and romance. By the time this film was made, Presley movies hardly ever played the larger burgs. But good ole country boys and their sweet mamas all over America, jam-packed the only movie house in town for such as these three-times-a-year releases. No more could they resist the occasion, than could a big city effete intellectual snob bypass the latest Ingmar Bergman flick. Between immersions Elvis sings "Yoga is As Yoga Does," "Love Machine," and the title tune. Elvis #23.

EASY RIDER (1969)

    D—Color
🎞 Peter Fonda, Dennis Hopper, Terry Southern
■ Dennis Hopper
▦ Bert Schneider
✇ COL
● 95m.
✪ Peter Fonda, Dennis Hopper, Jack Nicholson, Luke Askew
⊐ Phil Spector, Toni Basil, Karen Black (billed as Karen Marmer)
◑ Dunhill

    Two hippies (Fonda and Hopper) polish off a cocaine deal, then take off on their motorcycles for the New Orleans Mardi Gras. Along the way they meet up with an alcoholic Southern lawyer (Nicholson). Eventually the three of them are murdered by rednecks. One of the most well-received films (critically AND financially) ever pitched to the youth market—so much so that attendance for it went way beyond the original targeted audience. *Easy Rider* was the film phenom of its year, opening the floodgates for a spate of youth-oriented films. Fonda and Hopper's Kerouac-inspired travels are counterpointed by soundtrack rock including: "The Pusher" and "Born to be Wild" (Steppenwolf), "Wasn't Born to Follow" (The Byrds), "The Weight" (The Band) and "Ballad of Easy Rider" (Roger McGuinn).

EAT THE DOCUMENT (1972)

    R—Color
🎞 Bob Dylan
■ Bob Dylan and Howard Alk
✇ Leacock-Pennebaker
● 55m.
✪ Bob Dylan
⊐ The Hawks (The Band)

    Rarely-shown Dylan project—too short for widespread theatrical exhibition—consists mostly of footage of the singer's '66 European tour. Filmed by Pennebaker, and then later assembled by Dylan and actor-director Howard Alk into a kind of home movie collage, the highlight of the film is the gleanings from a Royal Albert Hall concert, featuring The Hawks, later known as The Band. Dylan seen singing "Leopard Skin Pillbox Hat," "Just Like Tom Thumb's Blues," and many others, just after he'd entered his "electric" phase.

ELEKTRA GLIDE IN BLUE (1973)

    D—Color
🎞 Robert Boris

- James William Guercio
- James William Guercio
- UA
- 113m.
- Robert Blake, Elisha Cook, Jr.
- UA

Motorcycle policeman (Blake) gets drawn into a murder investigation in this film with a cops-vs-hippies theme. Producer/director Guercio, who masterminded the group Chicago, also wrote the score for this cynical, downbeat film. "Most of All" by the Marcels heard on soundtrack.

ELVIS (1979)

D—Color
- Anthony Lawrence
- John Carpenter
- Dick Clark, Anthony Lawrence
- Dick Clark Films
- 119m.
- Kurt Russell, Shelley Winters
- DCP

Serviceable TV movie (shown theatrically outside U.S.) traces high points of Elvis Presley's life and career up until the occasion of his Las Vegas comeback. Director Carpenter worked on this project in between the filming of his two movie successes, *Halloween* and *The Fog*. Russell's (playing Presley) singing voice dubbed by Ronnie McDowell. Songs include: "Mystery Train," "Love Me Tender," "Pledging My Love" and "Lawdy Miss Clawdy," Vocal backing by The Jordanaires, and musical direction by Joe Renzetti. Elvis' discoverer, Sam Phillips, acted as a special consultant for the film.

ELVIS ON TOUR (1972)

R—Color
- Pierre Adidge, Robert Abel
- Pierre Adidge, Robert Abel
- Pierre Adidge, Robert Abel
- MGM
- 93m.
- Elvis Presley
- The Sweet Inspirations, Vernon Presley, Jackie Kahane.
- RCA

Documentary of 1971 cross country tour by Elvis finds him still thoroughly in control of the situation, with the dissolution that finally did him in seen creeping in only around the edges. Crafted by the same filmmakers responsible for Joe Cocker's *Mad Dogs and Englishmen*, with an assist from "montage supervisor" Martin Scorsese (!), this film employs even more split-screen and Dolby than the pathbreaking Cocker film. Lots of backstage footage, and everywhere Presley travels the out-front crowd is never less than lovingly hysterical. Elvis' last two films were concert movies, and this second of the two shows him in good form as he zips through 29!—count 'em—29? numbers including: "Johnny B. Goode," "C.C. Rider," "That's Alright Mama," "Suspicious Minds," "Burnin' Love," "Mystery Train," "I Got a Woman" and "Ready Teddy." Elvis #33.

ELVIS—THAT'S THE WAY IT IS (1970)

R—Color
- Denis Sanders
- Herbert F. Solow
- MGM
- 107m.
- Elvis Presley
- The Sweet Inspirations
- RCA

By the time this documentary on Elvis was made, his career was in a definite downswing. He was still the king, alright, but his recordings weren't selling nearly as well as they did before, and his film activity was bottoming out. This movie was but one part of a several-pronged attempt to bring the star's popularity level back up to its former state. This, then, is a permanent record of Elvis' so-called "Vegas comeback." Here we have, to use Lenny Bruce's phrase, "show business heaven" personified, as we see Elvis strut his stuff not only before the fascinated eyes of the likes of Cary Grant, Sammy Davis, Jr. and (!) Xavier Cugat, but also of average Joes just like you 'n me. Twenty-seven songs are featured, including "That's All Right Mama," "Can't Help Falling In Love With You," "Suspicious Minds," "Blue Suede Shoes," "Heartbreak Hotel" and "Mystery Train." Elvis #32.

ENO (1973)

R—Color
- Alfons Sinniger
- Alfons Sinniger
- Alfons Sinniger
- Fair Enterprises
- 24m.
- Eno, Chris Spedding, Phil Manzanera
- Roxy Music

This brief documentary portrait of one of the most influential figures in techo-rock, follows him from his days with Roxy Music to his split from the group and subsequent emergence as a solo performer. Songs performed include "The Paw Paw Negro Blowtorch" and "Needles in The Camel's Eye." Roxy Music seen and heard performing "Remake/Remodel."

ERIC CLAPTON AND HIS ROLLING HOTEL (1980)

R—Color
- Rex Pike
- Rex Pike
- Angle Films Ltd.
- 60m.
- Eric Clapton
- Muddy Waters, Elton John, George Harrison

Film of a 1979 German tour by Eric Clapton and musical company. "The Rolling Hotel" of the film's title is a luxury train built by the Third Reich's Goering, and it serves as the transportation for Clapton and crew on their German blitz. Muddy Waters was also along for the ride, and can be seen singing "Got My Mojo Working" and "Mannish Boy." Clapton does "Layla," "Lay Down Sally," "Tulsa Time" and others, and is joined for one of his concert encores by George Harrison and Elton John.

EVERYDAY'S A HOLIDAY (see SEASIDE SWINGERS)

EXPERIENCE (1969)

R—Color
- Peter Neal
- Austin John Marshall
- Pomegranate Films
- 29m.
- Jimi Hendrix
- Noel Redding, Mitch Mitchell
- Bull Dog

Good live performances of "Purple Haze" and "Wild Thing" by Jimi and the band, highlight this British short. Additionally, "Foxy Lady," "Castles Made of Sand," "May This Be Love" and "Voodoo Chile" heard accompanying visuals of backstage activity, and the like.

EXPRESSO BONGO (1960)

M—B/W
- Wolf Mankowitz
- Val Guest
- Val Guest
- Continental
- 108m.
- Laurence Harvey, Sylvia Sims, Cliff Richard
- A small-time agent (Harvey) moves into the highest reaches of show business when he discovers a young rock singer (Richard) in a coffee bar. Cliff sings "The Shrine On The Second Floor" in this lightweight rock satire—echoes of which can be seen in the recent *The Idolmaker.*

FAME (1980)

M—Color
- Christopher Gore
- Alan Parker
- David de Silva, Alan Marshall
- MGM
- 133m.
- Irene Cara, Barry Miller, Paul McCrane, Linda Clifford, Laura Dean
- RSO

Episodic musical/drama of four years in the life of a group of students at New York's High School For the Performing Arts. If you're wondering whatever happened to Lesley ("It's My Party") Gore, she's alive and well and writing songs for the likes of this update of the old MGM Mickey-Judy musicals. Several hit songs by Michael and Lesley Gore and Dean Pitchford (including "Hot Lunch Jam," "Out Here On My Own," "Red Light" and the title tune) all originated from this film/soundtrack album package.

FAMILY JEWELS, THE (1965)

- M—Color
- Jerry Lewis, Bill Richmond
- Jerry Lewis
- Jerry Lewis
- PAR
- 98m.
- Jerry Lewis, Donna Butterworth
- Gary Lewis and The Playboys

For her selection of a guardian, a child heiress (Butterworth) has a choice of five distinctly different uncles—all played by Lewis. Barely makes it under the wire as a rock movie, for just a snatch of "This Diamond Ring" is seen and heard as proud papa Jerry opens a closet door and out tumbles son, Gary Lewis, and The Playboys. One of Jerry's funniest!

FAMILY WAY, THE (1966)

- D—Color
- Bill Naughton
- the play *All in Good Time* by Bill Naughton
- Roy Boulting
- John Boulting, Roy Boulting
- WB
- 114m.
- Hayley Mills, Hywel Bennett
- London

Serio-comic British drama details the consequences of an innocent young man's (Bennett) inability to "perform" on his wedding night. The film's score by Paul McCartney was one of the first pieces of work any of The Beatles ever did away from the group.

FASTBREAK (1979)

- M—Color
- Sandor Stern
- a story by Marc Kaplan
- Jack Smight
- Stephen Friedman
- COL
- 107m.
- Gabe Kaplan, Harold Sylvester
- Motown

A basketball coach at a college in Nevada (Kaplan) wants so desperately to win the big game that he imports most of his players from the streets of New York City. Film has the ho-hum quality of made-for-TV movie. Billy Preston and Syreeta got a hit recording out of one of their soundtrack vocals for this comedy—"With You I'm Born Again." The pair also soloed and dueted on several other of the film's songs, which were written by David Shire, Carol Connors and James Di Pasquale.

FASTEST GUITAR ALIVE, THE (1968)

D—Color
- Robert E. Kent
- Michael Moore
- Sam Katzman
- MGM
- 87m.
- Roy Orbison, Sammy Jackson
- MGM

A group of Confederate soldiers (led by Orbison) rob the San Francisco mint, then discover that the Civil War is over. Film's main action concerns their attempts to return the gold to the U.S. government, while being pursued by a band of cutthroat thieves. Plot here is nearly a carbon copy of Elvis' first film, *Love Me Tender*; and this was originally intended as his second film. Finally, though, good sense prevailed; producer Katzman waited a while, then, called upon Orbison to play the part. Title comes from Roy's guitar which converts into a weapon whenever the varmints come into view. Sam the Sham (Scaduto), minus the Pharohs appears in a small part. Songs co-written (with Bill Dees) and sung by Orbison, include: the title tune, "Pistolero," "Good Time Party," "Medicine Man" and "Rollin' On."

FERRY 'CROSS THE MERSEY (1965)

M—B/W
- David Franden
- Jeremy Summers
- Michael Holden
- UA
- 88m.
- Gerry and The Pacemakers, Cilla Black
- The Fourmost

◔   United Artists

    Typical birth-of-a-band fairy tale as Gerry and the group make a grab for the brass ring and gold records, told in typical movie bio fashion. Songs include: "It's Gonna Be All Right," "I Like It," "I'll Be There" and eleven others.

FESTIVAL (1970)

    R—Color
■   Murray Lerner
▦   Murray Lerner
♋   Peppercorn-Wormser
●   98m.
✪   Bob Dylan, Donovan, Joan Baez, Howlin' Wolf, Paul Butterfield Blues Band, Mike Bloomfield, Judy Collins

    Documentary of Newport Folk Festivals, circa 1963-66. Bob Dylan shocked his folk fans when he let loose with the all-rocking "Maggie's Farm" at the 1966 Newport gig. Unfortunately this film shows only part of that historic performance, and doesn't examine any of its (then) earth-shattering implications to the pop music scene.

FILLMORE (1972)

    R—Color
■   Richard T. Heffron
▦   Herbert F. Decker
♋   TCF
●   105m.
✪   The Grateful Dead, It's a Beautiful Day, Jefferson Airplane, Santana, Hot Tuna, Cold Blood, Boz Scaggs, Elvin Bishop, New Riders of the Purple Sage, Stoneground, Quicksilver Messenger Service, Tower of Power
◔   Fillmore Records

    Concert film of the last days of San Francisco's Fillmore West rock emporium, interleaved with entrepreneur Bill Graham's reminiscences of the heyday of the S.F. "scene." Not all the groups listed in the credits are seen with complete versions of songs, but those who do include: Santana ("In a Silent Way"), The Grateful Dead ("Casey Jones"), Jefferson Airplane ("We Can Be Together") and Cold Blood ("You Got Me Humming").

FINGERS (1978)

    D—Color
✎   James Toback
■   James Toback
▦   George Barrie
♋   Brut
●   90m.
✪   Harvey Keitel, Tisa Farrow, Jim Brown

    A concert pianist (Keitel) doubles as gambling bet collector for the mob until his relationship with a young girl (Farrow) makes him decide to burn his bridges violently behind him. Keitel walks about with a portable tape recorder playing such golden oldies as "Summertime Summertime" by The Jamies, "Baby Talk" by Jan and Dean, and many others in this overly florid Mailer-by-way-of-Bernardo-Bertolucci film noir.

FIVE SUMMER STORIES (1973)

R—Color
- Greg MacGillivray, Jim Freeman
- Greg MacGillivray, Jim Freeman
- Greg MacGillivray, Jim Freeman
- MacGillivray-Freeman Films
- 100m.

Billed as "the last surfing movie," this is a compilation of the directors' previous hang ten efforts (*Waves of Change, The Sunshine Sea*, etc.), plus some new footage. Abundant use of classic Beach Boys "surfarias" on soundtrack, including: "California Girls," "Surfin' Safari," "Surf's Up," "Good Vibrations" and several others. Additional music by the group, Honk.

FLAMING STAR (1960)

D—Color
- Clair Huffaker, Nunnally Johnson
- Don Siegel
- David Weisbart
- TCF
- 87m.
- Elvis Presley, Barbara Eden, Dolores Del Rio

Elvis plays a half-breed Indian torn between his Native American culture and the white man's, in this almost musicless Presley film. Only the title song is heard in Siegel's sincere, but confused try, to change the pace for singer Presley. ELVIS #6.

FLASH GORDON (1980)

D—Color
- Lorenzo Semple, Jr.
- characters created by Alex Raymond
- Michael Hodges
- Dino Di Laurentis
- UI
- 110m.
- Sam J. Jones, Melody Anderson
- Elektra

Flashy and successful updating of the old comic strip and movie serial. Music by Queen (the title tune, etc.), plus a non-rock, symphonic score by Howard Blake.

FM (1978)

M—Color
- Ezra Sacks
- John A. Alonzo
- Rand Holston
- UI
- 105m.
- Martin Mull, Eileen Brennan, Cleavon Little
- Linda Ronstadt, Tommy Petty and The Heartbreakers, REO Speedwagon, Jimmy Buffet
- MCA

Dee-jays at a progressive rock radio station go on strike when they're threatened with a conservative record playlist. Film overflows with numerous parallel sub-plots and "wacky" goings-on. Appearances by Linda Ronstadt ("Poor, Poor Me," "Love Me Tender"), Jimmy Buffet ("Livingston Saturday Night"), REO Speedwagon ("Ridin' The Storm Out") and Tom Petty ("American Girl," "Breakdown"). Ironically, more people bought the soundtrack album from this film, than actually saw the movie. And no wonder! For every nook and cranny of *FM*'s story is permeated by music from the likes of Neil Young, Billy Joel, Warren Zevon, B.B. King, Steve Miller and The Eagles.

FOLLOW THAT DREAM (1963)

- M—Color
- Charles Lederer
- the novel *Pioneer Go Home*, by Richard Powell
- Gordon Douglas
- David Weisbart
- UA
- 110m.
- Elvis Presley, Anne Helm
- RCA

OR, *The Lauderdale Hillbillies* as Elvis and his family belligerently homestead on valuable Florida real estate in this standard Presley comedy-musical. Elvis sings the title tune, "What a Wonderful Life," "I'm Not the Marryin' Kind" and several others. ELVIS #9.

FOUR STARS (★ ★ ★ ★) (1967)

- D—B/W
- Andy Warhol
- Andy Warhol
- Filmmaker's Co-op
- 1,500m.
- Viva, Ondine, Nico, Patrick Close, Brigid Polk, Taylor Mead, Edie Sedgwick, Alan Midgette
- The Velvet Underground

Warhol extravaganza with occasional on-screen music by The Velvet Underground shown in its entirety on only one occasion. A two hour version also exists. No 15-record soundtrack album is available, but Nico's "It Was a Pleasure Then" from her *Chelsea Girl* album was written for and first performed in this film. The superimposed photographs of Nico on the cover of that album suggests the visual style of this epic project.

FOXES (1980)

- D—Color
- Gerald Ayres
- Adrian Lynes
- David Puttnam and Gerald Ayres
- UA
- 108m.
- Jodie Foster, Sally Kellerman, Adam Faith
- Casablanca

A San Fernando valley teenager (Foster) and her friends face modern adolescent problems (sex, drug use) compounded by parental neglect. The ads ("Daring To Do It!") were a sleazy come-on, for the film itself, though unsuccessful, is at least thoughtful. Foster's scene with her father (Faith) is a high point of this contemporary youth drama whose background sounds include songs by Janis Ian ("Fly Too High"), Cher ("Bad Love"), Bob Seger ("Ship of Fools") and Donna Summer (the film's haunting title theme, "On The Radio"). Other music by Giorgio Moroder.

FRANKIE AND JOHNNY (1966)

M—Color
- Alex Gottlieb
- Frederick de Cordova
- Edward Small
- UA
- 87m.
- Elvis Presley, Nancy Kovack-Mehta
- RCA

Period riverboat setting for Presley musical based on the old barroom ballad—only this time out F & J live happily ever after. Film represents a temporary upswing over most Elvis movie vehicles from around this period. Songs include the title tune, "Come Along" and "Petunia." ELVIS #21.

FREE (1973)

R—Color
- Bert Tenzer
- Bert Tenzer
- Bert Tenzer
- Indie-Pix
- 80m.
- Jimi Hendrix, Mountain, Van Morrison, Steppenwolf, Dr. John

Documentary of the 1970 Randall's Island (New York) Music Festival PLUS staged re-enactments of the volatile goings-on that surrounded the event. The film's press releases described *Free* as the first "musical docu-drama" (whatever that is), but the technique proves less than breathtaking as one waits for the next rock act (Hendrix, Morrison, et al.) to sweep away the fake drama from the screen.

FRIENDS (1971)

D—Color
- Jack Russell, Vernon Harris
- Lewis Gilbert
- Lewis Gilbert
- PAR
- 102m.
- Sean Bury, Alice Adams
- PAR

Two alienated teenagers fall in love and run away together, only to face harsher realities. This treacly tale of teen trysting has a soundtrack score written by Elton John and Bernie Taupin.

FUGS (1965)

- R—Color
- ■ Edward English
- ▦ Edward English
- ● 12m.
- ✪ The Fugs

Stone-age shock-rockers Ken Weaver, Ed Sanders and Tuli Kupferberg, collectively The Fugs, *epater* a bunch of tired-looking businessmen at a Waldorf-Astoria luncheon by singing "Slum Goddess," "Doin' Alright," "Group Grope," "Kill For Peace," "Wet Dream" and "I Couldn't Get High."

FUN IN ACAPULCO (1963)

- M—Color
- ☰ Allan Weiss
- ■ Richard Thorpe
- ▦ Hal Wallis
- ✇ PAR
- ● 97m.
- ✪ Elvis Presley, Ursula Andress
- ↻ RCA

Elvis plays a singer/lifeguard enamored of femmatador, Andress, in this hands-across-the-border project. Elvis' films had been banned in Mexico for several years after showings of *G.I. Blues* caused riots; and this shot-on-location musical signalled rapprochement and a lifting of the ban. Among the songs: "El Toro," "Marguerita," "The Bullfighter Was a Lady" and the title tune. ELVIS #13.

GAS! OR IT BECAME NECESSARY TO DESTROY THE WORLD IN ORDER TO SAVE IT (1970)

- M—Color
- ☰ George Armitage
- ■ Roger Corman
- ▦ Roger Corman
- ✇ AIP
- ● 79m.
- ✪ Robert Corff, Elaine Giftos, Ben Vereen, Cindy Williams, Bud Cort, Talia Coppola (aka. Talia Shire)
- ↱ Country Joe McDonald
- ↻ American International

A mysterious poison gas causes all those over the age of twenty-five to die. The survivors, however, soon find themselves facing the same set of problems they had assumed resulted from the "generation gap;" *Beach Party* meets Bertolt Brecht in Roger Corman's teenybopper apocalypse. This penultimate Corman directorial effort never got the wide release it deserved. Not that it would have been a box office bonanza, but its "head comics" nuttiness was a welcome relief from the solemn tone of the other "youthsploitation" flicks that were coming out at the same time. Songs by Country Joe and the Fish include "Please Don't Bury My Soul," "Maybe It Wasn't Really Love" and "Don't Chase Me Around." Country Joe playing a character called "A.M. Radio" appears on-screen at an end-of-the-world rock concert singing "World That We All Dreamed Of."

GENESIS—A BAND IN CONCERT (1976)

```
     R—Color
▪    Tony Maylam
▪    Tony Maylam
▦    Michael Samuelson
✿    EMI
●    45m.
✪    Genesis
```

Random clips of war, H-bombs and chase scenes share center stage with footage of Genesis in concert (Bingley Hall, Stafford, summer of 1976). To the end, the band is all but upstaged by this sort of zip-zap-zoomery.

GET YOURSELF A COLLEGE GIRL (1964)

```
     M—Color
▪    Robert E. Kent
▪    Sid Miller
▦    Sam Katzman
✿    MGM
●    88m.
✪    Nancy Sinatra, Joan O'Brien
�ড    The Animals, The Dave Clark Five, The Standells, Freddie Bell and The Bellboys
✪    MGM
```

A college student (O'Brien) gets into hot water over some spicy song lyrics she has written, but support from a sympathetic politician saves the day for this misunderstood miss. Late entry in the jukebox musicals sweepstakes, and a film whose uncertainty is reflected in the various title changes it went through before producer Katzman settled on the final and baffling one. (At different times during production the film was also known as: *The Swingin' Set* [its final U.K. title], *The Go-Go Set* and *Watusi a Go-Go*.) Further confusion evidenced by the film's mixed bag of rock *and* jazz (Stan Getz, Jimmy Smith and Astrid Gilberto) artists. The Dave Clark Five sing "Whenever You're Around" and "Thinking of You Baby," The Animals sing "Around and Around" and "Blue Feeling."

GHOST GOES GEAR, THE (1966)

```
     M—Color
▪    Roger Dunton, Hugh Gladwish
▪    Hugh Gladwish
▦    Harry Field
✿    Warner-Pathe (England)
●    41m.
✪    The Spencer Davis Group and Stevie Winwood
➢    Acker Bilk
```

Beatle-esque romp from Great Britain, trimmed for release by about half its original length, leaving only a sketchy story about a haunted house and, toward the conclusion, a garden party min-pop fest.

GHOST IN THE INVISIBLE BIKINI, THE (1966)

M—Color
- Louis M. Heyward and Elwood Ullman
- Don Weis
- James H. Nicolson and Samuel Z. Arkoff
- AIP
- 82m.
- Tommy Kirk, Deborah Walley, Nancy Sinatra, Boris Karloff, Francis X. Bushman
- The Bobby Fuller Four

Beach Party meets *Blithe Spirit* in this typically frothy AIP concoction about a restless ghoul (Karloff) who finds his mansion invaded by rock and rollers. Film represents the only screen appearance by legendary California rocker Bobby Fuller who died under somewhat mysterious circumstances not long after its making. Songs include "Geronimo," "Swing-A-Ma-Thing," "Don't Try To Fight It Baby," and "Make The Music Pretty."

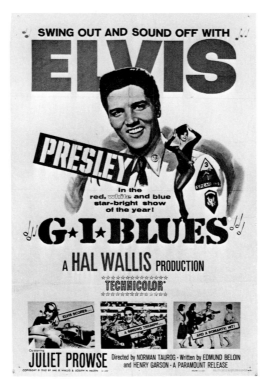

G.I. BLUES (1960)

M—Color
- Edmund Belan, Henry Garson
- Norman Taurog
- Hal Wallis
- PAR
- 104m.

⊗ Elvis Presley, Juliet Prowse
◎ RCA

Elvis is a singing G.I. chosen by his mates as their candidate in a race to see who can get a date with the notoriously undatable Prowse. When Elvis was drafted in 1958 many felt the time away from his fans would kill his career. Colonel Parker, however, gambled all by imposing a total recording blackout for the two years the singer was away. It worked! *G.I. Blues,* Elvis' first post-service film was almost as major a movie event as his first movie, *Love Me Tender.* This re-launch vehicle plays around with much of the myth surrounding Private Elvis Presley, but a demystification process is in operation here, for unlike before, he portrays someone not larger than life, but only a guy who *just happens* to be able to sing. *The New York Times'* film critic, Bosley Crowther, wrote of Elvis' return film, "gone is the wiggle, the lecherous leer, the swagger, the unruly hair, the droopy eyelids and the hillbilly manner of speech." Lest you think this was criticism on the writer's part, it was not! It was *praise.* Elvis *did* seem less threatening here, and *G.I. Blues'* hitless musical package ("Wooden Heart," "Pocketful of Rainbows," "Big Boots" etc.) was another sign that a downhill movie slide had begun. ELVIS #5.

GILDA LIVE (1980)

R—Color
🎬 Anne Beatts, Lorne Michaels, Marilyn Suzanne Miller, Don Novello, Michael O'Donoghue, Gilda Radner, Rosie Shuster, Paul Schaeffer and Alan Zweibel
▪ Mike Nichols
▦ Lorne Michaels
⚡ WB
● 96m.
⊗ Gilda Radner, Father Guido Sarducci
⇥ Rouge
◎ WB

Film of Gilda Radner's revue (staged at New York's Winter Garden theatre) based on characters she created on television's *Saturday Night Live.* Filtered through several layers of media, comedienne Radner's rag mop charm loses some of its spontaneity. Her two rock satire bits retain all of their force however. First is "Rhonda Weiss and the fabulous Rhondettes," a Shangri-las type group bewailing the F.D.A.'s banning of sugar substitute with "Goodbye Saccharine." Then, best of all, she's "Candy Slice" (a devastating parody of rocker Patti Smith) flinching and burping her way through "Gimme Mick"—a tribute to the leader of The Rolling Stones, penned by Radner and Paul Schaeffer.

GIMME SHELTER (1971)

R—Color
▪ David Maysles, Albert Maysles, Charlotte Zwerin
▦ Ronald Schneider
⚡ Cinema V
● 90m.
⊗ The Rolling Stones
⇥ Ike and Tina Turner, The Jefferson Airplane

Documentary of notorious 1969 Stones concert at Altamont, California. (We discuss this controversial film in depth in the text.) Most everybody, of course, remembers the real life snuffout climax, but what is often forgotten is how much good, well-filmed footage of The Rolling Stones is contained in this film—especially the early Madison Square Garden portion. It's ironic that these self-styled high priests of anarchy should be so totally at a loss when confronted by the real thing: the crowd at Altamont. Aside from the moral issues revolving around actually showing the murder, this is a manual for cliche-avoidance in rock filmmaking. Tina Turner is seen doing a spectacular version of "I've Been Loving You Too Long;" and songs by the Stones include: "Jumpin' Jack Flash," "Satisfaction," "You Gotta Move," "Wild Horses," "Brown Sugar" and (while the much-publicized killing is taking place just a few dozen yards away) "Sympathy For The Devil."

GIRL CAN'T HELP IT, THE (1956)

M—Color
- Frank Tashlin, Herbert Baker
- a story by Garson Kanin
- Frank Tashlin
- Frank Tashlin
- TCF
- 99m.
- Jayne Mansfield, Tom Ewell, Edmund O'Brien
- Fats Domino, Gene Vincent and The Blue Caps, The Platters, Little Richard, Eddie Fontaine, The Chuckles, Julie London, Nino Tempo, April Stevens, Eddie Cochran.

O'Brien plays a gangster who can't bear the thought that his girlfriend (Mansfield) is a "nobody," and so he hires press agent Ewell to turn her into an overnight superstar. In true screen fashion Ewell and Mansfield flip over each other, and before its happily-ever-after fadeout this delirious comedy presents some of the best-looking rock and roll ever (before or since) on a movie screen. Mansfield, here, is a succulent A-Bomb just waiting to explode (with rock music as the detonator) in this satire of record industry hucksterism—and the 1950's in general. The performers on hand, among them Fats Domino, Little Richard and Gene Vincent, constitute a virtual master class on how to rock and roll. And the *look* of the film is just right! Not like the earlier black-and-white rock musicals, but with Cinemascope, stereophonic sound and Technicolor you can eat with a spoon. Mansfield, playing a talentless would-be singer, was the ultimate fifties sexual commodity and the aura she exuded works in perfect complement to the hit-and-run 2:32 sec. foreplay-to-orgasm viscerality of the (then) "new sound." Music includes: the title tune and "She's Got It" (Little Richard); "Blue Monday" (Domino); "Be Bop A Lula" (Vincent) and "Twenty Flight Rock" (Cochran).

GIRL HAPPY (1965)

	M—Color
☰	Harvey Bullock, R.S. Allen
◼	Boris Sagal
▦	Joe Pasternak
☭	MGM
●	96m.
✪	Elvis Presley, Shelley Fabares
◎	RCA

Elvis plays a girls' college chaperone in this frothy musical whose numbers include: "Do the Clam" (bet you thought that was from *Clam Bake*), "Spring Fever," "Ft. Lauderdale Chamber of Commerce" and "She's Evil." ELVIS #18.

GIRL ON A MOTORCYCLE (1968)

D—Color
Ronald Duncan
the novel by Andre Pieyre de Mandiagues
Jack Cardiff
William Sassoon
Claridge
91m.
Marianne Faithfull, Alain Delon
Tetragrammaton

A gone-straight housewife (Faithfull) just can't hack her new way of life and reverts to her former wild lifestyle and lover (Delon). Wonderful unmitigated trash. Picture this! Pop icon, Marianne Faithfull, swaddled in black leather from head to toe, roars toward the camera astride a chopper. She screeches to a halt. Cut to next shot. Faithfull excitedly rushes into a room, exhorting Delon (no mean icon himself) to, "SKIN ME!" If this whets your appetite, there're ninety beautifully photographed minutes more in this movie whose title, in some markets, was changed to the rather blunt one of *Naked Under Leather*. Score by Les Reed.

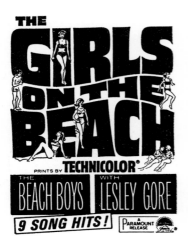

GIRLS ON THE BEACH, THE (1965)

M—Color
David Malcolm
William M. Witney
Harvey Jacobson
PAR
85m.
Noreen Corcoran, Martin West
The Beach Boys, The Crickets, Leslie Gore

A group of college girls are conned into believing that The Beatles are all set to make an appearance at a benefit for a sorority house. When the band proves "no show", the girls take matters in hand and successfully impersonate the fab four themselves.   Between cracks in the plot, The Crickets romp through the sand singing "La Bamba;" The Beach Boys sing the title tune and "Little Honda" and Lesley Gore trills "Leave Me Alone" and "It's Gotta Be You."

GIRL'S TOWN (1959)

- D–B/W
- Robert Smith
- Charles Haas
- Albert Zugsmith
- MGM
- 92m.
- Mamie Van Doren, Mel Torme
- The Platters, Paul Anka

Van Doren plays a good/bad girl who gets hit with a bum murder rap and is sent to a prison run by some kind of "nuns." There, she experiences some *sotto* (and not so *sotto*) "lez" stuff, and so terrified is she by her ordeal that she *nearly* "gets religion." *Variety* said, "scenes of Miss Van Doren in the tightest of costumes exchanging badinage with nuns are in dubious taste to say the least." Anka plays a singer whose big numbers in the film are "Lonely Boy" AND "Ave Maria;" and while Mamie *serves* time, The Platters *keep* time to "Wish it Were Me" in this *klassic* which also bears the yummy alternate title of *The Innocent and the Damned*.

GO-GO BIG BEAT (1965)

- R–Color
- Kenneth Hume, Frank Gilpin (uncredited)
- Kenneth Hume
- Eldorado
- 82m.
- Millie Small, The Animals, The Four Pennies, Lulu and The Luvvers, The Merseybeats, The Wackers, The Hollies

Strictly the old shell-and-pea game, for contrary to the implications of the ad campaign, The Beatles didn't actually appear in this film. In fact, Beatle manager Brian Epstein instituted legal action, for all that this British production contained was some sub-*West Side Story* ballet dancing (from a film short, *Mods and Rockers*) to the tune of music BY The Beatles. (But you had to look at the ads *very* closely to figure this out.) The other billed performers, shot in customary tilt-angled TV concert fashion, *do* appear, however. Songs include: "Here I Go Again," "Baby That's All" (Hollies); "My Boy Lollipop" (Small); "Shout" (Lulu) and "Baby Let Me Take You Home" (Hollies). Beatles songs: "Please, Please Me," "From Me To You," "She Loves You" and four others, performed by The Cheynes.

GO GO MANIA (*orig.* POP GEAR) (1965)

- M–Color
- Frederic Goode
- Harry Field
- AIP
- 70m.
- The Animals, The Beatles, Herman's Hermits, The Spencer Davis Group, The Nashville Teens, Billy J. Kramer and The Dakotas, Peter and Gordon, Susan Maughan, The Rockin' Berries, The Four Pennies, The Fourmost, The Honeycombs, Sounds Incorporated

A mock concert film, i.e. shot on stark, brightly lighted sets, with lip sync-ing and dubbed-in audience shrieks and applause. Top Brit rock jock, Jimmy Saville (bearing a remarkable resemblance to comic Marty Feldman), does the emcee honors as most of the acts go through the motions to one or two of their hit records. The one exception is The Beatles who are seen in good

quality color newsreels doing "Twist and Shout" and "She Loves You." For a while it's fun to watch, but after a time even the most ardent of British Invasion fans will probably begin to twitch. Performances include: "House of the Rising Sun," "Don't Let Me Be Misunderstood" (The Animals); "World Without Love" (Peter and Gordon); "Little Children" (Billy J. Kramer) and "I'm Into Something Good" (Herman's Hermits). Note: *Go Go Mania*'s cinematographer was the late Geoffrey Unsworth, whose more distinguished credits include: *2001, Tess, Superman* and *Murder on the Orient Express*.

GO, JOHNNY, GO (1959)

	M—B/W
▦	Paul Landres
▦	Alan Freed
✪	Hal Roach
◔	75m.
✪	Alan Freed, Jimmy Clanton
⇥	Chuck Berry, Ritchie Valens, Jackie Wilson, Eddie Cochran, Harvey Fuqua, Jo Ann Campbell, The Cadillacs, The Flamingoes
◑	Chess (partial)

Extremely minimal storyline of Clanton as a young singer competing in an Alan Freed talent contest allows for generous helpings of music from the estimable likes of Berry ("Maybellene"), Clanton ("Just A Dream"), Wilson ("Lonely Teardrops"), Cochran ("Come On Everybody") and (billed here as) "the late Ritchie Valens" ("La Bamba").

GOIN' SOUTH (1978)

- D—Color
- 🎬 John Herman Shaner, Al Ramus, Charles Shyer and Alan Mandel
- 🎞 Jack Nicholson
- 📽 Harry Gittes and Harold Schneider
- ⟳ PAR
- ⬤ 108m.
- ✪ Jack Nicholson, Mary Steenburgen, Christopher Lloyd, John Belushi, Veronica Cartwright

A broken-down outlaw escapes the gallows when an "unattached woman of property" claims him in accordance with local law. Basically "The African Queen Goes West," this comedy, by turns antic and sluggish, did little to enhance Jack Nicholson's reputation as an actor or director. It did however introduce audiences to the delightful Mary Steenburgen in the plum role of the bandit's feisty wife. Music by the gray eminence of southern California "Salon Rock," Van Dyke Parks, and Perry Botkin Jr. "Available Space" written and performed by Ry Cooder.

GONKS GO BEAT (1965)

- M—Color
- 🎬 Jimmy Watson, Robert Hartford-Davis and Peter Newbrook
- 🎞 Robert Hartford-Davis
- 📽 Peter Newbrook and Robert Hartford-Davis
- ⟳ WB
- ⬤ 92m.
- ✪ Kenneth Connor, Frank Thornton, Barbara Brown
- ⤴ The Long and The Short, The Nashville Teens, Lulu and the Luvvers, The Troles, Ray Lewis and The Trekkers, The Vacqueros, The Graham Bond Organization, Elaine and Derek, Alan David

Intergallactic ambassador stops warfare between "Beatland" and "Balladisle" by sparking a Romeo and Juliet romance between a boy and a girl of each of the communities. The Ballads outweigh the Big Beat numbers in what's basically a TV-style parade of British soft-rock acts.

GOOD TIMES (1967)

- M—Color
- 🎬 Tony Barrett
- 🎞 William Friedkin
- 📽 Lindsley Parsons
- ⟳ COL
- ⬤ 91m.
- ✪ Sonny and Cher, George Sanders, Edy Williams
- ⟳ ATCO

Tarzan movies, westerns and detective films are satirized in this mildly likeable movie(s)-within-a-movie. Story has Sonny and Cher, playing themselves, fantasizing about the various possible approaches to take in making their movie debut. Directed by William Friedkin (*The Exorcist, The French Connection*), *Good Times* is one of several rock films to have given some now-famous directors (Lester, Boorman, et al.) their first break. Nine songs, including: "I Got You Babe" and "Bang Bang."

GRADUATE, THE (1967)

D—Color
- Calder Willingham, Buck Henry
- the novel by Charles Webb
- Mike Nichols
- Lawrence Turman
- Avco-Embassy
- 105m.
- Dustin Hoffman, Anne Bancroft, Katharine Ross
- COL

Youth (Hoffman) just out of college becomes involved with a predatory older woman (Bancroft) AND THEN her daughter (Ross). A box office success *so* tasteful there was never a sequel. The film made rock movie soundtracks respectable and proved them a viable proposition. The songs, written by Paul Simon and sung by Simon and Garfunkel, mixes the old ("Scarborough Fair," "Sound of Silence") with the new ("Mrs. Robinson") to create a comfortable framework for this amiable rites-of-passage romance.

GRATEFUL DEAD, THE (1967)

R—Color
- Robert Nelson
- Robert Nelson
- Robert Nelson
- Canyon Cinema
- 7m.
- The Grateful Dead

Beautifully done featurette showing the group arriving, performing and departing (by helicopter) from an outdoor concert using varying degrees of speed-up motion and faster-than-the-eye-can-see editing devices. As the sound is speeded up like the images, it's impossible to make out what songs The Dead are playing. Still, this film captures much of the excitement surrounding the group in its early days.

GRATEFUL DEAD MOVIE, THE (1977)

R—Color
- Jerry Garcia
- Ron Rakow
- Monarch-Noteworthy
- 131m.
- The Grateful Dead
- Bill Graham

More a gathering of the tribe than mere concert movie, this over-two-hours affair captures "The Dead" at a five night 1974 San Francisco stand, running down a few dozen of their more popular anthems—the introduction of each one being met with knowing and adoring frenzy by the crowds on hand. A long, dazzling animation sequence by Gary Guiterez opens the film.

GREASE (1978)

M—Color
- Bronte Woodard

- ■ the musical play by Jim Jacobs and Warren Casey
- ▣ Randal Kleiser
- ▦ Robert Stigwood, Allan Carr
- ✆ PAR
- ● 110m.
- ✪ John Travolta, Olivia Newton-John, Jeff Conaway, Stockard Channing
- ⊐ Frankie Avalon, Sha-Na-Na
- ✺ RSO

Most of the harmless cliches about teen life in the 50's are trotted out in this homage to that era, as seen through the eyes of an on-again, off-again romantic duo, Danny (Travolta) and Sandy (Newton-John). On the Broadway stage this long-running cartoon-ish replay of "The Way It Was" was a thin but tolerable entertainment—harmless 50's rock and roll revisionism. But *Grease*, the movie, tends to get pulled out of shape in a distorted effort to make the doo-wop past at one with the disco present. Original music by Jim Jacobs and Warren Casey ("You're The One I Want," "Beauty School Dropout" and "Look At Me I'm Sandra Dee", etc.). The title tune, written especially for the film by Barry Gibb, is sung on the soundtrack by Frankie Valli. *Grease* contains extensive use of vintage atmosphere-inducing songs as "Hound Dog," "Tears On My Pillow" (Sha-Na-Na) and "Love Is A Many Splendoured Thing." Also heard, Cindy Bullens and Louis St. Louis.

GREAT ROCK AND ROLL SWINDLE, THE (1980)

   R—Color / B/W
- ▬ Julian Temple
- ▣ Julian Temple
- ▦ Jeremy Thomas, Don Boyd
- ✆ Virgin Films
- ● 105m.
- ✪ The Sex Pistols
- ⊐ Malcolm McLaren, Nancy Spungen, The Black Arabs and Jerzimy, Irene Handl, Tenpole Tudor
- ✺ Virgin

The anti-Beatles, The Sex Pistols, in the dark side of *A Hard Day's Night*, i.e. a heavily fantastical version of how The Pistols came to pass. Originally the group's premier film effort was supposed to be a vehicle entitled (with Russ Meyer set to direct) *Who Killed Bambi?* Then, it is said, Johnny Rotten balked, and Sid Vicious was arrested for killing his girlfriend Nancy Spungen. Then Vicious died, and both the project and group fell apart. The Svengali and manager of these punk innovators, Malcolm McLaren, was undaunted however, and so he set about concocting *this* fictional docu-cartoon of HOW IT ALL BEGAN, using scraps left over from the aborted film, together with any footage of The Sex Pistols he could lay his hands on, plus animated material also done for "Bambi." Because of this—Mclaren's undisguised hucksterism—*Swindle* turns out to be one of the most honest rock films of them all. Songs include "God Save The Queen," "Anarchy in the U.K.," "No Feelings," "Pretty Vacant," "Holidays in the Sun," (Sid's hilarious version of) "My Way" and "Johnny B. Goode"—or bits and pieces thereof. Note: In an unprecedented move, British censors forced the distributors of the film to *add* (not delete as per usual) footage with moralistic title cards heavy-handedly pointing out the deaths of Sid Vicious and Nancy Spungen.

GROUPIES (1970)

   R—Color
- ▬ Robert Dorfman, Peter Nevard

- Robert Dorfman, Peter Nevard
- Robert Weiner
- Maron
- 92m.
- Miss Harlow, Cynthia P. Caster, Andrea Whips
- Joe Cocker and the Grease Band, Ten Years After, Terry Reid, Spooky Tooth

More exhibitionistic than informative, this docu on sixties phenomenon of rock and roll camp followers concentrates on interviews with the wacked-out likes of Whips and Caster. Only musical sequence of note is Cocker singing "Delta Lady."

GURU, THE (1968)

- D—Color
- Ruth Prawer Jhabvala and James Ivory
- James Ivory
- Ismail Merchant
- TCF
- 112m.
- Michael York, Rita Tushingham, Aparna Sen, Madhur Jaffrey
- Twentieth Century-Fox

Maharishi-mania and eastern music fadism are given a gentle ribbing in this charming comedy in which York plays a musician suspiciously remindful of Beatle George Harrison. Music by Ustad Vilayat Khan.

HAIR (1979)

- M—Color
- Michael Weller
- the Broadway musical of the same name
- Milos Forman
- Lester Persky, Michael Butler
- UA
- 118m.
- John Savage, Treat Williams, Nicholas Ray, Beverly D'Angelo, Annie Golden
- RCA

Screen adaptation of the famed Broadway "tribal love-rock musical," with the big hits from the original ("Let The Sun Shine In," "The Age of Aquarius," "Black Boys/White Boys" etc.) blasting forth from the screen in teeth-rattling Dolby sound. Lyrics by Gerome Ragni and James Rado. Music by Galt MacDermot.

HARD DAY'S NIGHT, A (1964)

- M—B/W
- Alun Owen
- Richard Lester
- Walter Shenson
- UA (now UI)
- 87m.
- The Beatles, Wilfred Brambell, Victor Spinetti, Norman Rossington, John Jukin, Anna Quale
- United Artists

The Beatles (playing themselves) make a TV variety show appearance, but the broadcast is complicated by both their adoring hysterical fans and Paul's "grandfather" (Brambell), whose tart tongue keeps getting the boys into scrapes. Ringo, encouraged by granddad, wanders off for a "lark" just before the scheduled TV show. But in the nick of time the Beatles' drummer is found and everything goes as planned—to the relief of a much-harried TV director (Spinetti). Not much of a plot, but the success of The Beatles' debut film caught nearly everyone by surprise for its deliverance of the rock musical from the bondage of exploitation to the realm of "serious" entertainment and even (dare we say it?) *Art*. Richard Lester's antic direction and Alun Owen's witty script combined to make this film not only a top flight musical, but one of the most important films of the sixties as well. Original songs composed for the film include "I'm Happy Just To Dance With You," "And I Love Her," "If I Fell," "Tell Me Why," "Can't Buy Me Love" and the title tune. "She Loves You," "I Wanna Hold Your Hand," "I Should Have Known Better" and "Any Time At All" are also heard. When the film was re-released in 1981 a song not included in the original—The Beatles singing "I'll Cry Instead" over a montage of photos—was added to the opening of the film.

HARDER THEY COME, THE (1972)

D—Color
Perry Henzell, Trevor Rhone
Perry Henzell
Perry Henzell
International Films
110m.
Jimmy Cliff, Carl Bradshaw
Mango

Tragic tale of musician (Cliff) who comes to Kingston, Jamaica, from the outlands, only to become, briefly, a recording star and an unwitting political martyr. The "third world" implications of this extraordinary work are inescapable by the time Cliff is gunned down by villains. If regular-hour moviegoers didn't know a good thing when they saw it, a more adventuresome crowd did, for this Jamaican feature was one of the first weekend midnight movie hits. Cliff portrays a purist reggae star concerned with protecting his country's music from commercial exploitation—in what amounts to nearly a tract for Jamaican nationalism, i.e. the pop star as cultural guerilla. Soundtrack album from the film is, perhaps, *the* essential reggae album. Cliff sings "You Can Get It If You Really Want," "Many Rivers To Cross," "Sitting In Limbo" and the title tune, with additional atmospheric use of music by The Maytals, The Melodians, The Slickers, Desmond Dekker and Scotty.

HARUM SCARUM (1965)

    M—Color
- Gerald Drayson Adams
- Gene Nelson
- Sam Katzman
- MGM
- 95m.
- Elvis Presley, Fran Jeffries
- RCA

American pop star, Johnny Tyronne (Presley), is abducted to the country of "Lunarkand" while on tour in the Middle East, and swept up in political intrigue. All ends well, however, as he eventually resurfaces hale and hearty in, where else?, Las Vegas. By this point Elvis was (bump 'n) grinding films out at the rate of *exactly* three per year. And it shows! Dozens of extras running around in jalabas and Frederick's of Hollywood leftovers in (what appears to be) L.A.'s Griffith Park, a poor substitute for the film's alleged Mid-East locations. The brains behind this seven day wonder? None other than producer Sam (*Rock Around The Clock*) Katzman. Songs include: "Harem Holiday" (the film's British title), "Golden Coins," " My Desert Serenade" and "Kismet." Elvis #19 .

HAVING A WILD WEEKEND (*orig.* CATCH US IF YOU CAN) (1965)

	D–B/W
◼	John Boorman
▦	David Deutsch
✇	WB
●	85m.
✪	The Dave Clark Five, Barbara Ferris
◐	Epic

Clark and his group portray fringe members of Britain's entertainment industry who chuck it all and hit the road to see "the real world." But their adventure turns out to be all rather much of a letdown, as they end up back at square one after their outing. When first released, "Weekend" managed to carve out a little cult niche for itself. Which means no one went to see it. And small wonder! For director Boorman's (*Point Blank, Deliverance*) first feature represented rock revisionism of the first rank, painting a bleak and Byronic picture of rock high times. Dave and the Five don't do any on-screen singing here, nor do they portray musicians. But as the characters they play to flee the *ennui* of "swinging London," they are ever-accompanied by the strains of "Catch Us If You Can," "It's Gonna Be Alright," "I Like It," "Move On" and four other songs.

HEAD (1968)

	M–Color
▬	Jack Nicholson and Bob Rafelson
◼	Bob Rafelson
▦	Bob Rafelson, Jack Nicholson and Bert Schneider
✇	COL
●	86m.
✪	The Monkees (Micky Dolenz, David Jones, Mike Nesmith, Peter Tork), Annette Funicello, Timothy Carey
➔	Frank Zappa, Carol Doda, T.C. Jones, Sonny Liston, Teri Garr, Jack Nicholson and Bob Rafelson
◐	Colgems

A day in the life of the self-confessed "plastic pop group," The Monkees. Created for television to capitalize on the appeal of the Beatles, the Monkees had a number of top ten hits and (for awhile) a teenybopper following. Their popularity, however, was fast fading by the time this film–their *8½* as it were–reached the screen. Six new songs are shoehorned in between parody vignettes (Maria Montez movies, *Golden Boy*), pseudo-surrealistic segments (a romp through Victor Mature's hair), clips from old movies (*Dracula, Gilda*) and stock footage. Musical numbers include "Porpoise Song" (by Carole King and Gerry Goffin), "As We Go Along" (by Carole King and Toni Stern), "Daddy's Song" (by Nilsson), and "Can You Dig It" (by Peter Tork).

HEARTLAND REGGAE (1980)

R—Color
- J.P. Lewis, John Sutton Smith
- J.P. Lewis
- J.P. Lewis
- Crawley Films Ltd.
- 87m.
- Bob Marley and The Wailers, Peter Tosh, U-Roy, Jacob Miller, Rassless Morris, Dennis Brown, U-Roy, The I-Threes

Canadian-produced reggae documentary of the One Love Peace Concert held in Kingston, Jamaica in 1978. In addition to the music, a highlight of this film is the return to Jamaica of Bob Marley after a 16-month hiatus following an attempt on his life. As if that weren't enough to get the crowd excited, Marley can be seen here bringing on stage, for handshakes and rapproachment, staunch Jamaican political foes, Michael Manley and Eddie Seaga.

HEAT (1971)

D—Color
- Paul Morrissey, John Hollowell
- Paul Morrissey
- Andy Warhol
- Factory Films
- 103m.
- Joe D'Allesandro, Sylvia Miles

D'Allesandro, as a hustler, takes up with a fading movie queen, Miles, in this giddy *Sweet Bird of Youth* meets *Sunset Boulevard* send-up. The usual "who, exactly, is using whom?" questions form the backbone of this Warhol movie, with music by John Cale (including his "Days of Steam").

HEAVY METAL (1981)

M—Color
- Dan Goldberg and Len Blum
- comic book of the same name
- Gerald Potterton
- Ivan Reitman
- COL
- 86m.
- Asylum/Full Moon

Animated cartoon feature based on the "adult" comic strip of the same name, consists of five loosely connected episodes all of which revolve around extra-terrestials fighting for control of a magically powered secret substance. It was William Burroughs in *Naked Lunch* who first used the scientific term "heavy metal" as part of "hip" argot, replacing "too much," "out of sight" and the like. He probably never suspected it would eventually come to stand for a strain of hard rock music—not to mention the laser-gun carrying ample breasted women of this big screen "head" fantasy. Background sounds provided by such "heavy metal" exponents as Blue Oyster Cult ("Veterans of The Psychic Wars"), Black Sabbath ("Mob Rule"), Nazareth ("Crazy?"), Trust, ("Prefabricated"), Grand Funk Railroad ("Queen Bee") and Sammy Hagar (the title tune).

HEAVY TRAFFIC (1973)

	M—Color
🎬	Ralph Bakshi
■	Ralph Bakshi
🎞	Steve Krantz
⚡	AIP
●	75m.
↻	Fantasy

Animation. A kind of *Fantasia* for "the age of anxiety" as an artist unleashes his personal furies and demons at the drawing board. Live action and rotoscope animation underscored by use of Simon and Garfunkel's "Scarborough Fair," Chuck Berry's "Mabelline," "Twist and Shout" by the Isley Brothers, some jazz and Vivaldi.

HEDY (1965)

	M—B/W
🎬	Ronnie Tavel
■	Andy Warhol
🎞	Andy Warhol
⚡	Filmmakers Co-op
●	70m.
☻	Maria Montez, Mary Woronov, Jack Smith
⮑	The Velvet Underground

Half-spoken, half-sung, all-improvised on-screen musical accompaniment by Lou Reed, John Cale and company in this fantasy re-enactment of Hedy Lamarr's shoplifting arrest, trial and conviction. "She was a great woman!" says Smith as one of Hedy's (Montez) husbands in the finale of this Warhol lark also known as *The Fourteen Year-Old Girl*, *The Most Beautiful Woman in The World*, and *The Shoplifter*.

HELP! (1965)

	M—Color
🎬	Marc Behm, Charles Wood
■	Richard Lester
🎞	Walter Shenson
⚡	UA
●	92m.
☻	The Beatles
⮑	Leo McKern, Eleanor Bron, Victor Spinetti, Roy Kinnear
↻	Capitol

The Beatles' second film finds them again playing themselves and here they are pursued by members of an Eastern religious cult (led by Bron and McKern), a crazy scientist (Spinetti) and his bumbling assistant (Kinnear), all of whom are after a magically-endowed ring that has inadvertently come into the lads' possession. Director Lester, who shepherded the Beatles through their first film effort, *A Hard Day's Night*, for their second lets all the famed "Lesterian" touches get a trifle out of hand—so much so that at times the real stars of the film appear to be the bigger budget and the Technicolor camera, not the Beatles. But it's still plenty of fun, and the Beatles continue to shine in this shaggy-dog-tale about zealots who'll stop at nothing to remove the ring from Richard Starkey's finger. Songs: "Help," "Night Before," "You've Got To Hide Your Love Away," "Ticket To Ride," "I Need You," "You're Gonna Lose That Girl" and "Another Girl." Score by George Martin.

HERE WE GO ROUND THE MULBERRY BUSH (1967)

D—Color
- Hunter Davis
- the novel by Hunter Davis
- Clive Donner
- Larry Kramer
- Lopert
- 96m.
- Barry Evans, Judy Geeson
- The Spencer Davis Group
- United Artists

Amiable British trifle about a frustrated teenage virgin (Evans) who fumbles numerous opportunities to "prove his manhood." Music by Stevie Winwood and Traffic, and The Spencer Davis Group, who also appear. Songs include: the title tune and "Utterly Simple," by Traffic and "Every Little Thing," "Taking Out Time," "Looking Back" and "Picture of Her," by the Spencer Davis Group.

HEY, LET'S TWIST (1961)

M—B/W
- Greg Garrison
- Harry Romm
- PAR
- 80m.
- Joey Dee, Zohra Lampert
- The Peppermint Loungers, Teddy Randazzo, Jo Ann Campbell.
- Roulette

The ads for Dee's (as opposed to Chubby Checker's) movie version of the birth of the twist convey the sum and substance of the film's plot—Right Out of New York's Peppermint Lounge—Where It All Began! Dee sings: "Hey, Let's *TWIST*," "Mother Goose TWIST," "I Wanna TWIST," and others, in this choreographic special.

HIGH SCHOOL CONFIDENTIAL (1958)

D—B/W
- Lewis Meltzer, Robert Blees
- Jack Arnold
- Albert Zugsmith
- MGM
- 85m.
- Russ Tamblyn, Mamie Van Doren
- Jerry Lee Lewis

Plain clothes cop (Tamblyn) is called in to try and restore order at the "high school" in question where in addition to the basic 3R's, advanced courses in the 3 D's, drag racing, depravity and drug addiction, also are offered. The advertising copy for this film ("Behind these nice school walls . . . A TEACHERS' NIGHTMARE! A TEENAGE JUNGLE! Your own kids will never tell you, some won't . . . others DARE NOT!"), and the film itself, set the pace for an entire *school* of teen exploitation filmmaking. (See Chapter Four.) In the film's opening shot Jerry Lee Lewis memorably appears and pumps out the title tune for this zany classic of 50's teen attitude.

HOLD ON! (1966)

M—Color
- James B. Gordon
- Arthur Lubin
- Sam Katzman
- MGM
- 86m.
- Peter Noone (and Herman's Hermits), Sue Ann Langdon
- MGM

Re-hash of *Hard Day's Night* formula finds Pete and the Hermits as British rockers making their first U.S.A. tour—a swing-through that comes off so well the boys get a Gemini rocket named after themselves. It's a preposterous notion but director Lubin was an old hand at this sort of thing, for years earlier he'd helped guide actress Maria Montez through her various incarnations as jungle princesses and high priestesses. Songs include: the title tune, "A Must To Avoid," "Leaning On a Lampost" and eight others.

HOLLYWOOD KNIGHTS, THE (1980)

M—Color
- Floyd Mutrux
- Floyd Mutrux
- Richard Lederer
- COL
- 91m.
- Fran Drescher, Tony Danza, Robert Wuhl, Leigh French
- Polygram

Fraternity house members have a wild night of hi-jinks in commemoration of the closing of their beloved hang-out "Tubby's" drive-in. Writer-director Floyd Mutrux, known for giving familiar material a fresh approach (e.g. *American Hot Wax*) sticks to formula this time, and strikes out. It's literally *Animal House* meets *American Graffiti* with soundtrack golden oldies like Martha and the Vandellas "Heat Wave" sounding more than a bit shopworn from overuse in other "nostalgia" films. Other music by The Brooklyn Bridge who also sing the title tune.

HORROR OF PARTY BEACH, THE (1964)

M—B/W
- Richard L. Hilliard
- Del Tenney
- Del Tenney
- TCF
- 78m.
- John Scott, Alice Lyon
- The Del-Aires

In what was billed as "the first movie monster musical," radioactive monsters from the deep square off against twistin' nubile teens over possession of sandy turf. Lots of M.S.T. (monster screen time) in this *The Thing* meets *Beach Party* cautionary tale. For just as "making out" gets good, The Horror rears its ugly head. The reviewers said such insensitive things as "horrible" and "half-witted," but none of this negativism has deterred "Party Beach" in its decade-and-a-half quest for movie cult classic status. The Del-Aires sing "The Zombie Stomp" and several other equally "horror-ible" ditties in this Golden Turkey. Other music by Bill Holmes.

HOT ROD GANG (1958)

D—B/W
- Lou Rusoff
- Lew Landers
- Buddy Rogers
- AIP
- 72m.
- John Ashley, Gene Vincent

Poor little rich boy tale of young heir who, against his family's wishes, only wants to race cars and be a rock and roll star. As his best friend, Vincent (and the Blue Caps) sings "Baby Blue," "Dance To The Bop," "Dance In The Streets" and "Lonely Loretta."

HOUND DOG MAN (1959)

D—Color
- Fred Gipson, Winston Miller
- the novel by Fred Gipson
- Don Siegel
- Jerry Wald
- TCF
- 87m.
- Fabian, Stuart Whitman

Uneventful, low-key drama centering around the coming of age of young man in southern backwoods America. Twentieth-Century-Fox learned the hard way, here, that shoving a teen heartthrob (Fabian) into a period film (1912) didn't necessarily pay off (as with Elvis' *Love Me Tender*) at the box office. *Hound Dog Man* went straight to the dog pound. Songs: "What a Big Boy," "This Friendly World" and "Single."

HOW I WON THE WAR (1967)

D—Color
- Charles Wood
- the novel by Patrick Ryan
- Richard Lester
- Richard Lester
- UA
- 109m.
- Michael Crawford, John Lennon

Absurdist war film about an ill-equipped troop leader (Crawford) and his band of misfit soldiers, The Third Troop of The Fourth Musketeers. When John Lennon signed up for a dramatic part in this non-musical it was read as a sign confirming that the Beatles were all but *kaput*. Later, Lennon said that this first taste of freedom away from the other three was a capper on his decision to leave the group. At any rate, neither the film nor Lennon's performance in this erratically conceived anti-war movie set the world on fire back in '67. Music by Ken Thorne.

HOW TO STUFF A WILD BIKINI (1965)

M—Color
- William Asher, Leo Townsend
- William Asher

- 🎬 James H. Nicholson, Samuel Z. Arkoff
- 🎞 AIP
- ⏱ 93m.
- 🎭 Dwayne Hickman, Annette Funicello, Buster Keaton, Frankie Avalon
- 🎵 The Kingsmen
- 🔊 Wand

Avalon (unbilled in the official credits list) plays a young naval reservist who calls upon the services of a witch doctor (Keaton) to find out if his girl (Funicello) is remaining true to him while he's away. More nonsense than usual in this fourth in the AIP "beach" series—witchcraft, telepathy and astral projection, all in cartoony fashion, are on display here, along with music by The Kingsmen. Songs include: "Give Her Lovin'," "After the Party" and the title tune.

I LOVE YOU ALICE B. TOKLAS (1968)

- M—Color
- ✍ Paul Mazursky and Larry Tucker
- 🎥 Hy Averback
- 🎬 Charles Maguire
- 🎞 WB
- ⏱ 93m.
- 🎭 Peter Sellers, Leigh Taylor-Young
- 🔊 WB

An uptight Los Angeles lawyer (Sellers) thinks about changing his life-style when he meets a free-spirited hippie (Young). Harper's Bizzare sing the title song for this very funny Peter Sellers comedy.

I WANNA HOLD YOUR HAND (1978)

- M—Color
- ✍ Robert Zemeckis, Bob Gale,
- 🎥 Robert Zemeckis
- 🎬 Steven Spielberg, Tamara Asseyev, Alex Rose
- 🎞 UI
- ⏱ 104m.
- 🎭 Nancy Allen, Bobby Di Cicco, Marc McClure, Susan Kendall Newman
- 🎵 Murray the "K"

Four teenagers attempt to crash a Beatles TV performance, with the ensuing events and interactions altering, irreversibly, the course of their lives. This film from the team of Zemeckis and Gale (*1941, Used Cars*) isn't about the Beatles, per se, but the phenomenon of Beatlemania, and as such it is a loving momento of a week's worth of madness in the life of New York City—those few zany days when almost none of its inhabitants could escape even the most miniscule detail of the Great British Invasion. Liberal use of all early Beatles hits on soundtrack including: "I Wanna Hold Your Hand," "Please, Please Me," "I Saw Her Standing There," "Love Me Do" and thirteen others.

IDOLMAKER, THE (1980)

- M—Color
- ✍ Edward Di Lorenzo
- 🎥 Taylor Hackford
- 🎬 Gene Kirkwood and Howard W. Koch, Jr

- ✪ UA
- ● 116m.
- ✪ Ray Sharkey, Peter Gallagher, Paul Land, Tovah Feldshuh
- ● A&M

A sharp-eyed record promoter puts two unknowns on the road to 60's pop music stardom, but can't find personal satisfaction. Master rock record producer, Phil Spector, was reportedly originally set as musical adviser for this thinly disguised tale of the watershed years in the life of Robert Marucci, that dross-into-gold discoverer/mentor/manager of Frankie Avalon and Fabian. (Marucci acted as "technical adviser" on the film.) If, in fact, Spector was initially on board, but then split (for whatever reasons), it's too bad. For just the only quibble one can have about *The Idolmaker* is that most of the music is closer to the 80's present, instead of evoking the 60's era that's being dramatized. All else, though, is rather dazzlingly effective, especially Ray Sharkey as the Marucci-like "Vinnie Vacarri." Songs by Jeff Barry include the hit "Here is My Love," "Sweet Little Lover" and "Oo Wee Baby." Jesse Fredericks ghosted the singing voice of Paul Land (who played the Avalon-type crooner). Peter Gallagher (as the Fabian-styled heartthrob) did his own singing. Soundtrack musicians include Spector-veteran Darlene Love (whose singing on "Oo Wee Baby" comes closest to 60's verisimilitude) and Nino Tempo.

IF IT AIN'T STIFF, IT AIN'T WORTH A . . . (1977)

R—Color
- ▪ Nick Abson
- ▦ Dave Robinson, Angie Sanders
- ✪ Stiff Records
- ● 50m.
- ✪ Ian Dury, Wreckless Eric, Elvis Costello, Nick Lowe, Dave Edmunds, Terry Williams, Larry Wallis
- ● Stiff

Documentary of 1978 British tour by Stiff Records artists. Edmunds, Lowe and Williams (Rockpile) do "I Knew the Bride;" Wreckless Eric reprises "Semaphore Signals;" Larry Wallis is seen with his "Police Car" and Dury chews up the screen working out on "Wake Up and Make Love With Me."

IMAGINE (1972)

R—Color
- ▬ John Lennon, Yoko Ono
- ▪ John Lennon, Yoko Ono
- ▦ John Lennon, Yoko Ono
- ✪ Apple Films
- ● 81m.
- ✪ John Lennon, Yoko Ono
- ⮣ George Harrison, Phil Spector, Dick Cavett
- ● Apple

Performances of various Lennon & Ono compositions ("Imagine," "Crippled Inside," "Jealous Guy," "Power to the People," "Oh My Love" and others) interspersed with home movies, TV clips and collage. Also appearing on screen are such diverse celebrities as filmmaker, Jonas Mekas, Fred Astaire and Jack Palance. Most of the music comes from either John's *Imagine* album, or Yoko's *Fly*.

INNER SCAR (La Cicatrice Interieure) (1971)

D—Color

🎬 Philippe Garrel
🎞 Philippe Garrel
📽 Philippe Garrel
☡ Zanzibar
● 58m.
✪ Pierre Clementi, Nico
◑ Reprise

Probably the most spectacular *avant-garde* film ever made—with color and 'scope locations in Morocco, Iceland and the Canary Islands. Virtually plotless, this visual stunner follows the legendary Nico as she walks through flaming lava pits, sails between ice floes and rides across desert landscapes singing (on occasion) "Janitor of Lunacy," "Mutterlein," and "My Only Child." Soundtrack, co-produced by John Cale and Joseph Byrd (entitled *Desert Shore*), features Cale as well.

INVOCATION OF MY DEMON BROTHER (1969)

D—Color

🎬 Kenneth Anger
🎞 Kenneth Anger
📽 Kenneth Anger
☡ Filmmaker's Co-op
● 12m.
✪ Kenneth Anger, Bobby Beausoleil

Plotless experimental short, featuring strobe-like homoerotic imagery. Contains several shots of the Rolling Stones in performance, along with an original synthesizer score by Mick Jagger.

IT HAPPENED AT THE WORLD'S FAIR (1963)

M—Color

🎬 Si Rose, Seamon Jacobs
🎞 Norman Taurog
📽 Ted Richmond
☡ MGM
● 105m.
✪ Elvis Presley, Joan O'Brien
◑ RCA

But what *happens* isn't all that much, as Dondi-esque waif (Ginny Tiu) helps cement an affair between Elvis and girlfriend, played by O'Brien. "Take Me to the Fair," "Cotton Candy Land" and "Happy Ending" are amongst the musical numbers Elvis belts out in some on-location settings. ELVIS #12.

IT'S A BIKINI WORLD (1967)

M—Color

🎬 Charles S. Swartz, Stephanie Rothman

▇	Stephanie Rothman
▦	Charles S. Swartz
☏	Trans American
●	86m.
✪	Deborah Walley, Tommy Kirk
⤵	The Animals, The Castaways, The Toys, The Gentrys

When a BMOC (Kirk) finds out he has a reputation as a "phony blow-hard" he decides to masquerade as his non-existent milquetoast "brother." Director Rothman has an *auteur* rep in England for such films as *Group Marriage* and the womens' prison flick, *Terminal Island* and this, her first film, is considered terribly super-seminal to her *oeuvre*. Rothman said of this wonderfully-titled venture, "I became very depressed after making *It's a Bikini World.*" Music by Mike Curb and Bob Simmons performed by (The) Animals, Castaways, Toys and Gentrys.

IT'S TRAD DAD (*see* RING A DING RHYTHM)

IT'S YOUR THING (1970)

	R—Color
▇	Mike Gariguilo
▦	The Isley Brothers
☏	Medford Films
●	102m.
✪	The Isley Brothers, Patti Austin, The Five Stairsteps, The Edwin Hawkins Singers, Moms Mabley, Ike and Tina Turner, Brooklyn Bridge, Clara Ward

The Isley Brothers produced, and appear in, this film of an all-star soul show held in 1969 at New York's Yankee Stadium.

JAILHOUSE ROCK (1957)

	M—B/W
▬	Guy Trosper
▇	Richard Thorpe
▦	Pandro S. Berman
☏	MGM
●	97m.
✪	Elvis Presley, Judy Tyler
◐	RCA(EP)

Elvis (unfairly) spends time in the slammer on manslaughter charges. After he is sprung, he becomes a Presley-like singing sensation, thanks to the help of his manager (Tyler), with whom he gradually becomes romantically involved. One of the great iconographic moments in rock film history is Elvis' cootch dance to the title song—in an otherwise routine show-biz soaper. (Although the film stands head-and-shoulders above mid and late-period Elvis movie fare.) Nothing else is quite up to that dazzling title tune production number, but looking his dangerous and surly best Elvis does get off a few good lines like "Honey it's just the beast in me;" and he sings five fine songs: "Jailhouse Rock," "I Want To Be Free," "Baby I Don't Care" (all written by Jerry Leiber and Mike Stoller) "Don't Leave Me Now" and "Young and Beautiful." Brief on-screen appearance by Stoller. Elvis #3.

JAMBOREE (1957)

- M–B/W
- Lenard Kantor
- Roy Lockwood
- Max J. Rosenberg, Milton Subotsky
- WB
- 87m.
- Kay Medford, Paul Carr, Freda Holloway
- Jerry Lee Lewis, Fats Domino, Charlie Gracie, Buddy Knox, Carl Perkins, Frankie Avalon, Lewis Lymon and The Teenchords, Slim Whitman, Jodie Sands, The Four Coins, Rocco and The Saints, Count Basie, Joe Williams

Love duo, and recording stars, "Honey" and "Pete" spat and reconcile over and again as they rocket their way up the record charts. *Lots* of rock stars on hand, but the music they make only adds up to a handful of minutes in this heavily-plotted tale of retrograde teen stars. (They're kind of a road show Debbie and Eddie.) "Honey" (whose singing voice is ghosted by Connie Francis) and "Pete" solo and duet on what seems like five dozen songs. Most of the music is perfunctorily staged, but there is one memorable segment of Jerry Lee Lewis singing "Great Balls of Fire" that looks for all the world as if it were photographed by someone who knew what he was doing. Other music includes: "Wait and See" (Domino); "Cool Baby" (Gracie); "I'm Glad All Over" (Perkins); "Don't Wanna Be Teacher's Pet" (Avalon) and "Hula Love" (Knox).

JANIS (1975)

- R–Color
- Howard Alk, Seaton Findlay
- Howard Alk
- UI
- 97m.
- Janis Joplin
- The Kozmic Blues Band, Big Brother and The Holding Company, The Full Tilt Boogie Band
- Columbia

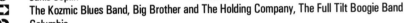

Documentary on the life and hard times of major rock force, Janis Joplin. Excerpts from *Monterey Pop* and *Woodstock*, as well as concert performances in Frankfurt, Calgary and Toronto are on display here, as well as some moving material on Janis, her freak flag flying, visiting her tenth high school reunion in Port Arthur, Texas. Also included is an excerpt from a touching TV interview with Dick Cavett. Although interest in Joplin has remained great even since her death, this Canadian-made venture came and went very quickly when it opened in '75. Songs include: "Ball and Chain," "Tell Mama," "Kozmic Blues," "Cry Baby" and "Move Over."

JAZZ ON A SUMMER'S DAY (1960)

- R–Color
- Arnold Perl, Albert D'Anniable
- Bert Stern
- Bert Stern
- New Yorker Films
- New Yorker Films
- 86m.
- Chuck Berry, Big Maybelle

Pathbreaking concert movie is nearly all jazz, but this pre-*Woodstock* venture laid down most of the ground rules for rock fest movies to follow. Memorable film of 1958 Newport Jazz Festival does dabble in rock, featuring nice segments with Chuck Berry singing "Sweet Little Sixteen" and Big Maybelle running down one of her winning, standard blues numbers.

JIMI HENDRIX (1973)

	R–Color
☰	Joe Boyd, John Head, Gary Weis
◪	Joe Boyd, John Head, Gary Weis
⌗	Joe Boyd
✪	WB
●	102m.
◯	Jimi Hendrix
◐	Reprise

Interviews with family, friends and an old army superior of Hendrix; plus familiar footage of the guitarist (*Woodstock, Experience,* etc.) mixed with some previously unshown musical material; and a rather-much-of-a-downer Hendrix/Dick Cavett TV interview all are seen in this assembled tribute to Jimi. Glimpsed briefly in various contexts and surroundings are such musicians as Little Richard, Lou Reed, Mick Jagger, Eric Clapton and Pete Townshend. All the various assemblings of the Experience and the Band of Gypsies (Cox, Miles, Mitchell & Redding) perform in whole (or in part): "Red House," "Machine Gun," "Johnny B. Goode," "In From the Storm," "Rock Me Baby," "Hey Baby," "Like a Rolling Stone," "Purple Haze" and (from *Woodstock*) "The Star Spangled Banner."

JIMI PLAYS BERKELEY (1971)

	R–Color
◪	Peter Pilafian
⌗	Michael Jeffrey
✪	Dor Jamm Films
●	45m.
◯	Jimi Hendrix
⤳	Mitch Mitchell, Billy Cox

Docu of a 1970 California concert by the Jimi Hendrix Experience. About ten minutes of the film are given over to extra-musical matters, such as newsreel footage of anti-Viet Nam rallies and interviews with "street people." But the remainder consists of vintage, well-photographed Hendrix. Songs include: "Purple Haze," "Voodoo Chile," "Johnny B. Goode," "Pass It On" and the inevitable "Star Spangled Banner."

JIVEASP (1975)

	R–Color
◪	Richard Kooris
⌗	Jack Canon
✪	Texas and Pacific Films
●	91m.
◯	Larry Raspberry and The Highsteppers
⤳	Professor Longhair, Jerry Lee Lewis, Leon Russell

Documentary of life on the road with Southwestern soul-stomp band, Larry Raspberry (ex of The Gentrys) and The Highsteppers—with stops along the way for visits with Russell, Lewis and Longhair.

JOHNNY CASH! THE MAN, HIS WORLD, HIS MUSIC (1969)

R—Color
- Robert Elfstrom
- Robert Elfstrom
- Arthur Barron, Evelyn Barron
- Continental
- 94m.
- Johnny Cash, Bob Dylan, Carl Perkins

Docu of singer Cash finds him reprising many of his recordings (including "Folsum Prison Blues" and "Ring of Fire") in concert performances, as well as a duet with Bob Dylan on "One Two Many Mornings." Carl Perkins sings "Blue Suede Shoes."

JOURNEY THROUGH THE PAST (1973)

R—Color
- "Bernard Shakey" (Neil Young)
- Frederic Underhill
- New Line
- 96m.
- Neil Young
- Crosby, Stills, Nash and Young, Buffalo Springfield

Combination home movie/concert film overseen by, and starring Young. Aims for something a little bit different and offbeat, but even Neil's most loyal followers and kindest critics couldn't come up with much in the way of encouraging words for his first movie effort. Instead, "puerile," "self-indulgent" and "pretentious" were the overwhelming reactions to this assemblage of old film clips (TV's *The Hollywood Palace*, etc.), staged fantasy sequences, random philosophizing and Young concert solo shots. This affair also features film and kinescopes of The Buffalo Springfield and Crosby, Stills, Nash and "Shakey," uh, Young, two groups with which the singer-guitarist has been associated. There's an appearance by actress, Carrie Snodgress, and the music includes a non-stop mixture of Young's songs such as "Find the Cost of Freedom," "The Needle and the Damage Done" and the title tune. Note: Young's record album of the same name bears little or no connection with this film project.

JUBILEE (1978)

D—Color
- Derek Jarman
- Derek Jarman
- Howard Malin, James Whaley
- Libra
- 104m.
- Jenny Runacre, Little Nell, Toyah Wilcox, Jordan & Adam Ant (of Adam and The Ants), Linda Spurrier, Wayne County, Lindsay Kemp, The Slits
- Polydor

Punk fantasy of Queen Elizabeth the First transported forward in time to roughly, the present, where what she sees makes the seditious behavior of *Clockwork Orange* look like a children's birthday party. While most everybody else was sitting around wondering whether or not punk rock was just a passing fad, former Ken Russell set designer, Derek Jarman, quickly cocktailed up this modish little psycho-fantasy. Though admired by the usually staid likes of *Variety* and *The British Film Institute Monthly Film Bulletin*, one party more closely connected with the production, namely Adam Ant, took strong exception to the film. Claimed Ant, in an interview in *Slash Magazine*, "*Jubilee* was made by a very sweet but very arty guy.... It was supposed to be 'street level' and it was all King's Road." Judge for yourself! Music mostly by Brian Eno, with an assist from Chelsea, Wayne County and The Electric Chairs, Siouxsie and The Banshees, Jerusalem, Suzi Pims and Amilcar. Songs include: "Right To Work" (Chelsea), "Love In a Void" (Banshees) and "Rule Britannia" (Pims).

JUST A GIGOLO (1979)

	D—Color
🎬	Joshua Sinclair, Ennio de Concini
🎬	David Hemmings
📺	Rolf Thiele
🎞	UA
⏺	105m.
✪	David Bowie, Marlene Dietrich, Kim Novak, Sydne Rome
◑	Ariola

Vice and violence in Weimar Germany is the background for this *Cabaret*-styled story of WW I veteran (Bowie) who takes up the life of the paid male escort and eventually meets doom and destruction. Although he doesn't sing in this most expensive German-made film since WW II, one of his works, "Revolutionary Song," is intoned by co-star, Rome. Other music by Manhattan Transfer and The Pasadena Roof Orchestra. Marlene Dietrich sings (actually, more of a recitative) the title tune.

JUST FOR FUN (1963)

	M—B/W
🎬	Milton Subotsky
🎬	Gordon Flyming
📺	Milton Subotsky
🎞	COL
⏺	84m.
✪	Mark Wynter, Cherry Roland
➡	Dusty Springfield, The Springfields, Bobby Vee, The Crickets, Freddie Cannon, Johnny Tillotson, Brian Poole, The Tremoloes, Sounds Incorporated, Ketty Lester, Jimmy Savile

The story line (something-or-other about teens demanding the right to vote) makes a few brief, perfunctory appearances here, but for the most part music holds center stage in this British slender-plot-premise special. Features a rare screen appearance by the great Dusty Springfield (with The Springfields); and also of interest is the fact that *Just For Fun* was photographed by Nicolas Roeg, later the director of *Performance* and *The Man Who Fell to Earth*. When this overseas entry opened in 1963 in New York City, notoriously indiscriminate teen moviegoers rioted and demanded their money back. Some *fun*!

KEEP ON ROCKIN' (1972)

	R—Color
🎬	D.A. Pennebaker

🖽 David McMullin, Peter Hansen, Mark Woodcock, Chris Dalrymple
🎬 Pennebaker Films
⏱ 102m.
✪ Chuck Berry, Little Richard, Jerry Lee Lewis, Bo Diddley, Jimi Hendrix, Janis Joplin, Big Brother and the Holding Company

Re-edited version of *Toronto Pop* (1970), with John Lennon and Yoko Ono, from the original version, being replaced by (due to legal reasons) vintage clips of Hendrix and Joplin/Big Brother from the earlier Monterey Pop Fest. Turns by Richard, Berry, Diddley and Lewis constitute an almost non-stop history of early rock and roll. Songs performed by the four greats before the crowd at Lennon and Ono's 1969 Toronto Peace Fest include: "I'm a Man," "Bo Diddley" (Diddley); "Great Balls of Fire," "Whole Lotta Shakin'Goin' On" (Lewis); "Johnny B. Goode," "Sweet Little Sixteen" (Berry) and "Tutti Frutti," "Long Tall Sally" (Richard).

KID GALAHAD (1962)

    M–Color
🎞 William Fay
◼ the 1937 Warner Brothers film, *Kid Galahad*
🎥 Phil Karlson
🖽 Hal Wallis
🎬 PAR
⏱ 95m.
✪ Elvis Presley, Lola Albright
⊘ RCA (EP)

Semi-musical remake of old Warner Brothers boxing drama finds Elvis portraying a reluctant championship fighter. During time-outs Kid Presley works his way through several musical numbers including: "King of the Whole Wide World," "This is Living," "Riding the Rainbow" and "I Got Lucky." ELVIS #10.

KIDS ARE ALRIGHT, THE (1979)

    R–Color / B/W
🎥 Jeff Stein
🖽 Bill Curbishley, Tony Klinger
🎬 New World
⏱ 96m.
✪ The Who
➜ Ringo Starr, Steve Martin, The Smothers Brothers, Ken Russell
⊘ MCA

Immensely satisfying compilation film of The Who's career. Old promo films, recent concert material, ancient concert footage, TV interviews and variety show appearances all heaved up on the screen in seemingly random fashion (with occasional quasi-narrational assist from Ringo Starr)—and yet despite this lack of a scheme, or perhaps because of it, this scattergun effort is one of the better and more useful theatrical rock films of recent years. SEE what appears to be a thousand guitars destroyed; HEAR The Who doing new versions of most of their biggest selling recordings; SEE Keith Moon (apparently) go all to pieces on nationwide British TV—in this docu-overview of four of the most influential rock 'n rollers of all time. Songs include: "Summertime Blues," a *Tommy* medley, "My Generation," "A Quick One" (from the unreleased "Stones" film, *Rock and Roll Circus*), "Won't Get Fooled Again" and "Who Are You?"

KIDS ARE UNITED, THE (1980)

R—Color
▪ Steve Barron
● 60m.
✪ The Jam, Ultravox, The Pirates, Penetration, Sham 69

Straight-ahead docu of 1978 Reading (England) Rock Festival features a standout set by The Jam.

KING CREOLE (1958)

M—B/W
▭ Herbert Baker, Micael Vincente Gazzo
▮ the novel, *A Stone For Danny Fisher*, by Harold Robbins
▪ Michael Curtiz
▩ Hal Wallis
▨ PAR
● 116m.
✪ Elvis Presley, Carolyn Jones, Walter Matthau
◐ RCA

Elvis is a night club singer who gets involved with some shady characters in yet another in a long line of movies he made about the show business school of hard knocks—and thanks to director Curtiz it all hangs together nicely. This is Elvis' last film before he entered the service, and after he returned to civilian life he rarely made another film even as good as this one. Elvis sings five Lieber/Stoller songs: "Crawfish," "You're The Cutest," "Let Me Be Your Lover Boy," "Danny Is My Name," the title tune, plus eight others. Elvis #4.

KINGDOM OF THE SPIDERS (1977)

    D—Color
- Richard Robinson, Allan Caillou
- Bud Cardos
- Igo Kantor, Jeffrey M. Sneller
- Dimension Pictures
- 95m.
- William Shatner, Woody Strode

Spiders, because of the usual ecological reasons, reproduce like mad and, eventually devour a small town. THE END! The only sci-fi film we know of where the pesky critters (in this instance trillions of 'em) continue to prevail at the film's climax. Before the final cobwebs descend, rockabilly great, Dorsey Burnette, gets the chance to sing three soundtrack songs: "Peaceful Verde Valley," "Things I Treasure" and "Green Side of the Mountain."

KISSIN' COUSINS (1964)

    M—Color
- Gerald Adams, Gene Nelson
- Gene Nelson
- Sam Katzman
- MGM
- 76m.
- Elvis Presley, Yvonne Craig
- RCA

Elvis as twins! He plays both an Air Force lieutenant and a down home country boy in this featherweight musical about the government's foiled attempts to build a missile site on some choice backwoods property. The Elvis*es* sing "There's Gold in the Mountains" and "Smokey Mountain Boy." ELVIS #14.

L.A., MY HOME TOWN (1977)

    R—Color
- Ian Whitcomb
- Geoff Haydon
- Barry Gavin
- BBC Films
- 52m.
- Ian Whitcomb, Peter Asher

L.A. travelog/film autobio made by Whitcomb, a rock and roller once referred to as "the Max Beerbohm of rock." Here, Ian is the writer, star and producer of a dandy little film about the British colony in Los Angeles. Record producer Peter Asher (formerly of the group Peter and Gordon) appears in one scene, and elsewhere Britisher Whitcomb reprises his one big 60's hit, "You Turn Me On," in addition to singing several English music hall ditties.

LA DOLCE VITA (1959)

    D—B/W
- Federico Fellini, Ennio Flaiano, Tullio Pinelli, Brunello Rondi
- Federico Fellini
- Giuseppe Amato

	AIP
	178m.
	Marcello Mastroianni, Anita Ekberg
	Nico
	RCA

Episodic story of a journalist (Mastroianni) in Rome, his personal problems and the more bizarre ones of the people he meets. "Ready Teddy" is sung by a Little Richard impersonator in a Roman night club. A pre-Velvet Underground Nico also turns up speaking what she claims to be "Eskimo" in this lavish Cook's Tour of European high and low life.

LADIES AND GENTLEMEN, THE ROLLING STONES (1974)

	R—Color
	Rollin Binzer
	Marshall Chess, Rollin Binzer, Bob Fries, Steve Gebhardt
	Dragon Aire
	83m.
	The Rolling Stones
	Nicky Hopkins, Bobby Keyes, Jim Price, Ian Stewart

Musical documentary of The Stones' '72 U.S. tour. Most unusual for a presentation of this sort, there are no interviews with the band, or fans, no behind-the-scenes poking and prodding by the cameras—just straight-ahead music, in a film that was lavishly presented in Quadrophonic Sound, at "hard ticket" prices. The Stones were lucky to have a slick concert film of their U.S.A. swing in reserve to counteract the bad publicity that surrounded their off-stage activities at the time. This record of their on-stage triumphs is a far cry from the sinister frolics captured by Robert Frank in his *Cocksucker Blues*, shot at the same time. The band slashes through fourteen uninterrupted numbers including: "Brown Sugar," "Bitch," "Gimme Shelter," "Tumblin' Dice," "Love in Vain," "Midnight Rambler," "Street Fightin' Man" and "Jumpin' Jack Flash."

LADY SINGS THE BLUES (1972)

	M—Color
	Terence McCloy, Chris Clark and Suzanne DePasse
	the book by Billie Holiday and William Dufty
	Sidney J. Furie
	Berry Gordy, Jay Weston, James S. White
	PAR
	144m.
	Diana Ross, Billy Dee Williams, Richard Pryor
	Motown

Singer Billie Holiday's rise from ghetto backstreets to Jazz stardom is complicated by drug addiction and romantic problems. While this elaborate musical drama has little to do with the actual facts of the great singer's life, Diana Ross' performance rings true, as does her singing. Wisely she doesn't try to imitate the Holiday sound, but instead works at capturing the flavor of "big band" vocal styling of the 40's. Songs include "God Bless The Child," "Good Morning Heartache," "Strange Fruit" and "My Man." Other music by Michel Legrand.

LAST WALTZ, THE (1978)

R—Color
■ Martin Scorsese
▦ Robbie Robertson
✪ UA
● 115m.
✪ The Band, Bob Dylan, Joni Mitchell, Neil Diamond, Emmylou Harris, Neil Young, Van Morrison, Ron Wood, Muddy Waters, Eric Clapton, The Staple Singers, Ringo Starr, Dr. John, Ronnie Hawkins, Paul Butterfield
⤵ Michael McClure, Lawrence Ferlinghetti
✪ Asylum

Documents The Band's (Robertson, Danko, Manuel, Hudson and Helm) Thanksgiving Day, 1976 farewell-as-a-group-concert at San Francisco's Winterland. Other musicians on hand for the occasion represent a veritable cross-section of a quarter-century of pop and rock and roll—from Waters to Butterfield, Dylan to Diamond, Morrison to Mitchell, etc. While the bulk of the film was shot at Winterland, the most stunning sequences (The Band, Harris, The Staples) were photographed on an MGM sound stage. Hands down, the most meticulously crafted concert film ever made. Director Scorsese left nothing to chance as he choreographed and storyboarded almost every musical sequence in the film in advance, down to the last detail. The end results more than justified all this fussiness in this beautifully-made concert film. Songs include: "Cripple Creek," "Stagefright," "The Night They Drove Old Dixie Down," "The Weight" (The Band); "Helpless" (Young); "Mannish Boy" (Waters); "Coyote" (Mitchell); "Baby Let Me Follow You Down," "I Shall Be Released" (Dylan, The Band, Starr and Wood) and "Mystery Train" (Butterfield).

LET IT BE (1970)

R–Color
🎬 Michael Lindsay-Hogg
📺 Neil Aspinall
🎞 UA
⏺ 81m.
✪ The Beatles
➡ Billy Preston
◐ Apple

Rehearsals and recording sessions for The Beatles' *Let It Be* album, plus an impromptu concert on the roof of the Abbey Road studios are the focus of this docu filmed only slightly before the group split up. The internal friction the band was experiencing when the film was made is obvious, with tension between George and Paul being especially noticeable. All the while the inscrutable Yoko Ono sits off to one side of the musical action, taking it all in expressionlessly. The mood only lightens during the latter half of the film when the boys go up on the roof for some mid-day serenading to a crowd that rapidly assembles down in the streets. One minute into the concert, and pandemonium sets in for blocks around—traffic stops, businessmen begin climbing over rooftops, etc. Songs include: "Don't Let Me Down," "Maxwell's Silver Hammer," "I've Got A Feeling," "Across The Universe," "I Me Mine," "The Long And Winding Road," "Shake, Rattle and Roll," "Kansas City," "Get Back" and "Let It Be."

LET THE GOOD TIMES ROLL (1973)

R–Color
🎬 Sid Levin, Robert Abel
📺 Gerald I. Isenberg
🎞 COL
⏺ 99m.
✪ Little Richard, Fats Domino, Chuck Berry, The Shirelles, The Five Satins, Bill Haley and His Comets, The Coasters, Bo Diddley, Danny and the Juniors, Chubby Checker
◐ Bell

A lively and largely successful try at doing something a little different with the concert film format. Colorful record of Richard Nader's rock revival shows mixes in newsreels of 50's fads and fashions, and through split-screen, juxtaposes old and new footage of various vintage rock stars running through "live" medleys of their classic recordings in front of widely receptive crowds.

LET'S ROCK (1958)

M–B/W
✍ Hal Hackady
🎬 Harry Foster
📺 Harry Foster
🎞 COL
⏺ 80m.
✪ Julius LaRosa, Phyllis Newman
➡ Paul Anka, Danny and The Juniors, The Royal Teens, Roy Hamilton, Wink Martindale, The Tyrones

A forties-style balladeer (LaRosa) finds his fame rapidly bottoming out, *until* he gets wise and hops on the rock and roll bandwagon. Helping to awaken the rock consciousness of LaRosa's washed-up crooner are Paul Anka (singing "I'll Be Waiting For You"), The Royal Teens (with "Short Shorts") and Danny and The Juniors (with their classic "At The Hop").

LIVE A LITTLE LOVE A LITTLE (1968)

M—Color
- Michael A. Hoey and Dan Greenburg
- Dan Greenburg's novel *Kiss My Firm But Pliant Lips*
- Norman Taurog
- Douglas Lawrence
- MGM
- 90m.
- Elvis Presley, Michele Cary, Rudy Vallee

Playful Michele Cary slips Elvis a tranquilizer that puts him to sleep for three days. But when he wakes up, he's *still* in an Elvis Presley picture. Rudy Vallee plays the boss of an advertising agency Elvis works for in his waking hours in this typical featherheaded Presley farce. Elvis sings "A Little Less Conversation." Music by Billy Strange. ELVIS #28.

LIVE AND LET DIE (1972)

D—Color
- Tom Mankiewicz
- the novel by Ian Fleming
- Guy Hamilton
- Albert Broccoli, Harry Saltzman
- UA
- 121m.
- Roger Moore, Jane Seymour
- United Artists

The title tune of this James Bond adventure was a big hit for Paul McCartney (the song's writer with his wife Linda), and his group, Wings. Score by George Martin.

LIVE IT UP (*see* SING AND SWING)

LISZTOMANIA (1975)

M—Color
- Ken Russell
- Ken Russell
- Roy Baird
- WB
- 105m.
- Roger Daltrey, Sara Kestelman, Paul Nicholas, Fiona Lewis
- Ringo Starr, Rick Wakeman
- A&M

Comic-strip style rendition of the life of composer Franz Liszt (Daltrey), takes him from the height of his popularity to his death (*and* beyond), touching on his super-active love life and relationship with his son-in-law Richard Wagner (Nicholas). Buoyed by his success with *Tommy*, director-extraordinaire Russell felt confident that he could *really* pull out all the stops with this follow-up (and when Russell pulls out all the stops . . . !) The premise of this baroque extravaganza is the frequently noted observation that composer-performer Liszt was the Elvis Presley of his day. But the heady brew that Russell offered proved too outrageous for intended audiences. Roger Daltrey cuts a flashy figure as Liszt (riding atop a block-long phallus in one indescribably weird dream sequence) and Ringo Starr appears briefly as the Pope. Rick Wakeman of "Yes," who gives Liszt's melodies "heavy metal" treatment on the film's soundtrack, also appears as the monster, evil musician-scientist, Wagner creates in his laboratory—Adolf Hitler! Songs include: "Chopsticks Fantasia," "Love's Dream," "Master Race" and "Rape, Pillage and Burn."

LONDON ROCK AND ROLL SHOW, THE (1973)

	R—Color
■	Peter Clifton
⌗	Peter Clifton
☚	Notting Hill
●	84m.
✪	Chuck Berry, Little Richard, Bill Haley and His Comets, Jerry Lee Lewis, Bo Diddley, Lord Sutch, Heinz, The Houseshakers
➲	Mick Jagger

Filmed record of 1973 rock and roll revival concert at Britain's Wembley Stadium. Stars do turns on the usual expected of their oldie goldies, interspersed with occasional comments by Mick Jagger.

LONELY BOY (1962)

R—Color
- Wolf Koenig, Roman Kroiter
- Roman Kroiter
- National Film Board of Canada
- 28m.
- Paul Anka

Singer Paul Anka at the beginning of his long and successful career is seen in appearances before crowds of screaming near-hysterical teenage fans, and in backstage moments in this much praised early *cinema verite* short. When filmmakers Koenig and Kroiter trained their cameras on young Anka, behind-the-scenes documentary films were something of a novelty. Though *Lonely Boy* has lost some of its initial freshness, it's still possible for contemporary viewers to sense the impact the film had when it was new, and see its influence on films like *A Hard Day's Night* (Anka-madness pre-figuring Beatlemania) and *Privilege* (the darker show biz slickness aspects). If you can hear it above the din, Anka sings "Diana," "Put Your Head On My Shoulder," "Mr. Wonderful" and the title tune.

LONG RIDERS, THE (1980)

D—Color
- Bill Bryden, Steven Phillip Smith, Stacy Keach, James Keach
- Walter Hill
- Tim Zinneman
- UA
- 100m.
- David Carradine, Stacy Keach
- Warner Brothers

Ry Cooder's score for this latest version of the Jesse James saga won the Los Angeles Film Critics Circle award for the best film score of 1980.

LOOKING FOR MR. GOODBAR (1977)

D—Color
- Richard Brooks
- the novel by Judith Rossner
- Richard Brooks
- Freddie Fields
- PAR
- 135m.
- Diane Keaton, Richard Gere, Tuesday Weld
- Columbia

Prim and proper—on the surface—school teacher (Keaton) gets involved with swinging singles scene to fatal end results. Disco, presented by Richard Brooks, the man who gave you "Rock Around The Clock" in *Blackboard Jungle,* is just as effective here as "Rock" was in that pioneer movie. Cuts by Thelma Houston ("Don't Leave Me This Way"), The O'Jays ("Back Stabbers"), Donna Summer ("Love To Love You Baby"), Diana Ross ("Love Hangover") and, among others, The Commodores, Bill Withers, Boz Scaggs and Giorgio Moroder, had sort of mix and fading in and out techniques that disco dee-jays use. Score by Artie Kaplan.

LORD LOVE A DUCK (1965)

	M–B/W
🎞	George Axelrod, Larry H. Johnson
▮	the novel by Al Hine
◼	George Axelrod
▦	Jack Fier, George Axelrod
☡	UA
●	105m.
✪	Tuesday Weld, Roddy McDowell, Harvey Korman, Lola Albright
◐	United Artists

Almost-grown nymphet (Weld) vamps everyone in sight and eventually secures movie stardom in a film called *Bikini Widow.* Classic satire begins as a send-up of youthsploitation movies, but rapidly rockets off into the anarchic stratosphere, taking pot-shots at Southern California lifestyles, parent-child relationships AND rock and roll. Back beat provided by Jordan Christopher and The Wild Ones singing the title tune—"HeyHeyHEY!" Other music by Neil Hefti.

LOVE AND MUSIC (*see* STAMPING GROUND)

LOVE ME TENDER (1956)

	D–B/W
🎞	Robert Buckner
◼	Robert Webb
▦	David Weisbart
☡	TCF
●	89m.
✪	Elvis Presley, Richard Egan, Debra Paget
◐	RCA(EP)

Confederate soldier (Egan) leads a band of men in robbing the U.S. mint (just as the Civil War concludes): meanwhile back on the farm his kid brother (Elvis) has just married the fiancee (Paget) of the presumed-dead Egan. Both plots strands, then, combine for a fittingly smashing climax. The biggest movie debut ever!—Elvis', and practically the greatest film sensation since Jolson talked. LMT hasn't aged particularly well, but it's light years beyond some of the later Elvis films like *Clambake.* In what's supposed to be the Civil War era, Presley anachronistically bumps and grinds his way through four songs: "Poor Boy," "We're Gonna Move," "Let Me" and the title tune. ELVIS #1.

LOVING YOU (1956)

	M–Color
🎞	Herbert Baker, Hal Kanter
◼	Hal Kanter
▦	Hal Wallis
☡	PAR
●	101m.
✪	Elvis Presley, Lizabeth Scott, Dolores Hart
◐	RCA

Unassuming country boy "Deke Rivers" (Elvis) is tapped for rock and roll stardom by enterprising manager, Scott. Things get complicated, though, when moral majority types get all riled up over "Deke's" indecency; but rock and roll finally wins out (in a climactic *Ed Sullivan Show*-ish finale), and "Deke" walks off *Scott*-free, hand-in-hand with the love of his life, Hart. Arguably Elvis' best film, and so close to the facts it could almost be called *The Elvis Presley Story*. Just about every possible facet of the Presley phenomenon is trotted out in this film, i.e. ELVIS as sensation, threat to the nation's youth, gimmick, etc. Scott as a kind of femme Colonel Parker mother-hens over Elvis as he impressively struts his stuff on such numbers as: "Hot Dog," "We're Gonna Live it Up," "Party," "Dancing on a Dare," "Lonesome Cowboy," "Fireworks," "Gotta Lotta Livin' To Do," "Dandy Kisses," "Mean Woman Blues," "Detour," "Teddy Bear" and the title tune. ELVIS #2 .

MAD DOGS AND ENGLISHMEN (1971)

	R–Color
🎬	Pierre Adidge
🎞	Pierre Adidge
📽	Pierre Adidge, Harry Marks, Robert Abel
⚡	MGM
●	118m.
✪	Joe Cocker, Leon Russell, and the Grease Band
◐	A&M

A shoot-the-works stereo, split-screen extravanganza of Cocker's 1970 tour, when the great R&B shaker and writher was at the height of his powers and popularity. "Delta Lady," "Feelin' Alright," "Something," "Cry Me A River" and "Bird On A Wire" are some of the Cocker classics given maximum-impact audio-visualization.

MADE IN U.S.A. (1966)

	D–Color
🎬	Jean-Luc Godard
📖	the novel *The Jugger* by Richard Stark (Donald Westlake)
🎞	Jean-Luc Godard
📽	Georges De Beauregard
⚡	Contemporary
●	90m.
✪	Anna Karina, Laszlo Szabo, Jean-Pierre Leaud
➔	Marianne Faithfull

Private detective Paula Nelson (Karina) comes to Atlantic City to find the murderers of her ex-lover Richard Politzer and becomes involved in a web of intrigue. Marianne Faithfull sings a haunting *a capella* version of "As Tears Go By" in a cafe scene of this beautiful and mysterious political thriller that is arguably Godard's best film.

MAGIC CHRISTIAN, THE (1970)

	M–Color
🎬	Terry Southern, Joseph McGrath, Peter Sellers
📖	the novel by Terry Southern
🎞	Joseph McGrath
📽	Denis O'Dell
⚡	Commonwealth-United
●	93m.

✪ Ringo Starr, Terry Southern, Spike Milligan, Christopher Lee
◑ Commonwealth United

Sporadically funny film of Terry Southern's novel about the fabulously wealthy "Grand Guy Grand" (Sellers) who uses his wealth for staging grand, grander and more outrageous put-ons. Finally with the aid of his adopted son (Ringo) he launches his *magnum opus,* the bedevilled cruise ship of the film's title. In one scene on board, Yul Brynner, in drag, sings Noel Coward's "Mad About The Boy" to Roman Polanski. Soundtrack score written and performed by Badfinger, who also have a go at a Paul McCartney tune, "Come and Get It."

MAGICAL MYSTERY TOUR (1967)

M–Color
■ The Beatles
▦ The Beatles
ℭ Apple Films
● 60m.
✪ The Beatles
⊐ The Bonzo Dog Band, Mal Evans, Mike McGear
◑ Capitol

Largely improvised film chronicles the adventures of The Beatles and friends as they take a ride on the MMT bus. One can guess why American TV execs refused to air this (at a time when The Beatles couldn't have been hotter) after previewing it. What was expected must've been a straightforward all-singing, all-dancing variety show, but what The Beatles delivered was a personal and thoughtful *statement.* Because of the surrealistic nightmarishness of some of MMT's scenes, the film is occasionally disturbing, but overall it is most charming in spite of its fragmented, herky-jerky mildly pretentious style. The songs written for, and visualized in, this rock *Un Chien Andalou* include: "I Am The Walrus," "Fool on the Hill" and the title tune.

MAHOGANY (1975)

D–Color
▬ John Byrum
■ Berry Gordy, Jr.
▦ Rob Cohen, Jack Ballard
ℭ PAR
● 109m.
✪ Diana Ross, Billy Dee Williams
◑ Motown

The rise and *rise* of a superstar designer/fashion model, "Mahogany" (Ross), is the focus of this trash maven's delight. So Diana Ross wants to do a moldy old Lana Turner-style fantasy! So what!? She's entitled! This enormously entertaining piece of Swiss cheese features Diana (heard) singing "Do You Know Where You're Going To?" Also on the soundtrack are, among others, The Temptations and Jermaine Jackson. Motown magnate, Gordy, replaced original director, Tony Richardson, part way through the filming. Score by Michael Masser.

MAN WHO FELL TO EARTH, THE (1976)

D–Color
▬ Paul Mayersberg
■ the novel by Walter Tevis

- ▨ Nicolas Roeg
- ▦ Michael Deeley, Barry Spikings
- ⅀ Cinema V
- ● 138m.
- ✪ David Bowie, Rip Torn

A visitor from a drought stricken planet (Bowie) comes to Earth and establishes an international electronics corporation to finance aid for his world. Gradually he is undone by U.S. corporate interests and his own emotional weaknesses. The cinematic answer to the old Bowie musical question, "Is there life on Mars?" Well, yes there is, and Bowie's it in this William Burroughsian sci-fi affair. While "the man who sold the world" doesn't sing here, he does manage to exploit all the mythical material of his songs in this fragmented narrative package based on Walter Tevis' novel. Critically well-received, still this film never managed to achieve much box office momentum when first released. Now, though, it is steadily played on the movie revival house circuit. Original music by Papa John Phillips and Stomu Yamashta. Also soundtrack usage of recordings by Roy Orbison ("Blue Bayou"), The Kingston Trio and many other non-rock artists like Artie Shaw and Louis Armstrong. Note: A truncated version of this film, less 20 minutes, was in release in the U.S. until 1981, at which time Roeg's original was put into circulation.

MASCULIN-FEMININ (1966)

D—B/W
- ▬ Jean-Luc Godard
- ▮ "La Femme de Paul" and "Le Signe" by Guy de Maupassant
- ▨ Jean-Luc Godard
- ▦ Jean-Luc Godard
- ⅀ COL
- ● 110m.
- ✪ Jean-Pierre Leaud, Chantal Goya, Marlene Jobert
- ➔ Brigitte Bardot, Francoise Hardy, Antoine Bourseiller

Goya, who later became a pop singer herself, stars as an *aspiring* one in Godard's study of restless youth in France in the sixties. Mixing essay (comments written on the screen in title cards), character study and Brechtian blackout sketch, Godard follows a young radical (Leaud) in his amorous adventures with Goya. "The children of Marx and Coca-Cola," is what the great French writer-director calls them. Standout sequence features the manufacture of a "ye-ye" hit in a recording studio. Music by J.J. Debout.

McVICAR (1980)

D—Color
- ▬ John McVicar, Tom Clegg
- ▮ the book *McVicar By Himself* by John McVicar
- ▨ Tom Clegg
- ▦ Roy Baird, Bill Curbishley, Roger Daltrey
- ⅀ Crown Int'l.
- ● 112m.
- ✪ Roger Daltrey, Adam Faith
- ◑ Polydor

Based on a non-fiction British best seller, *McVicar* features The Who's Roger Daltrey in the title role of a notorious recidivist. The Who produced the film, and perform (with orchestral augmentation) on the soundtrack. Songs by Jon Lind, Billy Nicholls and Russ Ballard. Musical director: Jeff Wayne. Songs include: "Free Me," "Just a Dream" and "White City Lights."

MEAN STREETS (1973)

D—Color
- Martin Scorsese, Mardik Martin
- Martin Scorsese
- Jonathan Taplin
- WB
- 110m.
- Robert DeNiro, Harvey Keitel

Study of drifters in New York's Little Italy features lots of soundtrack rock and roll, and not just for background. One sequence, for instance, uses The Stones' "Tell Me" as accompaniment to hero Keitel's strutting and preening entrance to his favorite hangout. Also heard, among many others, are The Chantels ("I Love You So"), The Marvelettes ("Please, Mr. Postman") and Johnny Ace ("Pledging My Love").

MEDICINE BALL CARAVAN (1971)

R—Color
- Francois Reichenbach
- Francois Reichenbach
- Francois Reichenbach, Tom Donohue
- WB
- 88m.
- The Youngbloods, Bonnie and Delaney, B.B. King, Stoneground, Alice Cooper, Sal Valentino, David Peel, Doug Kershaw
- WB

Itinerant docu of a 154-person bus and truck tour that set out to spread the gospel of flower power to the hinterlands of the U.S. in the Summer of 1970. (With Warner Brothers underwriting most of the expenses.) Travelling eastward across the country from San Francisco, every few hundred miles this band of gypsies give ad hoc concerts at stops along the way. Cameras capture not just the performances but, as well, the response of townies to the (then) rarefied likes of Cooper, Peel and company. Songs include: "Act Naturally" by The Youngbloods and "Free The People" by Bonnie and Delaney. Martin Scorsese acted as associate producer on this project which is also called *We Have Come For Your Daughters*.

MEDIUM COOL (1969)

D—Color
- Haskell Wexler
- Haskell Wexler
- Tully Friedman and Haskell Wexler
- PAR
- 111m.
- Robert Forster, Verna Bloom, Peter Bonerz
- The Mothers of Invention

A television news cameraman becomes involved with an Appalachian woman and her son during the 1968 Democratic national convention in Chicago. Photographer Wexler—here director and writer as well—put his impeccable liberal credentials to the test when making this film. He shot over twenty hours of footage of the tumultuous convention which was requisitioned by the U.S. Justice department for its investigation of what others described as "a police riot." The Mothers of Invention sing "Merry-Go-Round" in one sequence. Music by Mike Bloomfield.

MIDNIGHT COWBOY (1969)

- D—Color
- Waldo Salt
- the novel by James Leo Herlihy
- John Schlesinger
- Jerome Hellman
- UA
- 119m.
- Jon Voight, Dustin Hoffman
- RCA

Handsome country boy (Voight), seeking the bright lights of New York, meets up with lost soul (Hoffman). They link up in a kind of *Mice and Men* partnership in order to try and stay afloat. Together they experience both the high and low stratas of life in the great metropolis before their final and fateful bus journey away from the city. Fred Neil's "Everybody's Talkin'," sung by Nilsson, used recurringly throughout the film. Also soundtrack use of an early Warren Zevon song, "He Quit Me Man," sung by Lesley Miller, and music by Elephant's Memory. Additional music written and performed by Nilsson.

MIDNIGHT EXPRESS (1978)

- D—Color
- Oliver Stone
- the book by Billy Hayes
- Alan Parker
- Peter Guber
- COL
- 121m.
- Brad Davis, Randy Quaid, John Hurt
- Casablanca

An American college student arrested in Istanbul airport for attempting to smuggle hashish out of Turkey escapes a hellish Turkish prison after many trials and tribulations. Giorgio Moroder's driving disco-tinged electronic score for this manipulative and xenophobic adventure story won an Academy Award.

MRS. BROWN YOU'VE GOT A LOVELY DAUGHTER (1968)

- M—Color
- Thaddeus Vane
- Saul Swimmer
- Allen Klein
- MGM
- 95m.
- Herman's Hermits (with Peter Noone), Mona Washbourne
- MGM

A would-be pop group (the Hermits) moonlight as owners of a racing dog, the "Mrs. Brown" of the title. In between canine contests, the British group reprises a handful of their hits including the title tune, "I'm Into Something Good" and "A Must To Avoid."

MR. MIKE'S MONDO VIDEO (1979)

M—Color
- Michael O'Donoghue, Michael Glazer, Emily Prager, Dirk Wittenborn
- Michael O'Donoghue
- Michael O'Donoghue
- New Line
- 70m.
- Bill Murray, Gilda Radner, Larraine Newman, Michael O'Donoghue, Klaus Nomi, Sid Vicious

This offshoot of *Saturday Night Live* was initially shot as a TV special, but it was bounced by NBC and thrown into movie theatres instead. And we can see why. It's not very funny, though arid comedy spells are alleviated by Euro-rock "opera" singer Klaus Nomi's Yma Sumac-like screeching, and by Sid Vicious, at Paris' Olympia Theater, singing "My Way." (That same film footage also appears in *The Great Rock and Roll Swindle*.)

MISTER ROCK AND ROLL (1957)

M—B/W
- James Blumgarten
- Charles Dubin
- Ralph Siepe
- PAR
- 86m.
- Alan Freed, Teddy Randazzo
- Chuck Berry, Little Richard, The Moonglows, Clyde McPhatter, Frankie Lymon and The Teenagers, Brook Benton

Dee-jay Freed in the title role sets out to prove the preposterous premise to concerned citizens that rock and rock and roll isn't responsible for juvenile delinquency. His *aides-de-camp* include Chuck Berry, who sings "Oh, Baby Doll," and Little Richard, who gets the kids all riled up with "Lucille" and "Keep a Knockin'." Lots of music, little plot in this telethon-like quickie.

MODEL SHOP (1969)

D—Color
- Jacques Demy, Adrian Joyce
- Jacques Demy
- Jacques Demy
- COL
- 92m.
- Anouk Aimee, Gary Lockwood
- Spirit

A young drifter (Lockwood) who's just received his draft notice pursues a beautiful and mysterious woman (Aimee) around Los Angeles in a last chance effort at romantic fulfillment. Music and an on-screen appearance by the group, Spirit.

MONEY MADNESS (1977)

R—Color / B/W
- Michael Mason
- Michael Mason
- Michael Mason
- New Line Cinema
- 90m.
- Eddie Money

Attractively made behind-the-scenes documentary charts the rise of rocker Eddie Money (*née* Mahoney) from semi-obscurity to the bigtime. Interviews with Eddie's family and friends and Eddie himself. In clubs and studio sessions Eddie is seen singing "Payola," "Gamblin' Man" and his big hit "Two Tickets To Paradise."

MONKEY'S UNCLE (1965)

M—Color
- Tom August, Helen August
- Robert Stevenson
- Ron Miller
- Buena Vista
- 87m.
- Annette Funicello, Tommy Kirk
- The Beach Boys
- Buena Vista

Kirk is a boy genius who tries to upgrade the intellect of a simian friend in this standard Disney family comedy. Title tune sung by The Beach Boys and Annette during the credit sequence.

MONTEREY POP (1968)

R—Color
- D.A. Pennebaker
- D.A. Pennebaker, James Desmond, Barry Feinstein, Albert Maysles, Roger Murphy, Richard Leacock, Nick Proferes
- D.A. Pennebaker and Richard Leacock
- Leacock-Pennebaker
- 79m.
- Jimi Hendrix, Otis Redding, Jefferson Airplane, Janis Joplin and Big Brother and The Holding Company, Country Joe and The Fish, The Mamas and the Papas, The Animals, Canned Heat, Simon and Garfunkel, Booker T. and The M.G.'s, Ravi Shankar, The Who, Hugh Masakela
- (Partial—Redding & Hendrix only) Reprise

THE Big pre-*Woodstock* breakthrough concert film. In spite of some of the film's visual pretensions, there are still more than enough great performances to put this filmed record of the 1967 Monterey International Pop Festival over the top. Highlights include The Who ("My Generation") and Jimi ("Wild Thing")—both neck-and-neck in the amp-smashing sweepstakes, Janis ("Combination of the Two," "Ball and Chain") and Otis ("I've Been Loving You Too Long"). Other music includes: The Jefferson Airplane doing "Today" and Eric Burdon and The Animals singing "Paint It Black." The optical distortion of Redding almost beyond recognition is a typical example of the film's visual failings, but still in all *Monterey Pop* is required viewing.

MORD UND TOTSCHLAG (A DEGREE OF MURDER) (1966)

D—Color
- Volker Schlondorff, Gregor von Ressori, Niklas Frank and Arne Boyer
- Volker Schlondorff
- Rob Houwer Films
- 87m.
- Anita Pallenberg, Hans P. Hallswachs, Manfred Fischbeck

A waitress kills her lover during a fight and asks a total stranger for help in disposing of the body. One of Brian Jones' last efforts was providing the music for this brooding little thriller-cum-road-movie from German premier "New Wave" director Schlondorff.

MORE (1969)

D—Color
- Paul Gegauf, Barbet Schroeder
- Barbet Schroeder
- Barbet Schroeder
- Cinema V
- 116m.
- Mimsey Farmer, Klaus Grunberg
- Tower

One of the first films to blow the whistle on the supposed blissed-out benevolence of the "Summer of Love" drug culture. This harrowing study of heroin addiction features a standout performance by Farmer, an American actress who, like Jean Seberg, fared far better professionally on the other side of the Atlantic. Beautiful score by Pink Floyd.

MORE AMERICAN GRAFFITI (PURPLE HAZE) (1979)

D—Color
- W.B.L. Norton
- B.W.L. Norton
- George Lucas
- UI
- 111m.
- Candy Clark, Ron Howard, Cindy Williams, Mackenzie Phillips
- MCA

Failed sequel to George Lucas' hugely popular *American Graffiti*, updates, by a few years, the lives of most of the characters from the original film—one is now in Vietnam, others have become hippie dropouts and one couple has settled into suburban domesticity, etc. Therefore, the music heard here is a little spacier, a bit more "now" than the non-stop oldies parade (Haley, Berry et al) of the original film. This time around the *zeitgeist*-inducing sounds are by Hendrix, The Byrds and Dylan and other sixties stars.

MUSCLE BEACH PARTY (1964)

M—Color
- Robert Dillon
- William Asher
- James H. Nicholson, Robert Dillon

- ☡ AIP
- ● 94m.
- ✪ Annette Funicello, Frankie Avalon, Luciana Paluzzi
- ⛛ Stevie Wonder, Dick Dale and The Del Tones
- ↻ AIP Records

Visiting Italian countess (Paluzzi) goes ape for musclemen until suddenly smitten by Frankie's charms in this second entry in AIP's "Beach Party" series. Little Stevie Wonder makes a special appearance, along with musical regulars Dick Dale and The Del Tones. Songs include: "I Dream About Frankie," "Muscle Bustle" and the title tune.

NATIONAL LAMPOON'S ANIMAL HOUSE (1978)

- D—Color
- ☰ Harold Ramis, Douglas Kenney and Chris Miller
- ▦ John Landis
- ▦ Matty Simmons and Ivan Reitman
- ☡ UI
- ● 109m.
- ✪ John Belushi, Tim Matheson, John Vernon, Thomas Hulce, Donald Sutherland
- ↻ MCA

The most financially successful comedy ever made, this rowdy free-for-all details the frat house rivalry between super-straight "Omega House" and wild-and-crazy "Delta" at the mythical "Faber College." While most of this is fun, some scenes are in very questionable taste—especially one in which the kids visit an all-black night spot. There's rock and roll running through most of the action, "Louie Louie" by The Kingsmen functioning as the "Delts" personal anthem. Other songs heard include "Shout" by the Isley Brothers, "Twistin' The Night Away" by Sam Cooke, and "Tossin' and Turnin'" by Bobby Lewis. John Belushi tears his way into the R & B classic "Money" during a party scene. Non-rock music by Elmer Bernstein. Song, "Animal House" written and performed by Stephen Bishop.

NED KELLY (1970)

D—Color
- Tony Richardson, Ian Jones
- Tony Richardson
- Neil Hartley
- UA
- 103m.
- Mick Jagger, Allen Bickford
- UA

Tableau-styled musical-drama based on life and adventures of legendary late nineteenth century Australian outlaw, Kelly. Mick Jagger, in a straight dramatic part, plays Kelly, while the soundtrack abounds with a dozen Shel Silverstein compositions (sung by Waylon Jennings) which comment on the action. Mick sings "The Wild Colonial Boy."

NEVER TOO YOUNG TO ROCK (1975)

M—Color
- Ron Inkpen, Dennis Abey
- Dennis Abey
- Greg Smith, Ron Inkpen
- GTO (England)
- 99m.
- Freddie Jones, Peter Noone
- Mud, Slick, The Rubettes, The Glitter Band

A promoter searching for England's best groups is thwarted by mysterious saboteurs. Silly spy plot is the clothesline upon which some lower echelon glitter bands are hung out to dry. Songs include "Angel Face" (The Glitter Band), "Tiger Feet" (Mud), "Sugar Baby Love" (The Rubettes), and "The Boogiest Band in Town" (Slick).

NO NUKES (1980)

R—Color
- Julian Schlossberg, Danny Goldberg, Anthony Potenza
- Julian Schlossberg, Danny Goldberg
- WB
- 103m.
- The Doobie Brothers, Jackson Browne, Gil-Scott Heron, Crosby, Stills, Nash and Young, James Taylor, Carly Simon, Jessie Colin Young, Bruce Springsteen, John Hall, Bonnie Raitt, Nicolette Larsen
- Asylum

The above-listed stars (as well as many others not in this film) pooled their talents for a 1980 pro-solar, anti-nuclear benefit at New York's Madison Square Garden. This is a filmed record of that well-intentioned but, ultimately rather enervated parade of socially conscious rockers. Highlights include: "The Times They are a Changin'," "Mockin' Bird" (Taylor & Simon); "Runaway" (Raitt); "Teach Your Children," "Long Time Gone" (CSN&Y); "Lotta Love" (Doobies, Larsen); "Before the Deluge" (Brown); "Get Together" (Young); and "Stay," "Devil With the Blue Dress On" (Springsteen).

O LUCKY MAN (1973)

M/D—Color
David Sherwin
Lindsay Anderson
Michael Medwin, Lindsay Anderson
WB
174m.
Malcolm McDowell, Rachel Roberts, Ralph Richardson
Alan Price
WB

McDowell is a young man looking for a leg up in the business world. Quixotically, he stops at nothing to "get on," yet at the film's climax (after endless rejection and, finally, prison) he finds himself no better off than when he started out. A unique example of successfully integrating rock into a dramatic context—in fact, Alan Price's wonderful songs and on-screen singing often help to counteract the more pretentious aspects of this Brechtian *Pilgrim's Progress*. This sort-of sequel to Anderson's *If* was considerably cut for U.S. release.

ONE PLUS ONE (SYMPATHY FOR THE DEVIL) (1968)

R—Color
Jean-Luc Godard
Jean-Luc Godard
Micael Pearson, Ian Quarrier
New Line
99m.
The Rolling Stones
Anne Wiazemsky

The Stones rehearsing and recording "Sympathy For The Devil" in a studio used in counterpoint to Godard's commentaries on revolutionary politics. Unique in the opportunity it provides to see and hear the creation of a song/recording from the ground up. Godard never intended for the final mix to be heard, or for the song to become *One Plus One*'s central focus. You can just imagine his pique then, when co-producer Ian Quarrier slapped on the completed track at the end and changed the film's title to *Sympathy For The Devil*. Fortunately Godard's version is also still available.

ONE-TRICK PONY (1980)

D—Color
- Paul Simon
- Robert M. Young
- Michael Tannen
- WB
- 98m.
- Paul Simon, Marc Winningham, Lou Reed
- The B-52's, The Lovin' Spoonful, Sam and Dave, Tiny Tim
- (Simon only) Warner Brothers

Simon plays a rock musician whose popularity has diminished considerably but who, to the detriment of both his marriage and his sense of personal worth, keeps trying to re-kindle his career. Sixties superstars never faded even halfway to eighties oblivion the way Simon's "Jonah" does in this semi-autobio (?). And it's hard to swallow the idea of songs like "Late in the Evening" being deemed *passé* in the film, whereas in real life those same tunes are top ten hits. But even though Simon the screenwriter is annoying, Simon the actor is often charming. To help things along there's an appearance by rocker Lou Reed as a record producer and on-screen appearances by The B-52's ("Rock Lobster"), Sam and Dave ("Soul Man") and The Lovin' Spoonful ("Do You Believe in Magic?").

OUT OF SIGHT (1966)

M—Color
- Larry Hovis
- Lennie Weinrib
- Bart Patton
- UI
- 87m.
- Jonathan Daly, Karen Jensen
- Gary Lewis and The Playboys, Freddie and The Dreamers, The Turtles, Dobie Gray, The Astronauts, The Knickerbockers
- Decca

From the director who brought you the slightly deflated *Beach Ball* comes this equally dispirited romp about a teen driven daffy by exposure to way too much rock and roll. "Out of sync" turns by Freddie and The Dreamers, The Knickerbockers and others.

OVER THE EDGE (1979)

D—Color
- Charles Haas, Tim Hunter
- Jonathan Kaplan
- George Litto
- WB
- 95m.
- Matt Dillon, Michael Kramer, Pamela Ludwig
- Warner Brothers

The supposedly "ideal" community of "New Granada" proves to be something short of paradise when its teenagers go on a *Clockwork Orange*-style rampage. This teenage gang violence flick got less play than even *The Warriors*. Reportedly Warner Brothers was upset by audience reaction to a scene where the kids locked their parents in the gym during a P.T.A. meeting. Excellent "New Wave" rock soundtrack featuring Cheap Trick ("Speak Now," "Hello There," "Surrender."), The Cars ("Just What I Needed," "My Best Friend's Girl"), Little Feat ("All That You Dream") and The Ramones ("Lobotomy").

OWL AND THE PUSSYCAT, THE (1970)

	M—Color
☰	Buck Henry
■	the play by Bill Manhoff
▣	Herbert Ross
▦	Ray Stark
⚙	COL
●	96m.
✪	Barbra Streisand, George Segal
◐	Columbia

Funny neo-screwball comedy about a would-be writer (Segal) who falls in love with a hooker (Streisand) has a score by Chicago.

PAJAMA PARTY (1964)

	M—Color
☰	Louis M. Heyward
■	Don Weis
▦	James H. Nicolson and Samuel Z. Arkoff
⚙	AIP
●	82m.
✪	Tommy Kirk, Annette Funicello
⊐	Nooney Rickett Four

A Martian (Kirk) comes to Earth to plan an interplanetary invasion, but changes his mind after contact with teenage earthlings. The *Beach Party* formula gets a sci-fi twist in this typical bit of American-International insanity. The Nooney Rickett Four (!) sing "There Has To Be A Reason."

PARADISE HAWAIIAN STYLE (1966)

	M—Color
☰	Allan Weiss, Anthony Lawrence
■	Michael Moore
▦	Hal Wallis
⚙	PAR
●	91m.
✪	Elvis Presley, Suzanna Leigh, Donna Butterworth
◐	RCA

Elvis is co-owner of a fledgling helicopter service, and the ups and downs of this new venture plus a (*de rigeur*) bumpy love affair form the main elements of this routine musical. Songs include: "Drums of the Islands," "House of Sand" and (urrrp) "Queenie Wahine's Papaya." Elvis #20.

PAT GARRETT AND BILLY THE KID (1973)

- D—Color
- Rudolph Wurlitzer
- Sam Peckinpah
- Gordon Carroll
- MGM
- 106m.
- Bob Dylan, James Coburn, Kris Kristofferson
- Columbia

Peckinpah's enervated western (and easily his worst feature) details the events leading up to Garrett's (Coburn) fabled gunning down of Billy the Kid (Kristofferson). Dylan in his only dramatic appearance portrays Billy's taciturn and mysterious sidekick, "Alias." Peckinpah disowned the film since he did not get final cut on it. Dylan wrote the soundtrack music and songs, one of which, "Knockin' On Heaven's Door," became a best seller.

PATSY, THE (1964)

- M—Color
- Jerry Lewis and Bill Richmond
- Jerry Lewis
- Ernest D. Glucksman
- PAR
- 101m.
- Jerry Lewis, Ina Balin, Peter Lorre, John Carradine, Hans Conried, Keenan Wynn, Hedda Hopper, Lloyd Thaxton

When a famous comedian is killed in a plane crash, his associates attempt to replace him by turning an unknown (Lewis) into a star. Jerry does a rock parody, "I Lost My Heart In A Drive-In Movie" (by David Raksin and Jack Brooks), in a scene spoofing lip-syncing on *American Bandstand*-style TV shows in this rather bitter satire of "overnight success" in show business.

PATTI AND VALLI (1973)

- R—Color
- Patti Smith
- Sandy Daley
- Sandy Daley
- 30m.
- Patti Smith, Valli

Patti gets her kneecap tatooed by noted English-born bohemian, Valli. No music, but exhaustive off-screen commentary by Smith.

PAYDAY (1973)

- M—Color
- Don Carpenter
- Daryl Duke
- Ralph J. Gleason
- Cinerama Releasing
- 103m.
- Rip Torn, Ahna Capri, Elayne Heilveil

Twenty-four hours "on the road" with country and western singing star Maury Dann (Torn), detailing his drinking, drugging, sexual excesses and eventual death. There's a little bit of Maury Dann in every musical troubador. *Payday* may center on country and western music but it's accurate and often painful observations are equally applicable to the pop life. Underappreciated by audiences when it was first released, this film has since attained a loyal following. Almost every dramatic film about rock made afterwards, to one degree or another draws upon it for inspiration. As the Hank Williams-ish Dann, Torn—in the best performance of his career—does his own singing of the Shel Silverstein-composed songs which include "Lovin' You More," "Slow Fadin' Circle" and "Sunny Side of Life."

PERCY (1971)

	M—Color
🎬	Hugh Leonard
■	the novel by Raymond Hitchcock
▦	Ralph Thomas
▤	Betty Box
⌁	MGM
●	103m.
✪	Hywel Bennett, Elke Sommer
◑	Pye

British farce about world's first penis transplant . . . produced by, uh, Betty Box! The Kinks' "Willesden Green" (one of their first forays into country music) comes from their score for this good-taste-is-timeless special.

PERFECT COUPLE, A (1979)

	D—Color
🎬	Robert Altman, Allan Nicholls
■	Robert Altman
▤	Robert Altman
⌁	TCF
●	110m.
✪	Paul Dooley, Marta Heflin
⤴	Keepin 'em Off The Streets
◑	Lion's Gate

Uptight "straight" (Dooley) meets a young singer (Heflin) through a dating service. His family and her musician friends form the obstacles on their bumpy road to love. "Streets" (fronted by film's co-scripter, Nicholls), a rock-fusion group director Altman hoped to launch through this film, is the communal cornerstone around which revolves this pathetically outdated tale of the rock scene and turning on, tuning in and dropping out. Music laid down by the group is a bland amalgam of soul and fuzz-tone.

PERFORMANCE (1970)

	D—Color
🎬	Donald Cammell
■	Donald Cammell, Nicholas Roeg
▤	Sanford Lieberson
⌁	WB
●	102m.

⊙ Mick Jagger, James Fox, Anita Pallenberg, Michele Breton
◐ Warner Brothers

Chas (Fox), a petty hoodlum on the lam from gangsters he betrayed, takes refuge in the mansion of retired pop star, Turner (Jagger). Chas' experiences while dwelling in this "decadent" parallel universe constitute the main action in this hypnotic film. When the Warner Brothers brass first viewed this seminal cult classic, their reaction was said to have been apoplectic. With its fragmented narrative, extremes of sex and violence, drug-induced hallucinations and arcane literary references, *Performance* is clearly a film designed to disturb. Underneath its Borgesian surface and bisexuality, however, lies a simple gangster-on-the-run-meets-intellectual-outcast story straight out of *The Petrified Forest.* All Cammell, Roeg and company did was flesh it out in contemporary rock terms. In the Leslie Howard role, Jagger disarms the viewer as easily as he charms the slick teddy boy portrayed by Fox. But even the sociopathic hood Bogie played in *The Petrified Forest* would have been thrown off balance by rock recluse (*Sunset Boulevard* by way of Oscar Wilde) Turner.

Turning conventional notions of *macho* on its ear, Jagger struts, pouts and sulks only to pull back at the last moment into a trance-like state of *performance* that owes nothing to acting in the conventional sense, but everything to what rock and roll *persona*fication is finally all about. Music arranged and produced by Jack Nitzsche features soundtrack *performances* by Randy Newman ("Gone Dead Train"), Merry Clayton ("Poor White Hound Dog"), Ry Cooder, Buffy Sainte-Marie, The Last Poets AND (on screen) Mick singing "Memo From Turner," written by Jagger and Keith Richard. Musical direction by Randy Newman, for one of the most effective and achieved of all original rock movie scores.

PETULIA (1968)

D—Color
🎬 Lawrence B. Marcus
▌ the novel *Me and the Arch Kook Petulia* by John Haase
▐ Richard Lester
▩ Raymond Wagner
✇ WB
● 105m.
⊙ Julie Christie, George C. Scott, Richard Chamberlain
◐ (non-rock) Warner Brothers

The bored kooky wife (Christie) of a playboy (Chamberlain) makes a desparate stab at happiness by forging a relationship with a somewhat unwilling doctor (Scott). The aftershock of "the summer of love" rattles the windows of some of San Francisco's *nouveau* and not-so-nouveau rich in memorable satire directed by Beatles' film mentor, Lester. Brief on-screen appearances by Janis Joplin and Big Brother and the Holding Company, and The Grateful Dead. Non-rock score by John Barry.

PHANTOM OF THE PARADISE (1974)

M—Color
🎬 Brian De Palma
▐ Brian De Palma
▩ Edward R. Pressman
✇ TCF
● 92m.
⊙ Paul Williams, William Finley, Jessica Harper, Gerrit Graham
◐ A&M

A disfigured songwriter (Finley) takes revenge on the evil music promoter (Williams) who stole his work and kept him from his one true love (Harper). Brian De Palma's rock and roll send-up (which mixes in elements from *Faust* and *The Picture of Dorian Gray* as well as *The Phantom of The Opera*) never caught on with audiences, and hasn't acquired the cult following of a *Rocky Horror Picture Show*. Perhaps De Palma's underlying romantic sincerity has proved too off-putting for some viewers. In any event this is a marvelous film. Songs by Paul Williams include "Somebody Super Like You," "Life At Last" and "The Hell of It."

PICTURES AT AN EXHIBITION (1972)

    R—Color
- Nicholas Ferguson
- Lindsey Clennel
- Crown-International
- 95m.
- Emerson, Lake and Palmer

Extended version of the title tune forms the core of this videotaped, tricked-up coverage of ELP concert. Also visualized are "The Barbarian," "Take a Pebble," "Knife Edge" and "Nut Rocker."

PIED PIPER, THE (1972)

    M—Color
- Andrew Birkin, Jacques Demy, Mark Peploe
- a poem by Robert Browning
- Jacques Demy
- David Puttnam, Sanford Lieberson
- 90m.
- Donovan, Diana Dors, Donald Pleasence

The traditional fairy tale, by way of a poem by Browning, gets a thorough going over by Demy, with the end result being more in the vein *grand guignol*. Around the time this film was made, Donovan, who also wrote the score and sings in the film, ceased being such a hot pop star; thus the project only got limited U.S. distribution.

PINK FLOYD A POMPEII, LES (*aka* PINK FLOYD) (1971)

    R—Color
- Adrian Maben
- Michele Arnaud
- EMI
- 85m.
- Pink Floyd

One of the most frequently exhibited of all rockumentary films. The interviews and other non-musical goings-on get a bit obtrusive, but all this should matter little to the Floyd faithful as the group gets to work its way through seven *long* songs including "Dark Side of The Moon," "A Saucerful of Secrets" and "Set The Controls For The Heart of The Sun," shot audience-less at the deserted amphitheatre at Pompeii.

PIPE DREAMS (1976)

    D—Color
- Steven Verona

- Steven Verona
- Steven Verona
- Avco Embassy
- 89m.
- Gladys Knight, Barry Hankerson
- Buddah

Knight, in her dramatic debut, plays a woman who goes off to join her husband, who is on the Alaska Pipeline crew, in a try at saving her floundering marriage. This mildly enjoyable film was a real family affair, made by Knight's production company, co-starring her real-life husband, Hankerson, and has soundtrack music intoned by Gladys and The Pips. Songs include (no, they don't do "I Heard it Through the Pipeline"): "So Sad the Song," "Nobody But You" and "Pipeline."

PLATINUM HIGH SCHOOL (1960)

- D–B/W
- Robert Smith
- Charles Haas
- Albert Zugsmith
- MGM
- 93m.
- Mickey Rooney, Terry Moore
- Conway Twitty

An appearance by Conway Twitty (who also sings the title tune) in a film about "a very *exclusive* private school where money can buy everything . . . even murder."

PLAY IT COOL (1962)

- M–B/W
- Jack Henry
- Michael Winner
- Julian Wintle, Leslie Parkyn
- Allied Artists
- 82m.
- Billy Fury, Bobby Vee, Helen Shapiro
- Shane Fenton and The Fentones

Rock group, "Billy (Fury) and The Satellites," on their way to Brussels from England, meets up with an attractive, but stuffy, rich girl and then, the usual clash-of-lifestyles ensue. Fury, one of several sixties British Presley pretenders, is joined by Helen Shapiro, another U.K. "fave," for this lightweight fare about the liberation of a teen heiress. America's Bobby Vee also appears in this romp whose songs include: "Who Can Say?," "Cry My Heart Out" and "But I Don't Care."

POOR COW (1968)

- D–Color
- Nell Dunn, Kenneth Loach
- the novel by Nell Dunn
- Kenneth Loach
- Joseph Janni

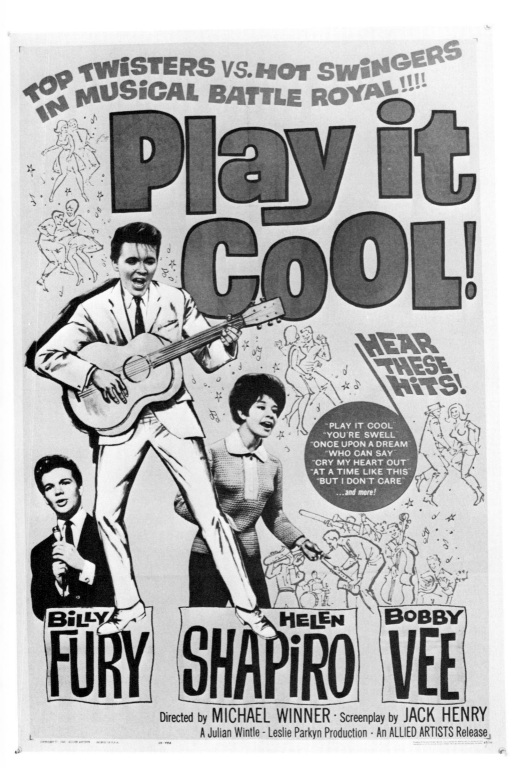

TOP TWISTERS VS. HOT SWINGERS IN MUSICAL BATTLE ROYAL!!!!

Play it COOL!

HEAR THESE HITS!

"PLAY IT COOL"
"YOU'RE SWELL"
"ONCE UPON A DREAM"
"WHO CAN SAY"
"CRY MY HEART OUT"
"AT A TIME LIKE THIS"
"BUT I DON'T CARE"
...and more!

BILLY FURY

HELEN SHAPIRO

BOBBY VEE

Directed by MICHAEL WINNER · Screenplay by JACK HENRY
A Julian Wintle - Leslie Parkyn Production · An ALLIED ARTISTS Release

    National-General
    104m.
    Carol White, Terence Stamp

A working class teenager's (White) marriage and (later) love affair are both shattered by her lovers being sent to prison. Eventually her husband (and the father of her child) returns and White resigns herself to a bleak and hopeless future. This British slice-of-life drama (influenced by French "New Wave" moviemaking) has an original score by Donovan. Songs include: "Be Not Too Hard," "Colours" and "Poor Love."

POP GEAR (see GO GO MANIA)

POPCORN—AN AUDIO-VISUAL THING (1970)

    R—Color
    Peter Clifton
    Peter Ryan
    Sherpix
    85m.
    The Rolling Stones, Otis Redding, Joe Cocker, The Bee Gees, Traffic, Jimi Hendrix, Vanilla Fudge
    The Emperor Rosco

The lure of the performers is certainly strong enough, but in some instances these stars can only be glimpsed in clips of varying quality culled from wide and varied sources. There're also snippets of funeral pyre cremations, hippie communes in Katmandu, Twiggy and A-Bomb blasts to contend with. A hodge-podge made all the more unsettling by its stabs at sociologese and artiness. The Small Faces are heard on soundtrack. Redding sings "Satisfaction"; Hendrix does "Wild Thing" and "Hey Joe"; and The Stones do "2,000 Light Years From Home" and "Jumpin' Jack Flash."

POPEYE (1980)

    M—Color
    Jules Feiffer
    characters created by E.C. Segar
    Robert Altman
    Robert Evans
    PAR
    118m.
    Robin Williams, Shelley Duvall, Wesley Ivan Hurt, Paul Smith, Ray Walston
    Van Dyke Parks, Klaus Voorman, The Steinettes
    Boardwalk

Popeye the sailor (Williams) arrives in the town of Sweethaven, falls in love with Olive Oyl (Duvall) adopts the foundling Sweet Pea (Hurt), defeats the villainous Bluto (Smith) and is reunited with his long-lost pappy (Walston). When this incoherent live-action version of the classic cartoon *Popeye The Sailor* was first released, songwriter Harry Nilsson said he would cut his own album of the film's songs, as the production did not do them justice. As of this writing no album has appeared. Beatles-session veterans Klaus Voorman and Van Dyke Parks (in his first screen appearance since *The Swan*), can be spotted as musicians in the amusement arcade scene where Williams growls out the song "I'm Popeye." Duvall singing "He's Large" is the best musical number, however, and the only memorable moment in this very disappointing film. Parks also served as musical arranger.

PRETTY THINGS, THE (1966)

       M—Color
-   Caterina Arvet
-   Caterina Arvet and Anthony West
-   Anthony West
-   Amanda (England)
-   14m.
-   The Pretty Things

A brief bit of sub-Richard Lester larking about (slow-motion, fast-motion, no motion) featuring the sixties "British Invasion" Pop ensemble.

PRIVILEGE (1967)

       D—Color
-   Norman Bogner, Peter Watkins
-   Peter Watkins
-   John Heyman
-   UI
-   103m.
-   Paul Jones, Jean Shrimpton
-   UNI

Watkins' futuristic vision of an England where an idolized rock singer (Jones) is employed as a force for keeping youth under the heel of the church (and away from confronting the establishment) was attacked as hysterical and paranoid at the time of its release, but many of the ideas in *Privilege* eerily portended the impact and approach of later mega-rockers like Bowie and Morrison. Director Watkins claims to have known little about rock when he made this film, and he credits the Paul Anka documentary *Lonely Boy* as a source for portions of his work. Score by Mike Leander. Songs (including "Free Me" and a version of "Onward Christian Soldiers") by Leander and Mark London.

PSYCH-OUT (1968)

       D—Color
-   E. Hunter Willett, Betty Ulius
-   Richard Rush
-   Dick Clark
-   AIP
-   88m.
-   Susan Strasberg, Jack Nicholson
-   The Strawberry Alarm Clock, The Seeds
-   Sidewalk

Jennie (Strasberg), a 17-year-old deaf girl, gets involved in the sixties Haight-Ashbury drug scene when she goes there searching for her missing brother. Crash pads, lots of acid-rock and trip-outs are the order of the day up to the climax which finds the brother commiting suicide and Strasberg trapped on the Golden Gate Bridge on a "bad trip." This grim, little shocker produced by, of all people, Dick Clark, features appearances by The Seeds ("Pushin' Too Hard") and The Strawberry Alarm Clock ("Incense and Peppermint"). Other music by Ronald Stein.

PUNK IN LONDON (1979)

R—Color
- Wolfgang Buld
- Wolfgang Buld
- HFF Productions
- 111m.
- The Clash, The Stranglers, The Jam, Rough Trade, Boom Town Rats, X-Ray Specs, The Lurkers, Anonymous Chaos, Subway Sect, The Adverts, The Kill Joys, Wayne County and The Electric Chairs, Chelsea, Jolt

German-made overview of London punk, circa '77. Interviews with retrograde Teddy Boys, pseudo-sociologists, scenemakers and the musicians themselves form the non-musical interludes. The nearly-random music made by the various groups comes mostly in bits and snatches. Narration in German.

PUNK ROCK MOVIE (1978)

R—Color
- Don Letts
- Peter Clifton
- Cinematic Releasing
- 86m.
- The Sex Pistols, The Clash, The Slits, Siouxsie and The Banshees, X-Ray Specs, Slaughter and The Dogs, Generation X, Subway Sect, Shane, Wayne County, Eater, Johnny Thunder and The Heartbreakers, Alternative TV

8mm-blown-up-to-35mm ad hoc coverage of London punk. Fittingly underlighted and overamplified, Letts' film technique for this occasion seems the logical filmic extension of punk—rites, drug rituals, razor blades and all. Filmed mostly at London's Roxy Club when that city's punk "scene" was at its peak.

QUADROPHENIA (1979)

D—Color
- Dave Humphries, Martin Stellman, Franc Roddam
- the record album of the same name, by The Who
- Franc Roddam
- Roy Baird, Bill Curbishley
- World-Northall
- 120m.
- Phil Daniels, Leslie Ash, Garry Cooper
- Polydor

Period 60's tale of mods and rockers in England—and specifically of one deeply anguished mod (Daniels) whose alienation, fueled by drugs, finally ends in self-destruction. Near perfect integration of rock and story. Film is based on The Who's 1973 album of the same name, and very effectively utilizes Who sounds, as well as atmospheric, evocative oldies by James Brown, The Kingsmen, The Ronettes, The Crystals, The Cascades and Booker T. and the M.G.'s. Soundtrack songs by The Who (executive producers of the film) include: "5:15," "I Am The Sea," "Love Reign Over Me" and "I Am One." Note: Daniels is leader of rock group, The Cross; and Sting, of The Police, appears in brief dramatic role.

RADIO ON (1979)

    D–B/W
- Chris Petit
- Chris Petit
- Keith Griffiths
- British Film Institute
- 101m.
- David Beames, Lisa Kreutzer

    Portrait of Britain in the late 70's emerges from this unresolved tale of a London dee-jay (Beames) who travels to the North of England to investigate the death of his brother. Associate producer of (and inspiration for) this Raymond Chandler-esque project is German filmmaker, Wim Wenders. Sting of The Police, has a small part as a gas station attendant hung up on Eddie Cochran. "Trans-Europe Express" by Kraftwerk is featured prominently on the soundtrack. Other music by David Bowie, Lena Lovich, Devo, The Rumor, Wreckless Eric, Ian Dury and Robert Fripp fills the air almost constantly in Petit's haunting, *noir* road movie.

RAGA (1971)

    R–Color
- Nancy Bacal
- Howard Worth
- Howard Worth
- New Line

	96m.
	Ravi Shankar, George Harrison
	Apple

Docu of Indian sitarist, Ravi Shankar, with a musical appearance (in a decidedly Eastern vein) by his protege, George Harrison.

RAINBOW BRIDGE (1971)

	D—Color
	Chuck Wein
	Chuck Wein
	Barry de Prendergast
	Alcyone Films
	108m.
	Pat Hartley, Jimi Hendrix
	Reprise

Last twenty minutes of this film features a Jimi Hendrix concert on the island of Maui, but the preceding hour-and-a-half about residents of an occult commune visited by concerned citizens from Venus, constitutes the cinematic equivalent of root canal work. A short non-musical sequence revolving around Hendrix is also highlighted. One of the most dreaded of all rock films, still this one surfaces with ominous regularity on the movie revival circuit because of Hendrix's performances of, among others, "Dolly Dagger," "A Roomful of Mirrors" and the inevitible "Star Spangled Banner."

REGGAE (1970)

    R–Color
- Horace Ove
- Horace Ove
- 60m.
- The Pyramids, The Pioneers, Black Faith, John Holt, Count Prince Miller, Millie, The Maytals, Desmond Dekker, Bob and Marcia, Darcus Owusu, Junior Lincoln, Dave Hatfield, Graham Goodall, Lee Gopthall, Graham Walker

    One of the first, if not in fact the very first, feature films about reggae. A *soupcon* of talk about the *significance* of the music is interspersed between generous coverage of the 1970 Carribbean Music Festival at Wembley.

REGGAE SUNSPLASH (1980)

    R–Color
- Stefan Paul
- Kino Aresenal Tubingen
- International Harmony
- 107m.
- Bob Marley and The Wailers, Peter Tosh, The Third World Band, Burning Spear

    German-made docu of the 1979 Sunsplash Festival II at Montego Bay alternates between coverage of this major reggae event, some potent rasta rapping and behind-the-scenes looks at Marley and Tosh.

RENALDO & CLARA (1978)

    R–Color
- Bob Dylan, Sam Shepard
- Bob Dylan
- Mel Howard, Jack Baran
- Lombard Street Films
- 232m.
- Bob Dylan, Joan Baez
- Sara Dylan, Ronnie Hawkins, Ronee Blakely, Jack Elliot, Harry Dean Stanton, Allen Ginsberg, David Blue, Roger McGuinn, Sam Shepard, Arlo Guthrie, Roberta Flack

    Much of this film was shot in and around Bob Dylan's '75 Rolling Thunder Review tour, and is given over to fantasies, improvs, man-on-the-street interviews, disguises, swapped identities, Pirandellian playlets AND feathers galore–but there is precious little straight-forward music making in this four-hour vanity production. Numerous other artists, musicians and cronies took part in Zimmerman's Folly. A hundred press agents working overtime can do terrifying things to the human spirit and, based on the evidence of this film, Dylan has decided that his public is now ready, once and for all, to pin down a mythic "Dylan For The Ages." However, when *R & C* opened in a few theatres in '78 it played to empty houses, and Dylan's subsequent re-cutting of it down to a more manageable length (112m.) proved fruitless. Baez sings "Suzanne;" McGuinn sings "Eight Miles High;" Ginsberg reads his *Kaddish* and Dylan is heard and/or seen singing (mostly portions of) numerous of his most famous songs including: "A Hard Rain's Gonna Fall," "It Ain't Me Babe," "She Belongs To Me," "Sad Eyed Lady of the Lowlands" and (with Blakely) "Just Like a Woman."

REVOLUTION (1969)

D—Color
- Jack O'Connell
- Jack O'Connell
- Jack O'Connell
- UA
- 90m.
- Today Malone
- Country Joe and The Fish, Quicksilver Messenger Service, The Steve Miller Band, Mother Earth
- UA

Pseudo-*cinéma vérité* view of San Francisco's Haight-Ashbury district around the so-called "Summer of Love." The film's star is an actress bearing the terrifically trippy name of Today Malone. Songs include: "Co'Dine" (Quicksilver), "Mercury Blues" (Miller) and the title tune sung by Tracy Nelson and Mother Earth.

RING A DING RHYTHM (*orig.* IT'S TRAD DAD) (1962)

M—B/W
- Milton Subotsky
- Richard Lester
- Milton Subotsky
- COL
- 73m.
- Chubby Checker, Gary (U.S.) Bonds, Gene Vincent, Del Shannon, Helen Shapiro, Craig Douglas, Gene McDaniels, The Brook Brothers
- Columbia

Shapiro and Douglas play small town British teens trying to overcome the *usual* local fogies' resistance to both pop/rock *and* trad jazz. Although several dozen notches below Lester's later *A Hard Day's Night,* his first film shows lots of little touches around the edges which finally sprang forth full-blown a couple of years later in that classic Beatles film debut. In *Ring a Ding,* the director tried to pump some visual energy into an otherwise standard British vaudeville—which called upon the services of, both, trad players *and* rockers, i.e. Shannon, Bonds, Checker and Vincent.

RIOT ON SUNSET STRIP (1967)

D—Color
- Orville H. Hampton
- Arthur Dreifuss
- Sam Katzman
- AIP
- 85m.
- Mimsey Farmer, Aldo Ray
- Tower

Cop (Ray) finds his patience strained when Sunset Strip hippie creeps drug and rape his teenage daughter (Farmer). Exploitation producer, Katzman, thought he had a potentially big hit on his hands with this ripped-from-today's-headlines special; but *Riot* ended up one of the bigger b.o. busts of the year. Music and appearances by Chocolate Watch Band and The Standells, who perform the title tune and "Get Away From Here."

ROADIE (1980)

M—Color
Michael Ventura, Big Boy Medlin
Alan Rudolph
Carolyn Pfeiffer
UA
103m.
Meat Loaf, Art Carney
Blondie, Alice Cooper, Roy Orbison
Warner Brothers

Picaresque (and strained) tale of Texas mechanic (Loaf) who gets swept up by a traveling rock band and hits the road. Orbison, Cooper and Blondie (doing "Ring of Fire") are on hand for musical diversion in this otherwise listless comedy. Soundtrack music by Cheap Trick, Jerry Lee Lewis, Pat Benatar and others.

ROBERT HAVING HIS NIPPLE PIERCED (1973)

R—Color
Patti Smith
Sandy Daley
Sandy Daley
Sandy Daley
40m.
Robert Mapplethorpe, Patti Smith

Self-descriptive title for film of noted New York photographer Mapplethorpe getting a bit of jewelry affixed to his person. Patti doesn't sing here, but her rambling stream-of-consciousness off-screen commentary is chock-full of information about her childhood and adolescence. A must for Smith fans.

ROCK ALL NIGHT (1956)

D–B/W
- Charles B. Griffith
- Roger Corman
- Roger Corman
- Allied Artists
- 65m.
- Dick Miller, Abby Dalton
- The Platters, The Blockbusters

"Shorty" (Miller) a regular at the "Cloud Nine" night club, gets picked on by the big guys. But when the club is held up by bandits, only "Shorty" shows enough nerve to stand up to them. He saves the day and wins the girl (Dalton). The Platters and The Blockbusters make brief singing appearances in this "Revenge of the 98 lb. Weakling" programmer from Roger Corman.

ROCK AROUND THE CLOCK (1956)

M–B/W
- Robert E. Kent, James B. Gordon
- Fred F. Sears
- Sam Katzman
- COL
- 77m.
- Bill Haley and His Comets, Alan Dale, Lisa Gaye, Alan Freed
- The Platters, Freddie Bell and His Bellboys, Ernie Freeman

"I like your sound," a city slicker (Dale) tells Haley when he stumbles upon the singer and his band (The Comets) wailing away at a small town sock hop. Dale likes it so much, in fact, that he helps launch Haley and his new "sound" (rock and roll) into the big time. Somewhere along the line influential dee-jay Freed (as himself) steps into the picture. And the rest is (rock and roll) history! This first-of-its-kind movie was an international box office bonanza. When Katzman's competition saw what the producer had wrought they (and just about every studio in town) jumped on the bandwagon to rush rock "product" into release. Katzman, though, understood the teen market better than just about anyone else, and over the next few years the veteran producer assumed the position of past-master of the rock musicals sweepstakes. Haley and his group zip through nine of their early big hits (the title tune, "Rudy's Rock," "Rock," "Mambo Rock," "Rock-a-Beatin' Boogie," "Happy Baby," "See You Later, Alligator," "Razzle Dazzle" and "ABC Boogie"), and mid-way through the film The Platters step in to harmonize on two of their big sides, "Only You" and "The Great Pretender."

ROCK AROUND THE WORLD (orig. THE TOMMY STEELE STORY) (1957)

M–B/W
- Norman Hudis
- Gerard Bryant
- Peter Rogers, Herbert Smith
- AIP
- 71m.
- Tommy Steele, Abby Dalton

Highly fanciful filmization of the "life story" of British rocker, Steele. Most Americans are only familiar with Tommy Steele as the star of musical comedies like *Half a Sixpence,* but to a generation of British teenagers he was a fifties rock demi-god—one of several so-called English "answers" to Elvis Presley. (Along with Cliff Richard, Adam Faith and other pretenders to the title.) This alleged bio was rushed into production at just about the time Steele peaked in his first incarnation. It is treacle of the highest order, but oh how it must have delighted hordes of frenzied U.K. youth at the time.

ROCK,BABY, ROCK IT (1957)

    M—B/W
- Murray Douglas Sporup
- J.G. Tiger
- Freebar
- 77m.
- Johnny Carroll, Kay Wheeler
- The Cell Block Seven, The Five Stars, Rosco Gordon, Preacher Smith and The Deacons, Don Coats, The Bon Airs, The Belew Twins

A group of musicians band together to try and stop their local hangout from being taken over by greedy gangsters. One of the most widely sought after, but seldom seen of all rock films. Produced on a shoestring budget, this curio's cult status arises as much out of its primitiveness, as from its bevy of somewhat obscure Southwest U.S. blues and rockabilly talents such as Carroll, The Belew Twins and The Five Stars. One of the stars, Kay Wheeler (billed as "the Queen of Bop and Rock"), was a bigwig in the International Elvis Presley Fan Club; and none of the 17 songs featured in this "sizzling story of hot rock as you have never seen it before" were anything more than minor regional hits. Still, this film does have a small but loyal following, if not because of its stars and songs (The Five Stars' "Hey, Juanita;" Carroll's "Wild, Wild Women" and "Crazy, Crazy Love;" The Cell Block Seven's "Hot Rock" etc.) *than* for reasons of *Rock, Baby, Rock It*'s elusiveness and sheer inaccessibility. The music is performed with, for the most part, "live" sound, and is surprisingly *quite* good. Gordon (one of the legendary Beale Street Boys), rockabilly kingpin Carroll and The Five Stars are the standouts in this must-see poverty row extravaganza. Filmed in Memphis, Tennessee.

ROCK CITY (*orig.* SOUND OF THE CITY) (1973)

    R—Color
- Peter Clifton
- Peter Clifton
- COL
- 104m.
- The Rolling Stones, Eric Burdon and The Animals, The Crazy World of Arthur Brown, Otis Redding, Peter Townshend, Cream, Stevie Winwood, Blind Faith, Cat Stevens, Jimi Hendrix, Donovan, Joe Cocker, Ike and Tina Turner, Pink Floyd, Rod Stewart, Faces

Much of the material seen here is utilized in two other similar compilation films by director Clifton: *Popcorn* and *Superstars in Film Concert.* (See separate entries.) The visual quality of the different sequences varies wildly inasmuch as they were shot in different locales. The patient rock fan, though, should have a field day. Among the various performances are: Hendrix doing "Hey Joe;" Redding's "Satisfaction" and The Stones with "We Love You," "2000 Light Years From Home" and "Have You Seen Your Mother, Baby?," plus an interview with Pete Townshend. Assembled and ready for release in 1973, *Rock City* didn't see the light of day until eight years later.

ROCK 'N ROLL HIGH SCHOOL (1979)

M—Color
Richard Whitley, Russ Dvonch, Joseph McBride
Allan Arkush
Michael Finnell
New World
93m.
P.J. Soles, Vincent Van Patten, Mary Woronov, Paul Bartel, The Ramones
Sire

A Hard Day's Night meets Jean Vigo's Zero For Conduct as the students of "Vince Lombardi High" stop at nothing to see their idols, The Ramones, in person—in spite of opposition from "Principal Togar" (Woronov) who claims The Ramones' music "makes mice explode." The film that asks the musical question, "Is There Life After High School?" If the pat and pastoral endings of 50's and 60's sock-hop musicals struck an unresolved anarchic chord in many of their viewers, then High School's fadeout of students burning to the ground their prison-of-a-learning-institution should warm their cockles. Every cliche and conceit from those wholesome, old teen rock musicals (and before them, the MGM Mickey-Judy musicals) is used as a springboard for some genuinely inspired satire. As western civilization goes up in flames, so to speak, Joey and The Ramones sing the title tune plus others, including: "Blitzkrieg Bop," "I Just Wanna Have Something To Do," "I Wanna Be Sedated," "I Wanna Be Your Boyfriend" and "Pinhead." Also heard over and under the action are such vintage favorites as: "Do You Wanna Dance" (Bobby Freeman); "Did We Meet Somewhere Before?" (Wings); "School Days" (Chuck Berry); "Come Back Jonee" (Devo) and "Rock and Roll" (The Velvet Underground).

ROCK, PRETTY BABY (1956)

M—B/W
Herbert Margolis, William Raynor
Richard Bartlett
Edmond Chevie
UI
89m.
Sal Mineo, John Saxon
Decca

Squeaky clean Universal-International musical of a high school rock band's trials and tribulations. Fans of rock and roll movies should beware, but pop sociologists will have a field day. The musicians (one of whom is portrayed by Rod McKuen) all have names like "Ox," "Sax" and "Fingers," and this film is entered for the record mainly because of the presence of "rock" in its title.

ROCK, ROCK, ROCK (1957)

M—B/W
Will Price
DCA
83m.
Alan Freed, Tuesday Weld, Teddy Randazzo
Frankie Lymon and The Teenagers, La Vern Baker, Chuck Berry, The Flamingos, The Moonglows, Johnny Burnette, The Three Chuckles
Chess (partial)

Teenager Weld suffers the torments of first love against the background of Alan Freed leading various rock acts in and out of the picture. In her movie debut, Weld's voice is dubbed by Connie Francis. Berry sings: "You Can't Catch Me," Lymon does "I'm Not a Juvenile Delinquent" and Baker works out on her hit "Tra La La."

ROCKERS (1978)

	D—Color
	Theodoras Bafoloukos
	Theodoros Bafoloukos
	Patrick Hulsey
	Rockers Film Corp
	100m.
	Leroy Wallace, Richard Hall
	Big Youth, Mighty Diamonds, Jacob Miller, Gregory Isaacs, Dillinger, Jack Ruby, Errol Brown, Prince Hammer
	Mango

This reggae feature covers much the same ground as did *The Harder They Come,* with musician (Wallace) taking on a criminal syndicate that is making things difficult for struggling rasta-rockers. In addition to the above-noted musicians, *Rockers* also uses music by Peter Tosh, The Heptones and other reggae stars on its soundtrack.

ROCKIN' THE BLUES (1957)

	M—B/W
	Arthur Rosenblum
	Fritz Pollard
	Austin Productions
	68m.
	Linda Hopkins, The Hurricanes, Four Wanderers, The Harptones, Connie Carrol

The appearance of proto-doowoppers The Harptones (of "Life is But a Dream" fame) should be of interest to rockophiles in this primitive throwback to forties filmed vaudeville. The group sings: "First Last and Only Girl," "Oowee Baby" and "Mambo Boogie." Entre-act turns by top R 'n B dee-jay, Hal Jackson and by beloved chittlin' circuit comics Mantan Moreland and Flournoy Miller. Carrol sings a prophetic ditty, "Rock and Roll's the Latest Fad."

ROCKSHOW (1980)

	R—Color
	MPL Communications
	Miramax
	105m.
	Paul McCartney and Wings

Perfunctory and uncinematic Wings concert movie. This feature-length *Wings' Greatest Hits* package features Paul, Linda, Jimmy McCulloch, Joe English and Denny Laine re-hashing old standbys like "Band on the Run" and "Jet," plus a dash of Beatles favorites for good measure.

ROCKY HORROR PICTURE SHOW, THE (1975)

	M—Color
	Jim Sharman and Richard O'Brien
	the stage musical, *The Rocky Horror Show* by Richard O'Brien

- Jim Sharman
- Lou Adler and Michael White
- TCF
- 101m.
- Tim Curry, Susan Sarandon, Barry Bostwick, Richard O'Brien, Jonathan Adams, Little Nell, Pat Quinn, Peter Hinwood, Charles Gray
- Meat Loaf
- Ode

When their car breaks down in a rainstorm, newlyweds Brad and Janet seek shelter in the mansion of Dr. Frank N. Furter, self-described "Sweet transvestite from transexual Transylvania." Numerous seductions and musical numbers ensue. This engaging rock and roll send-up of horror films began as a camp for homosexuals, but by now its become something of a rite-of-passage for precocious teenyboppers. Entering its second half-decade (with no signs of losing steam) of weekend midnight screenings at over 200 U.S. theatres, *Rocky Horror* has turned into the "counter-culture's" answer to *The Fantasticks*. To say that the showings are accompanied by "audience participation" would be the understatement of all time. Songs by Richard O'Brien include "Science-Fiction Double Feature," "Sweet Transvestite," "Toucha Toucha Touch Me" and "The Time Warp."

ROD STEWART AND FACES AND KEITH RICHARDS (1977)

R—Color
- Roger Grod

⠃⠃ Roger Grod
ↄ Apache Films
● 71m.
✪ Rod Stewart, The Small Faces, Keith Richards

Concert film of a 1974 Stewart appearance at the Kilburn State Theatre in London. The singer is backed by The Faces—Ron Wood, Ian McLagen, Kenny Jones and Tetsu Yamauchi, and also by Rolling Stone Keith Richards appearing here in a sideman capacity. Songs include: "Maggie May," "Twistin' the Night Away," "Bring It On Home to Me" and "You Send Me."

ROLLING STONES ON FILM. Just as with The Beatles (see "Beatles on Film"), in addition to major film productions listed elsewhere in this book, there are a number of other official and semi-official short films featuring The Stones (newsreels, videotape-to-film transfers, promo films, etc.). When theatres advertise a *Rolling Stones Special,* some or all of the following are likely to show up. *The Stones In The Park* (a.k.a. *The Stones in Hyde Park*) is a 45-minute Granada TV documentary of a Stones concert given in tribute to the just-deceased Brian Jones on July 5, 1969. (Jones had died on July 3rd.) Songs include: "Midnight Rambler," "Satisfaction," "I'm Free," "Monkey Man," "Jumpin' Jack Flash," "Honky Tonk Woman," "Love in Vain" and "Sympathy For the Devil." *The Rolling Stones Gather Moss* (1964) is a 6-minute Pathe color newsreel of The Stones backstage during a British tour. They are also seen singing "Around and Around." *The Rolling Stones Montreal Concert* is a 4-minute color film of Mick and company doing "Jumpin' Jack Flash." The band's section from *The TAMI Show* (see separate listing) is often excerpted and presented as *Live in Santa Monica.* They are seen, here, singing "Off the Hook" and "Time Is On My Side." *The Stones on Ed Sullivan* is a brief video clip of a 1969 TV performance of "Gimme Shelter." There is also a 1968 short descriptively titled *The Making of Beggar's Banquet,* featuring The Stones in recording session. Also cropping up from time-to-time are two Jagger interview films, one from 1965, *The Mick Jagger Interview;* the other from two years later is called *Jagger Jabber.* Early and mid-period promo films include: *Lady Jane* (filmed at Albert Hall in 1966), *Jumpin' Jack Flash, 2,000 Light Years From Home, Till The Last Goodbye* and *It's Only Rock and Roll.* More recent promo shorts include: *Miss You, She's So Cold* and *Emotional Rescue,* all shot on videotape.

ROLLING STONES ROCK AND ROLL CIRCUS, THE (1968)

R—Color
■ Michael Lindsay-Hogg
✪ The Rolling Stones, John Lennon, Yoko Ono, The Who, Led Zeppelin, Cream

Unreleased Stones movie (originally intended for U.S. TV) features a wealth of musical talent, all strutting their stuff at a psychedelic circus as Mick Jagger cracks the whip. The Who's segment of this film appears in *The Kids Are Alright.*

ROME '78 (1978)

M—Color
⬓ James Nares
■ James Nares
⠃⠃ James Nares
ↄ New Cinema
● 90m.
✪ Lydia Lunch, Eric Mitchell, James Chance

New York punk rockers swathed in bedsheets pose in front of Roman-looking New York monuments, and stab each other to death in best backyard playacting fashion in this very funny parody of Hollywood historical spectaculars. Music by James Nares.

ROOTS ROCK REGGAE (1977)

      R—Color
- Jeremy Marre
- Jeremy Marre
- Harcourt Films
- 55m.
- Bob Marley and The Wailers, Jimmy Cliff, The Heptones, Junior Murvin, The Gladiators, The Mighty Diamonds, Ras Michael, The Lewis Brothers, Jacob Miller, Scratch, Joe Higgs, U-Roy

Unconvincing docu of reggae music scene (shot in and around Kingston, Jamaica) marred by too much voiceover commentary and interruption. Songs include: "Trenchtown Rock," "Lively Up Yourself" (Marley); "From The Beginning" (Cliff); "When The Right Time Comes" (The Mighty Diamonds) and "Go There Natty Dread" (U-Roy).

ROSE, THE (1979)

      D—Color
- Bill Kerby, Bo Goldman
- Mark Rydell
- Marvin Worth, Aaron Russo
- TCF
- 134m.
- Bette Midler, Frederic Forrest, Alan Bates
- Atlantic

Overly familiar too-much-too-soon fable of galvanic sixties rock singer (Midler) and her rise and fall. Unresistant to the worst tendencies of movie biopics, the crafters of this *film a clef* of Janis Joplin manage to step into just about every dramatic license trap imaginable. The music's all wrong for the period, and the central character (as written) possesses about as much personal warmth as an iron foundry. One of the few saving graces herein is Bette's interesting, if somewhat overripe, performance in her dramatic debut. Songs include: Amanda McBroom's title tune (a big hit for Bette), "Sold My Soul to Rock And Roll," "Fire Down Below," "Midnight in Memphis" and "When a Man Loves a Woman." Musical arranger and supervisor: Paul Rothchild.

ROUSTABOUT (1964)

      M—Color
- Anthony Laurence and Allan Weiss
- John Rich
- Hal Wallis
- PAR
- 101m.
- Elvis Presley, Barbara Stanwyck
- RCA

Elvis plays a footloose singer/swinger who, when he joins a carnival run by Stanwyck, learns about the work ethic the *hard* way. Before extreme cost-cutting set in, one of the extra-added niceties in Presley's films was the lack of expenses spared in the casting of the customary "older woman" role, i.e. Lola Albright (*Kid Galahad*), Liz Scott (*Loving You*) and Hope Lange (*Wild in the Country*). Topping that list is the great Barbara Stanwyck, pluckily holding her own under less-than-ideal circumstances, in this musical of the carny life. Elvis sings "It's Carnival Time," "Carny Town," "Wheels on My Heels," the title tune and several others. ELVIS #16.

RUDE BOY (1980)

R—Color
- David Mingay, Ray Gange, Jack Hazan
- Jack Hazan, David Mingay
- Jack Hazan, David Mingay
- American Cinema Releasing
- 117m.
- The Clash, Ray Gange

Mixture of drama, concert movie and *cinéma vérité* in biographical study of real life Clash fan, Gange, the rude boy in question. Events depicted in the film go a long way toward demonstrating why our British cousins chatter on so much about "the class system." Even the most virulent of The Clash's anti-establishment rhetoric can seem ineffectual at combatting the economic system which perpetually represses the likes of Gange. Well-staged concert sections—and not just arbitrarily slotted into the storyline—feature memorable performances of "London's Burning," "White Riot," "The Prisoner," "Tommy Gun," "All The Young Punks," "Complete Control" and many others.

RUST NEVER SLEEPS (1979)

R—Color
- Bernard Shakey (Neil Young)
- L.A. Johnson
- International Harmony
- 103m.
- Neil Young
- Reprise

"Ol' Rust Eyes is Back," read the ad copy for this concert film of the San Francisco stop on Neil Young's '78 tour. Odd goings-on in the form of oversized props, roadies in strange disguises and other absurdist tacks (all a misguided attempt to make things more interesting) actually end up detracting from Young's performance. Also on display are snippets from *Woodstock*, including the scene of Jimi Hendrix playing the National Anthem. In spite of the presence of too much icing, Young is in good musical form on such numbers as: "Ride My Llama," "Welfare Mother" and "My My Hey Hey (Out of the Blue)."

SAN FRANCISCO (1968)

M—Color
- Anthony Stern
- Anthony Stern
- British Film Institute
- British Film Institute
- 15m.

Impressionistic "symphony of a city"-type documentary with much in the way of fast moving and single frames, using Pink Floyd's "Interstellar Overdrive" on the soundtrack.

SATURDAY NIGHT FEVER (1977)

D—Color
🎬 Norman Wexler
📄 a magazine article by Nik Cohn
🎞 John Badham
📺 Robert Stigwood
🎭 PAR
⏺ 118m.
✪ John Travolta, Barry Miller
🔂 RSO

By day a Brooklyn hardware store worker (Travolta) anonymously toils away, but come Saturday night he's king at the local disco. Still, an ambitious young secretary (Karen Lynn Gorney) makes him aware of an even better life that could be awaiting him on the shores of Manhattan. A mere magazine article in *New York Magazine* was the seed kernel of this movie-turned-empire way of life. One of the most successful motion pictures to ever call on the services of rock music for added box office assist, *Fever* (almost singlehandedly) established John Travolta as a star, re-invented disco, and resurrected the badly sagging career of The Bee Gees—not to mention making a fortune for producer Robert Stigwood that surely (one hopes) exceeded the wildest boundaries of even *his* imagination. The soundtrack album's sales were equal in impressiveness to the movie's grosses. The Bee Gees are musically assisted on the soundtrack by (among others) Yvonne Elliman, Trammps ("Disco Inferno"), Kool and the Gang ("Open Sesame") and K.C. and the Sunshine Band ("Boogie Shoes"). Bee Gees' titles include: "How Deep Is Your Love?," "Night Fever," "More Than A Woman" and "Stayin' Alive"—all massive singles sellers. Additional score by David Shire.

SAVAGE SEVEN, THE (1968)

D—Color
🎬 Michael Fisher
🎞 Richard Rush
📺 Dick Clark
🎭 AIP
⏺ 96m.
✪ Robert Walker, Adam Rourke, Duane Eddy
🔂 Atco

Rourke plays the leader of a cycle gang that forms an uneasy alliance with an Indian tribe against some bad guys. Duane Eddy, of the "twangy" guitar, plays a straight dramatic part in one-of-the-better motorcycle mellers. Original score by Iron Butterfly and Cream.

SAVE THE CHILDREN (1973)

R—Color
🎬 Matt Robinson
🎞 Stan Lathan
📺 Matt Robinson
🎭 PAR
⏺ 123m.
✪ Marvin Gaye, The Staple Singers, The Temptations, The Chi-Lites, Main Ingredient, The O'Jays, Isaac Hayes, Bill Withers, Curtis Mayfield, Roberta Flack, Gladys Knight and The Pips, Jerry Butler, The Jackson Five.
🔂 Motown

Rockumentary with the above performers pooling their talents for the 1972 Operation PUSH Concert in Chicago.

SCORPIO RISING (1963)

      M—Color
- Kenneth Anger
- Kenneth Anger
- Kenneth Anger
- Filmmakers Co-op
- 31m.
- Bruce Byron, Johnny Sapienza, Frank Carifi

Visual essay juxtaposing, through montage, the private rites of motorcycle cultists (dressing in leather gear, polishing their bikes, partying and racing), with the public icons that fascinate them (James Dean, Marlon Brando, Hitler, Christ.) One of the most influential films ever to surface from the "underground." It singlehandedly ripped the lid off the whole Pandora's box of previously taboo homoerotic material and iconically defined and fixed in place most of the signposts of motorcycle fetishism, (John Travolta in *Saturday Night Fever* readying for his big night out is based on a similar segment in Anger's film of a biker lovingly tending to his *toilette* to the strains of Bobby Vinton's "Blue Velvet"). Most importantly (for our purposes), Anger pioneered the use—several years prior to *Easy Rider*—of lyrically underscoring/accompanying/commenting on action through use of pre-existent rock recordings. Songs heard include "I Will Follow Him" (Little Peggy March), "Hit The Road Jack" (Ray Charles), "Wipe Out" (The Surfaris), "My Boyfriend's Back" (The Angels) and "Fools Rush In" (Kris Jensen). Others by Elvis Presley, The Rondells, The Crystals, Gene McDaniels and Claudine Clark.

SEASIDE SWINGERS (*orig.* EVERYDAY'S A HOLIDAY) (1965)

      M—Color
- Anthony Marriot, Jeri Matos, James Hill
- James Hill
- Maurice J. Wilson, Ronald J. Kahn
- Embassy
- 94m.
- Freddie and The Dreamers, Mike Sarne, John Layton
- The Baker Twins, The Mojos
- Mercury

British musical comedy exploiting the popularity of Freddie and The Dreamers ("Do the Freddie," "I'm Tellin' You Now," etc.). This romp 'n roller, shown but briefly in the U.S., also features Michael Sarne, later to direct the film of Gore Vidal's *Myra Breckenridge*. Freddie and The Dreamers sing "What's Cookin' " and "Don't Do That to Me."

SEBASTIANE (1976)

      D—Color
- Derek Jarman, James Waley and Jack Welch
- Derek Jarman and Paul Humfress
- James Waley and Howard Malin
- 86m.
- Leonardo Treviglio, Richard Warwick, Peter Hinwood, and Lindsay Kemp

In a remote outpost a Roman captain falls in love with one of his soldiers who is indifferent to his advances. Love quickly turns to hatred as the Captain orders the torture and execution of the man he desires. Brian Eno composed the moody electronic score for this homoerotic hot fudge sundae about the martyred Saint Sebastian. Muscular male nudity abounds in this specialized item with dialogue in Latin.

SECRET LIFE OF PLANTS, THE (1977)

R—Color
- Peter Tompkins, Wolon Green
- the book of the same name
- Wolon Green
- Michael Braun
- PAR
- 89m.
- Stevie Wonder
- Tamla

Botanical docu based on the best-selling book of the same name, with an original score by Stevie Wonder. This film seemed to have everything going for it, i.e. a pre-sold title and Wonder's music, but after it was finished, the film was almost never shown. And it's no big *secret* as to why, for *The Secret Life of Plants* is excruciatingly ponderous—with a quasi-metaphysical theme running through it that proves elusive to all but the most blissed-out of attendees. Stevie's music, however, is absolutely magnificent, in the variations-on-a-theme, classic film music mold. Very few "songs," per se, but an endless cascade of synthesizer and strings-styled program music, instead. Wonder appears on screen, briefly singing the title tune; also heard is The Beatles' "Here Comes The Sun."

SECRET POLICEMAN'S BALL, THE (1979)

R—Color
- Roger Graef
- Roger Graef, Thomas Schwalm
- Amnesty International
- 95m.
- Pete Townshend, Tom Robinson, Neil Innes
- John Cleese, Peter Cook, Clive James, Eleanor Bron, Michael Palin, Terry Jones
- Island

Film of 1979 Amnesty International Comedy Gala at London's Her Majesty's Theatre, with most of the funny business handled by members of the Monty Python comedy group. Musical interludes include a stunning acoustic version of "Won't Get Fooled Again" by Peter Townshend accompanied by classical guitarist, John Williams. Pete also performs "Pinball Wizard" and "Drowned," and Tom Robinson sings "Glad to be Gay" and "1967 (So Long Ago)."

SEPARATION (1967)

D—Color
- Jane Arden
- Jack Bond
- Jack Bond
- Continental

● 93m.
✪ Jane Arden, Joy Bang

Semi-surrealistic tale of older woman (Arden) contemplating taking her first younger lover. Music written for this film surfaced later as the first Procul Harum album. Shot in black-and-white on color stock, which makes for an extremely interesting visual look.

SGT. PEPPER'S LONELY HEARTS CLUB BAND (1978)

M—Color
▬ Henry Edwards
■ the musical play of The Beatles album of the same name, by Robin Wagner and Tom O'Horgan
▬ Michael Schultz
▦ Robert Stigwood
✿ UI
● 111m.
✪ The Bee Gees, Aerosmith, Alice Cooper, Earth, Wind and Fire, Billy Preston, Stargard, Peter Frampton, George Burns, Steve Martin
◐ RSO

Film (very) loosely based on songs in the classic Beatles album, with a nod in the direction of *Yellow Submarine*. The Lonely Hearts Club Band led by "Billy Shears" (Frampton) is infiltrated by villianous agents, "Mean Mr. Mustard" (Frankie Howerd) and company, who falls in love with "Strawberry Fields" (Sandy Farina) who. . . . For musical authenticity and quasi-officiality the film's makers called upon the service of Beatles producer emeritus, George Martin. So, on paper, it seemed as if there were simply no way this Robert Stigwood production could fail. But, lo and behold, when it opened in theatres, the film played to half-full houses. The two-record set soundtrack album did just as poorly, though Earth Wind and Fire did have a modest hit with their version of "Got To Get You Into My Life." Many notables appear in the grand finale, where "All You Need is Love" is sung—Donavan, Helen Reddy, Monte Rock III, Dr. John, Wilson Pickett, Minnie Riperton, Elvin Bishop, Tina Turner, and Frankie Valli among them. Other numbers in this "Pepper" oratorio include "Getting Better" (performed by Peter Frampton and the Bee Gees), "Fixing A Hole" (George Burns), "The Long and Winding Road" (Barry Gibb), "Get Back" (Billy Preston), "Maxwell's Silver Hammer" (Steve Martin), and 22 others.

SHAFT (1971)

D—Color
▬ Ernest Tidyman
■ the novel by Tidyman
▬ Gordon Parks
▦ Joel Freeman
✿ MGM
● 100m.
✪ Richard Roundtree, Moses Gunn
◐ Enterprise

A racketeer whose daughter is kidnapped enlists supersleuth Shaft (Roundtree) to help find her. All ends well, with Shaft aided in his successful search by so-called black militants. This popular Raymond Chandler-esque fable was instrumental in opening up floodgates of blacksploitation movies in the early seventies. Isaac Hayes, writing and directing *Shaft*'s musical score, laid down most of the ground rules for the funky satin sheet sounds essential to the genre.

He won the 1971 Oscar for best song, "Theme From Shaft." Other musicians on soundtrack include The Bar Kays and The Movement.

SHAFT IN AFRICA (1973)

	D—Color
≈	Stirling Silliphant
▣	John Guillerman
⊞	Roger Lewis
☡	MGM
●	112m.
✪	Richard Roundtree, Vonetta McGee
◐	MGM

In this sequel to the popular *Shaft*, the more-super-than-ever sleuth, "Shaft," gets kidnapped to Africa where he's forced to aid in the breaking up of a French slavery ring. Score by Johnny Pate, with the song, "Are You Man Enough?," sung by The Four Tops.

SHAKE, RATTLE AND ROCK (1956)

	M—B/W
≈	Lou Rusoff
▣	Edward L. Cahn
⊞	James H. Nicholson
☡	AIP
●	72m.
✪	Touch Connors, Lisa Gaye, Paul Dubov, Margaret Dumont, Sterling Holloway
⊐	Fats Domino, Joe Turner, Tommy Charles, Choker Campbell

A citizen's group wants to bar rock and roll from their Anytown, USA, but a courageous and persistent dee-jay (Connors) gets some dirt on one of the do-gooders and the day is saved for rock. The finale where the kids' music is on trial in a televised courtroom scene is a real howler. The ever-so-avuncular Fats Domino sings "Honey Chile," "I'm in Love Again" and "Ain't That a Shame," and Joe Turner belts out "Feelin' Happy" and "Lipstick, Powder and Paint" in this silly, but likeable quickie. One of the very first of the juve-rockers.

SHAMPOO (1975)

	D—Color
≈	Robert Towne, Warren Beatty
▣	Hal Ashby
⊞	Warren Beatty
☡	COL
●	110m.
✪	Warren Beatty, Julie Christie, Jack Warden, Goldie Hawn, Lee Grant, Tony Bill, Carrie Fisher

Twenty-four hours in the life of a Beverly Hills hairdresser who can't decide which of his many lady loves he really wants to settle down with. The Beach Boys' "Wouldn't It Be Nice" and The Beatles "Strawberry Fields Forever" are used to ironic effect in the background of the action of this devastating satirical farce of Beverly Hills mores circa the 1968 Presidential election. Score by Paul Simon.

SHELL SHOCK ROCK (1979)

- R—Color
- John Davis
- 50m.
- The Undertones, Stiff Little Fingers, The Idiots

Documentary of punk scene in Belfast, Northern Ireland. Remarkable for its detailing of the music's relationship to the ongoing political crisis. Alternates performance footage and telling interviews with fans and members of the general public. The Idiots sing "Teenager in Love."

SHINING STAR (orig. THAT'S THE WAY OF THE WORLD) (1975)

- D—Color
- Robert Lipsyte
- Sig Shore
- Sig Shore
- Marvin Films
- 99m.
- Harvey Keitel, Ed Nelson, Bert Parks
- Earth, Wind and Fire

Moderately engaging record biz exposé drama, with a musical seg featuring Earth, Wind and Fire, and a dramatic appearance by that group's Maurice White.

SIMON OF THE DESERT (1965)

- D—B/W
- Luis Bunuel
- Luis Bunuel
- Gustavo Alatriste
- Contemporary Films
- 45m.
- Sylvia Pinal, Claudio Brook

The Devil (Pinal) asks St. Simon (Brook) to join her in a dance called the "Radioactive Flesh" at a New York disco in the apocalyptic finale of this cheerfully mordant satire about a man of God tempted by the pleasures of the flesh. "It will be the last dance!" the Devil promises with a smile as she rocks and rolls with abandon. Music by Raul Lavista.

SING AND SWING (orig. LIVE IT UP) (1963)

- M—B/W
- Lyn Fairbanks
- Lance Comfort
- Lance Comfort
- UI
- 75m.
- David Hemmings, Veronica Hurst, Steve Marriott
- Gene Vincent, The Outlaws, Sounds Incorporated

Pleasant British musical about a struggling rock band and its bid for stardom. Hemmings portrays a guitarist with the group.

SING, BOY, SING (1958)

D–B/W
- Claude Binyon
- the NBC TV production *The Singing Idol*
- Henry Ephron
- Henry Ephron
- TCF
- 90m.
- Tommy Sands, Edmund O'Brien
- Capitol

This story of the rise of a simple country boy to the top of the show business heap bears more than a passing resemblance to the life and times of Elvis Presley. The film began life as a *Kraft TV Playhouse* entry and was so successful in that form that TCF turned it into a big screen musical. The centerpiece of both versions was singer Tommy Sands, and for about 15 minutes he was a serious contender in the who-will-be-the-next-Elvis sweepstakes. Songs include: the title tune and "Teenage Crush."

SING SING THANKSGIVING (1974)

R–Color
- David Hoffman, Harry Wiland
- Harry Wiland
- Varied Directions
- 78m.
- Joan Baez, B.B. King, Joe Williams, Mimi Farina, The Voices of East Harlem

Filmed memento of a 1974 Thanksgiving Day concert at Sing Sing Penitentiary given by Joan Baez and musical friends.

SIR HENRY AT RAWLINSON END (1980)

M–B/W
- Viv Stanshall
- the song and radio show by Viv Stanshall
- Steve Roberts
- Tony Stratton Smith
- Charisma Films
- 75m.
- Trevor Howard, Patrick Magee

Episodic *Goon Show*-like comedy about the title character (Howard) who resides in a mansion populated by ghosts, his mother's corpse and a band of W.W. II German P.O.W.'s. Whacked-out film version of a story-song (and subsequent radio serial) that originally cropped up on an old Bonzo Dog Band album—written by that group's Viv Stanshall. Trevor Howard has said (perhaps with a note of irony?) that of all the films of his illustrious career, this is the one he'll best be remembered for. Script by Stanshall, who also wrote musical score.

6.5 SPECIAL (1957)

R–B/W
- Alfred Shaughnessy

🏠	Herbert Smith
🎬	Anglo
⏱	88m.
✪	Petula Clark, Lonnie Donnegan, Dickie Valentine, Jim Dale, Cleo Laine, Jackie Dennis, The John Barry Seven

British film based on the popular TV musical series of the same name. There's very little that qualifies as rock and roll in this 1957 feature, but if you look hard enough you can see *the scene* just beginning to emerge.

SKI PARTY (1965)

	M–Color
🎞	Robert Kaufman
🎥	Alan Rafkin
🏠	Gene Corman
🎬	AIP
⏱	90m.
✪	Frankie Avalon, Dwayne Hickman
⮕	Leslie Gore, James Brown

Hickman and Avalon spend an inordinate and embarrassing amount of time in drag in this AIP try at duplicating *Beach Party* success on the ski slopes. In between all the swishing and shushing, merciful musical interludes are provided by Brown and Gore.

SKIDOO (1968)

	M–Color
🎞	Doran William Cannon
🎥	Otto Preminger
🏠	Otto Preminger
🎬	PAR
⏱	98m.
✪	Jackie Gleason, Carol Channing, John Phillip Law, Frankie Avalon, Burgess Meredith, Cesar Romero, Alexandra Hay
⮕	Groucho Marx, Donyale Luna, Nilsson and Stone Country
🎵	RCA

A retired gangster faces trouble from his mobster past, until the hippie friends of his daughter come to his aid. Jackie Gleason on Acid! Carol Channing doing a musical number about "free love!" They weren't ready for it in 1968, and they *still* aren't. A "guilty pleasure" for even hard-core Preminger fans, *Skidoo* is the closest thing to *The Girl Can't Help It* produced in the '60's. Music and Lyrics by Nilsson of the southern California soft-rock variety; "I Will Take You There," "Garbage Can Ballet" and "The Cast and Crew" being the highlights.

SLAP SHOT (1977)

	M–Color
🎞	Nancy Dowd
🎥	George Roy Hill
🏠	Robert J. Wunsch, Stephen Friedman
🎬	UI

● 122m.
✪ Paul Newman, Michael Ontkean

A down-and-out hockey team regains its momentum when its coach decides to play dirty. Rock and roll (Maxine Nightingale's "Right Back Where We Started From," Leo Sayer's "You Make Me Feel Like Dancin'," Fleetwood Mac's "Say That You Love Me" etc.) pours out of every juke box and radio the characters come into contact with in this knockabout comedy.

SLAUGHTER'S BIG RIP-OFF (1973)

D—Color
▬ Charles Johnson
■ character created by Don Williams
■ Gordon Douglas
▦ Don Williams
𝕮 AIP
● 93m.
✪ Jim Brown, Ed McMahon, Don Stroud, Gloria Hendry
◐ Polydor

Music by the Godfather of Soul, Soul Brother Number One, Mr. Dy-no-mite himself James Brown and the J.B.'s for this blacksploitation melodrama about a one-man army fighting an international crime syndicate. "How Long Can You Keep It Up?" sung by Lyn Collins.

SON OF DRACULA (1974)

M—Color
▬ Jay Fairbanks
■ Freddie Francis
▦ Ringo Starr
𝕮 Cinemation
● 90m.
✪ Harry Nilsson, Ringo Starr
◐ RCA

Comic version of Dracula legend stars Harry Nilsson, who also wrote score. The producer of the film, Ringo Starr, is also on hand in this fumbled musical spoof of Hammer films. Ironically, the director of this effort is old Hammer standby, Freddie Francis.

SON OF STIFF TOUR MOVIE (1981)

R—Color
■ Jeff Baynes
▦ Dave Robinson, Phillip McDonald
𝕮 Stiff Records
● 60m.
✪ Any Trouble, Dirty Looks, Ten Pole Tudor, The Equators, Joe "King" Carrasco and The Crowns
◐ Stiff

The first Stiff Records tour film, *If it Ain't Stiff, it Ain't Worth a...*, contained such powerhouse performers as Nick Lowe, Elvis Costello and Ian Dury, but this second edition's musical lineup is not nearly as impressive. Generally shown in tandem with the first film, this sequel's performances include: "Betty's World" (Carrasco), "Turning Up the Heat" (Any Trouble) and "There Are the Boys" (Tudor).

SONG REMAINS THE SAME, THE (1976)

R—Color
Peter Clifton and Joe Massot
Peter Grant
COL
136m.
Led Zeppelin

A documentary of Led Zep's 1973 Madison Square Garden concert with a few fictional interludes (the group dressed as gangsters, Robert Plant rescuing a damsel in distress) and bits of off-stage pre and post-concert activity. Songs include "Stairway To Heaven," "Whole Lotta Love," "Dazed and Confused," "Black Dog" and "No Quarter."

SORCERER (1977)

D—Color
Walon Green
the film *The Wages of Fear,* by Henri Georges Clouzot
William Friedkin
William Friedkin
UI/WB
122m.
Roy Scheider, Amidou
MCA

Prisoners in a Latin American labor camp volunteer for a dangerous mission—transporting trucks of nitrogylcerine through a dense jungle rainforest. Tangerine Dream's techno-rock score is one of the most effective elements in this dramatically murky, though visually arresting, melodrama by the director of *The Exorcist.*

SOUL TO SOUL (1971)

R—Color
Denis Sanders
Richard Bock, Tom Mosk
Cinerama
95m.
Wilson Pickett, Ike and Tina Turner, Santana, Willie Bobo, Roberta Flack, Eddie Harris, The Staple Singers, The Voices of East Harlem, The Isley Brothers
Stax

14th anniversary of Ghana's independence celebrated by visiting American soul stars and local musicians in *Woodstock*-style documentary.

SOUNDS OF THE SEVENTIES (1971)

R—Color
Richard W. Jackman

☯   Fair Ent. (England)

●   42m.

✳   Santana, It's A Beautiful Day, Johnny Winter, Taj Mahal

Four American acts captured "live" at England's Royal Albert Hall in a blurry tape-to-film transfer. Music includes: "Riverside," "Oh Susannah" (Mahal); "Johnny B. Goode," "Downhill Daughter" (Winter); "White Bird" ("Day") and "Soul Sacrifice" (Santana).

SPACE MOVIE, THE (1980)

R—Color

▬   Tony Palmer

■   Tony Palmer

☷   Richard Branson

☯   Virgin Films

●   80m.

Compilation film of outer space NASA footage has "space symphony" accompaniment by Mike Oldfield.

SPARKLE (1976)

D—Color

▬   Joel Schumaker

■   Sam O'Steen

☷   Howard Rosenman

☯   WB

●   98m.

✳   Irene Cara, Dawn Smith, Lonette McKee

Rise from the ghetto to superstardom of "Supremes"-like group features excellent musical material written by Curtis Mayfield, sung by Cara and McKee. *Sparkle* sporadically shines, but finally succumbs to blacksploitation formula. Songs include: title tune, "Hooked on Your Love," "Look Into Your Heart" and "Rock With Me."

SPEEDWAY (1968)

M—Color

▬   Phillip Shuken

■   Norman Taurog

☷   Douglas Laurence

☯   MGM

●   94m.

✳   Elvis Presley, Nancy Sinatra

✹   RCA

Heading round the final turn toward the finish line of his film career Elvis plays what seems like his umpteenth part as a race car driver. This time out he's a stock car papa who falls in love with an I.R.S. agent (Sinatra) who's hot on his tail over back taxes. Like most of the later Elvis movies this one comes with all the requisite trimmings of speed, sex, silliness and song, including a duet with Sinatra on "Your Groovy Self." Solo, Elvis sings "There Ain't Nothin' Like A Song." Not to be confused with *Spinout*. Elvis #27.

SPINOUT (1966)

- M—Color
- Theodore J. Flicker, George Kirgo
- Norman Taurog
- Joe Pasternak
- MGM
- 90m.
- Elvis Presley, Shelley Fabares
- RCA

Silly musical about a singing race car driver (Elvis) and his various romantic involvements. Not to be confused with *Speedway*. Songs include: "Stop, Look and Listen," "Adam and Evil" and the title tune. ELVIS #22.

STAMPING GROUND (*orig.* LOVE AND MUSIC) (1971)

- R—Color
- Jason Pohland
- Wolf Schmidt, Sam Waynberg
- 101m.
- Santana, Al Stewart, Canned Heat, The Byrds, It's A Beautiful Day, Country Joe and the Fish, Pink Floyd, Dr. John, Family, Quintessence, T-Rex, The Flock, Soft Machine

Film of a 1970 pop fest in Rotterdam comes off as a Dutch sub-*Woodstock*. "Airplane's" version of "White Rabbit," a standout in this West German film, received only limited U.S. distribution. Additional performances include The Byrds doing "Old Blue," the "Floyd" stretching out on "Heart of the Sun" and "Saucerful of Secrets" and Al Stewart singing "Zero She Flies."

STAR IS BORN, A (1976)

- M—Color
- John Gregory Dunne, Joan Didion and Frank Pierson
- a story by William Wellman and Robert Carson
- Frank Pierson
- Jon Peters
- WB
- 140m.
- Barbra Streisand, Kris Kristofferson, Paul Mazursky, Gary Busey
- Booker T., Vanetta Fields and Clydie King
- Columbia

A rock superstar on his way down (Kris) helps a young singer on her way up (Barbra), but her love can't save him from self-destruction. This is the second remake of the classic Hollywood tale (not counting an early incarnation entitled *What Price Hollywood?*) and easily the most florid. Moving the action from the movies to the recording industry serves to make it not only louder but *bigger*. People travel by helicopter, ambulance and mile-long limos over vistas so vast and imposing even de Mille would find them a bit "much." As a rocking and rolling "Norman Maine"—here called "John Howard Norman," Kristofferson seems as much confused by the scale of his surroundings as anything in the plot. Streisand, on the other hand, appears quite at home. Music penned for the film includes material by Kenny Asher and Paul Williams ("Woman on The Moon," "With One More Look At You"), Rupert Holmes ("Queen Bee"), Leon Russell and Barbra Streisand ("Lost Inside of You") and Kenny Loggins and Marilyn and Alan Bergman ("I Believe In Love"). Williams and Streisand co-authored "Evergreen" which won the 1976 Oscar for Best Song.

STARDUST (1974)

M—Color
- Ray Connolly
- Michael Apted
- David Puttnam and Sandy Lieberson
- COL
- 111m.
- David Essex, Adam Faith, Larry Hagman, Keith Moon, Dave Edmunds, Paul Nicholas, Edd Byrnes, Karl Howman
- Arista

Jim Maclaine (Essex) and his group (the Stray Cats) become an international pop music sensation. Jim, however, is the real drawing card and he soon splits to become an even more successful solo act. Success brings isolation and paranoia fed by drugs, eventually leading the young star to an early grave. Sixteen minutes were lopped off for the American release of this rise-of-a-rock-star musical drama from Britain, thus somewhat diminishing its overall effectiveness. What remains—even in the truncated version—is still extremely affecting. Very close to being a bio of the Beatles (although elements of the careers of other superstars are interleaved) it captures much of the atmosphere of splendorous seclusion of the higher echelons of the rock world. Faith's portrayal of Essex's sexually ambiguous manager is a standout in this sequel to the far more modestly scaled *That'll Be The Day.* Music and songs by Dave Edmunds and David Puttnam.

STAY AWAY JOE (1968)

M—Color
- Michael Hoey
- Peter Tewksbury
- Douglas Laurence
- MGM
- 102m.
- Elvis Presley, Joan Blondell

"He's an Indian who prefers necking to scalping . . . Elvis goes west . . . and the west goes wild (and that's no sitting bull)," reads the ad copy for this banal feature-length sitcom. Elvis sings the title tune. ELVIS #26.

STEPPIN' OUT (1979)

R—Color
- Lyndall Hobbs
- Lyndall Hobbs
- Lyndall Hobbs
- TCF
- 26m.
- The Merton Parkas, Secret Affair

Disco docu of night life in London in the late seventies—lots of (in the words of cartoonist William Hamilton) "kicky knits and deep-vented shaped suits in an environment of chrome, smoky plastic and mirrors." With on-screen appearances by The Merton Parkas, and a soundtrack infused with the musical likes of Millie Small, Brian Ferry, Sylvester and The Who.

STEVE MILLER BAND (1968)

R–Color
- Ben Van Meter
- Capitol Records
- 6m.
- Steve Miller Band

Miller's record label produced and released this promo film of Steve singing "Hey Little Girl" and "Roll With It."

STONY ISLAND (1978)

M–Color
- Richard Davis
- Andrew Davis
- Andrew Davis, Tamar Hoffs
- World-Northal
- 97m.
- Richard Davis, Gene Barge
- Glades

Hey-let's-do-the-show-right-here type story about the birth and evolution of a Chicago band; with a young musician (Davis), finding his star players in the unlikeliest of places when he sets out to recruit players for the group. The makers of the film touted it as a jazz movie, with the phrase "rock and roll" never once uttered anywhere in the course of *Stony Island*. One of its stars, Gene Barge (also co-composer and co-producer), just so happens to be the fellow who did all those ripping sax breaks of the Gary U.S. Bonds *rock* classics like "Quarter To Three" and New Orleans, so how could this film's music consist of anything *but* rock and roll? Or, at least, rock-fusion. Beautifully photographed by Tak Fujimoto and, all things considered, one of the better independently made (under $400,000) features of the recent past. On-screen players include Barge, Davis and Patrice Rushen. Dramatic score (also in a rock vein) by David Matthews.

SURF PARTY (1964)

M–Color
- Harry Spalding
- Maury Dexter
- Maury Dexter
- TCF
- 68m.
- Bobby Vinton, Jackie DeShannon
- The Astronauts, The Routers

This is only one of many "surfrolics" which cropped up in the wake of AIP's success with *Beach Party*. Star Vinton claims he was paid exactly $750 for his appearance, and from the look of things that figure just might've been the single highest budgetary outlay . . . in other words *Surf Party* is a far cry from the craftsmanship of the Funicello/Avalon Coppertone rockers.

SUPERSTARS IN FILM CONCERT (1971)

R–Color
- Peter Clifton

▩ Peter Clifton
♧ National Cinema
● 105m.
❖ The Rolling Stones, Ike and Tina Turner, Eric Burdon and The Animals, Donovan, Paul Jones, Zoot Money, Arthur Brown, Jimi Hendrix, Procol Harum, Ten Years After, Otis Redding, Traffic, John Lennon, Yoko Ono, Jethro Tull, Joe Cocker

This hodge-podge of clips from divergent sources (and of varying quality) is similar to, and contains much the same footage as the compilation films *Popcorn* and *Rock City* (see separate entries). The Stones do "Have You Seen Your Mother, Baby;" Ike and Tina perform "River Deep, Mountain High;" Hendrix lays down yet another version of "Hey Joe" for film posterity; Otis Redding renders a smashing "Satisfaction" . . . and much more in this interesting but erratic effort.

SUSPIRIA (1976)

    D—Color
▨ Dario Argento and Dario Nicolodi
▣ Dario Argento
▩ Salvatore Argento
♧ TCF
● 97m.
❖ Jessica Harper, Joan Bennett, Alida Valli, Udo Kier, Stefania Casini
◉ Attic

Eerie techno-rock score by Dario Argento and Goblin for this stylish horror film about a series of bizarre murders at an exclusive European dancing school run—the heroine (Harper) discovers—by a coven of witches. American Ballet Theatre it ain't!

SWAN, THE (1956)

    D—Color
▨ John Dighton
■ the play by Ferenc Molnar
▣ Charles Vidor
▩ Dore Scharyl
♧ MGM
● 112m.
❖ Grace Kelly, Alec Guinness
⇥ Van Dyke Parks

Grace Kelly's last film—Van Dyke Parks' first—is a frothy romantic comedy about a royal love triangle. Parks, started out as a child actor, and when this film was made the twelve-year-old probably hadn't even begun work on his legendary and influential album *Song Cycle*. Famed L.A. session musician Parks ("Eight Miles High," "Smiley Smile," "Tape From California," etc.) does lend back-up support here too, but in this instance it's for Princess Grace, not Brian Wilson.

SWINGIN' ALONG (*orig.* DOUBLE TROUBLE) (1961)

    M—Color
▨ Arthur Morton
▣ Charles Barton
▩ Jack Leewood

≈ Lippert
● 74m.
✪ Peter Marshall, Tommy Noonan, Barbara Eden
⊐ Bobby Vee, Ray Charles

Noonan, an amateur songsmith, and Marshall, a con man, combine their talents and resources to walk off with first prize in a songwriting contest. This feature was first released as *Double Trouble.* It was such a bomb, though, that the Charles and Vee sequences were shot and inserted as a last ditch try at pumping some life into it. Alas it didn't fare any better as *Swingin' Along,* but Charles' "What'd I Say" is a knockout.

SWINGIN' SUMMER, A (1965)

M—Color
≈ Leigh Chapman
■ Robert Sparr
⬚ Reno Carell
≈ United Screen Arts
● 80m.
✪ James Stacy, William Wellman, Jr.
⊐ The Righteous Brothers, The Rip Chords, Donnie Brooks, Gary Lewis and The Playboys, Jody Miller
◐ Hanna-Barbera

"They're Lovin', Laughin' and Livin' it up and for kicks, playing CHICKEN ON WATER SKIS! So spread out the beach towels . . . grab your gals. It's gonna be. . . .": a) Edward D. Wood, Jr.'s *Glen or Glenda* b) Sergei Eisenstein's *Battleship Potemkin* c) *Lawrence of Arabia* d) none of the above. First prize winner gets two free tickets to National Talent Consultants latest production *A Swingin' Summer.* Second prize is, of course . . . four free tickets to same. "SEE AND HEAR 7 Great New Songs Hits: "A Swingin' Summer," "Justine," "Penny the Poo," "Nitro," "Ready To Groove," "Out To Lunch" and "Red Hot Roadster." Film introduces 'TV's *Hollywood Palace* billboard girl, Raquel Welch."

SYMPATHY FOR THE DEVIL (*see* ONE PLUS ONE)

TAKE ME HIGH (1973)

M—Color
≈ Christopher Penfold and Kenneth Harper
■ David Askey
⬚ Kenneth Harper
≈ MGM
● 90m.
✪ Cliff Richard, Debbie Watling, Hugh Griffith, George Cole

Cliff Richard, returning to the screen after some six years of intense involvement with Chrisianity plays a merchant banker on his way up in this British variation of *How To Suceed in Business Without Really Trying.* Songs written by Tony Cole include "It's Only Money," "The Anti-Brotherhood of Man," "Winning" and "Love is The Word."

TAKING OFF (1971)

D—Color
Milos Forman, John Guare, Jean-Claude Carriere, John Klein
Milos Forman
Alfred W. Crown
UI
93m.
Buck Henry, Lynn Carlin, Audra Lindley
Ike and Tina Turner, Carly Simon
Decca

Serio-comic generation gap tale of middle-class parents and their daughters' flirtation with the "summer of love." Ike and Tina Turner have a memorable guest shot pounding out "Goodbye So Long," and Carly Simon does a brief turn as an auditioning singer (with a song called "Long Term Physical Effects"). The Incredible String Band is also heard briefly singing "Air."

TAMI SHOW, THE (1965)

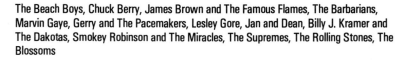

R—B/W
Steve Binder
Lee Savin; Exec Prod: Bill Sargent
AIP
96m.
The Beach Boys, Chuck Berry, James Brown and The Famous Flames, The Barbarians, Marvin Gaye, Gerry and The Pacemakers, Lesley Gore, Jan and Dean, Billy J. Kramer and The Dakotas, Smokey Robinson and The Miracles, The Supremes, The Rolling Stones, The Blossoms

One for the time capsules! The greatest gathering of rock performers ever assembled for one film, *Woodstock* and *Monterey Pop* withstanding. All in performance at the Santa Monica (California) Civic Auditorium, October 24, 1964. While the original videotape stock of this film (which is discussed more fully in the main text of this book) lacks a *Woodstock*'s visual resources, *"TAMI"* makes up for these failings with its own wit, verve and talent. Musical highlights include: The Supremes' "Where Did Our Love Go?" and "Baby Love;" The Stones' "Around and Around" and "Off The Hook;" Brown's "Please, Please Me;" Berry's "Johnny B. Goode;" Gaye's "Can I Get A Witness" and Smokey's "Mickey's Monkey." Note: Currently circulating versions of *"TAMI"* lack the Beach Boys sequence, which has been deleted due to contractual reasons.

TEENAGE MILLIONAIRE (1961)

M—B/W
H.B. Cross
Lawrence Doheny
Howard B. Kreitsek
UA
84m.
Jimmy Clanton, Zasu Pitts
Chubby Checker, Jackie Wilson, Dion, Bill Black Combo

This film's slender plot pemise entirely dispenses with exposition. For the only way the writer of this could figure out how to integrate music into the action was to have the star (Clanton) *imagine* the musical sequences. Otherwise, the story revolves around a poor little rich boy who only wants to be a rock and roll star. He gets his big chance . . . The End. There's a brief appearance here by TV *Superman*'s "Jimmy Olson," Jack Larson, in a movie that's so bedraggled it makes you wanna take it home and give it some chicken soup.

TEN FROM YOUR SHOW OF SHOWS (1973)

M−B/W
■ Max Liebman
▦ Max Liebman
❦ Walter Reade
● 92m.
✪ Sid Caeser, Carl Reiner, Howard Morris

Hilarious (and pioneering) rock parody as "The Three Haircuts" (Caeser, Reiner and Morris) sing "I Got a Rock in My Hand and a Roll in My Mouth" in a segment from this compilation film of legendary early-fifties TV series.

TEN GIRLS AGO (1962)

M−Color
🖎 Peter Farrow, Diane Lampert
■ Harold Daniels
▦ Edward A. Geluin
❦ Am-Can
✪ Dion, Buster Keaton, Eddie Foy, Jr., Bert Lahr

Unreleased Canadian feature starring Dion, with comedy support by Keaton, Lahr and Foy. No other information available.

THANK GOD IT'S FRIDAY (1978)

M−Color
🖎 Barry Armyan Bernstein
■ Robert Klane
▦ Rob Cohen
❦ COL
● 100m.
✪ Donna Summer, The Commodores
🡒 Paul Jabara
◔ Casablanca

This disco slice-of-life special zooms in on the comings and goings on a *typical* Friday night at a Hollywood dance spot, i.e. the big dance contest, guys who dress like girls (and vice versa), the heartbreak and laughter, drugs, etc. Summer, in her screen debut, plays an aspiring singer yearning for her big break in show business in this floperoo musical that failed to tap the "SatNitFvr" market for which it was intended. Summer's hit, "The Last Dance" was introduced in this film which also features on-screen performances by The Commodores ("Too Hot To Trot," "Easy" and others) and a nearly non-stop mix of disco sounds such as "I Am What I Am" (The Village People), "I Wanna Dance" (Marathon) and "Lovin', Livin' and Givin' " (Diana Ross). Note: "The Last Dance" won the 1978 Academy Award for best song.

THAT'LL BE THE DAY (1973)

D—Color
- Ray Connolly
- Claude Whatham
- David Putnam and Sandy Lieberson
- Mayfair Films
- 91m.
- David Essex, Billy Fury, Keith Moon, Ringo Starr
- Ronco

Essex plays a lower class British worker with a wife and child who tries to settle down, but who finally succumbs to the chancy and itinerant life of a rock musician. Not as much music in this film as in the smash sequel, *Stardust*, with the tone being more along the lines of a standard "kitchen sink" drama of lower class conflict and aspiration. At the film's climax, the Essex character has just made the decision to chuck his marriage for a go at music. In *Stardust* his dreams are realized beyond his wildest hopes. A non-stop parade of "oldies": everything from Buddy Holly's "That'll Be the Day" to Brian Hyland's "Sealed With a Kiss," floods the soundtrack, with additional music supervision by Keith Moon and Neil Aspinall. Ringo and Fury are absent from the sequel.

THAT'S THE WAY OF THE WORLD (*see* SHINING STAR)

THIEF (1981)

D—Color
- Michael Mann
- Michael Mann
- Michael Mann
- UA
- 122m.
- James Caan, Tuesday Weld
- UA

A safecracker (Caan) makes plans for leading a normal life, but is thwarted by his criminal accomplices. Tangerine Dream's high-tech electro-rock, so effective in *Sorcerer,* proves totally destructive here. Played at an ear-splitting pitch, it completely overwhelms the drama.

THIS IS ELVIS (1981)

R—Color/B/W
- Malcolm Leo, Andrew Solt
- Malcolm Leo, Andrew Solt
- Malcolm Leo, Andrew Solt
- WB
- 111m.
- Elvis Presley
- RCA

Staged dramatic sequences, newsreel footage, and movie and TV clips combine for the first, but surely not the last, major movie project on the life and music of Elvis Presley. (Made with the cooperation of Presley manager, Colonel Tom Parker.) At one and the same time one of the best, and the absolute *worst* rock documentaries ever produced. First the good news! *This is Elvis* contains "Jailhouse Rock" and "Teddy Bear" (from *Loving You*), inarguably Elvis' two best movie production numbers, complete and intact. This tribute also has portions of the classic kinescopes from the TV shows of Ed Sullivan, Frank Sinatra, Milton Berle and Tommy and Jimmy Dorsey, plus a "Revealing" and seldom seen interview from a mid-fifties TV show hosted by columnist Hy Gardner . . . and much more, of interest to even the casual Elvis fan. BUT! in an effort to lend the project unnecessary "scope," "point of view," "perspective" etc., Malcolm Leo and Andrew Solt (makers of the excellent TV docu *Heroes of Rock and Roll*) made the disastrous choice of staging (with actors portraying Elvis at different ages) various highlights of the singer's life. Furthermore, the affair is narrated by Elvis soundalike, singer Ral Donner, telling his "story," so to speak, from the grave. Thus before you get to the real Presley you have to sit through fifteen minutes of the mawkish and embarrassing film of Elvis as a child and adolescent. Often spectacular renditions of such songs as: "Hound Dog," "Love Me Tender," "Don't Be Cruel," "Heartbreak Hotel," "Blue Suede Shoes," "Suspicious Minds," "That's When Your Heartaches Begin" and many others.

TICKLE ME (1965)

	M—Color
🎬	Elwood Ulman, Edward Bernds
📽	Norman Taurog
🎞	Ben Schwalb
⚙	Allied Artists
●	90m.
✪	Elvis Presley, Julie Adams
◐	RCA

Elvis plays a worker at an all-femme dude ranch. Late-period Presley movies tended toward the feature of curvaceous cuties literally draped in all the sets like fixtures, and this entry is certainly no exception. Includes "It Feels So Right," "I'm Yours" and "Put the Blame on Me." Elvis #17.

TIMES SQUARE (1980)

	M—Color
🎬	Jacob Brackman
📽	Alan Moyle
🎞	Kevin McCormack
⚙	AFD
●	102m.
✪	Robin Johnson, Trini Alvarado, Tim Curry
◐	RSO

Laughably conceived Patti Smith-like punk rocker (Johnson) leads a privileged adolescent runaway (Alvarado) through the lower depths of New York's Times Square, where the worst things that happen are a little dirt and noise, BUT no drugs, prostitution, "chickenhawks" or death. Pseudo-punk, on-screen performances by Johnson permeate this egregious effort from the Stigwood Organization which actually tries to paint a picture of the runaway life as the good life. Those groups and performers lending their recordings for a soundtrack collage spun by a dee-jay (Curry) on-screen include: The Pretenders, Roxy Music, The Ramones, Lou Reed, Garland Jeffreys, The Patti Smith Group and Desmond Child and Rouge.

TO RUSSIA . . . WITH ELTON (1979)

- R—Color
- ⊟ Dick Clement, Ian La Frenais
- ◾ Dick Clement, Ian La Frenais
- ▦ Allan McKeown, Ian La Frenais
- ● 77m.
- ✪ Elton John

Elton John sings for the borscht and babushka set in docu of singer's '79 tour of Soviet Union. Film narrated by Dudley Moore, features E.J., feathers and all, doing "Crocodile Rock," "Rocketman" and, fittingly, "Back in the U.S.S.R.," and other hits, before austere and confused-looking crowds in Moscow and Leningrad.

TOMMY (1975)

- M—Color
- ⊟ Ken Russell
- ◾ the rock opera of the same name by Pete Townshend and The Who
- ◾ Ken Russell
- ▦ Robert Stigwood and Ken Russell
- ⚡ COL
- ● 111m.
- ✪ Ann-Margret, Roger Daltry, Oliver Reed, Robert Powell, Jack Nicholson
- ⊐ Tina Turner, Elton John, Eric Clapton, Keith Moon, Pete Townshend, John Entwistle, Arthur Brown, Paul Nicholas.
- ✪ MCA

A blind, deaf and dumb pinball champion becomes the leader of a religious cult. Initially growing out of a Who jam session, the first stage was the recording—the first (so-called) "rock opera." Then it went through several theatrical metamorphoses (a ballet and quasi-musical) and became an even bigger phenomenon. Then it touched down on the stage of New York City's Metropolitan Opera in a performance by The Who themselves. A film, then, was inevitable; and *who* but Ken Russell could have created the form that finally transformed the project into the maddest, most eccentric movie musical since *Yolanda and The Thief.* Somehow this all star rock gala just manages to *work*—even down to the shot of Ann-Margret (who plays Tommy's mother) rolling around in a veritable lava flow of baked beans pouring out of a busted television set. Elton John's rendition of "Pinball Wizard" (in giant platform shoes) is a musical high point, and Tina Turner simply IS "The Acid Queen" in the most genuinely *terrifying* production number ever made. Other hits include "See Me Feel Me," "I'm Free," "We're Not Gonna Take It" and "Eyesight To The Blind" (which unlike the other Who-penned numbers was written by Sonny Boy Williamson). Ann-Margret's number "The Day It Rained Champagne" was especially written by The Who for this film.

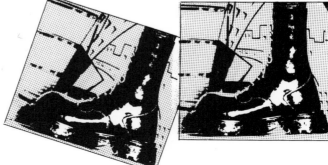

TOMMY STEELE STORY, THE (*see* ROCK AROUND THE WORLD)

TONITE LET'S ALL MAKE LOVE IN LONDON (1967)

R–Color
- Peter Whitehead
- Peter Whitehead
- Peter Whitehead
- Lorrimer
- Michael Caine, Edna O'Brien, Vanessa Redgrave
- Eric Burdon and the Animals, Andrew Loog Oldham, the Rolling Stones, Julie Christie, David Hockney, Donyale Luna, Pink Floyd, (and the voice of Alan Ginsberg).
- Immediate

Pseudo-sociological documentary look at mid-sixties "swinging London." Explication, demonstration, observation, confession and syncopation by the on-screen likes of the above-noted musicians, artists and actors . . . plus others. Appearances by "the Floyd" (who also did the film's score), along with the Animals and the Stones. Additional music by Chris Farlowe and the Small Faces.

TOOMORROW (1970)

M–Color
- Val Guest
- Val Guest
- Harry Saltzman
- Rank

● 95m.

✪ Olivia Newton-John, Benny Thomas, Vic Cooper, Karl Chambers

Ready-Steady-Go-type quickie about a pop group, "Toomorrow" (composed of by the film's four stars) kidnapped by aliens from another planet, the Alphoids, fascinated by the new sound of something called a "tonaliser." The titles of some of "Toomorrow's" and Newton-John's songs, "If You Can't Be Hurt You Can't Be Happy" and "Happiness Valley" are a dead giveaway to the level of music aspired to in this featherweight British entry. Co-produced by Don Kirshner.

TOUCHABLES, THE (1968)

     D—Color

🎬 Ian La Frenais, David and Donald Cammell and Robert Freeman

🎞 Robert Freeman

🎼 John Bryan

🎫 TCF

● 94m.

✪ Judy Huxtable, David Anthony, James Villiers, Michael Chow

🔵 Twentieth Century Fox

Four young girls kidnap a pop star and keep him prisoner in a plastic bubble. Easily the most insane of the "swinging London" Pop/Op art fantasy flicks. Title song by Steve Winwood and Jim Capaldi of Traffic, sung by Nirvana. Other music by Ken Thorne.

TOUCHED BY LOVE (1980)

     D—Color

🎬 Hesper Anderson

🎞 the book *To Elvis With Love* by Lena Canada

🎞 Gus Trikonis

🎼 Michael Viner

🎫 COL

● 90m.

✪ Deborah Raffin, Diane Lane

A teacher of handicapped children (Raffin) breaks through to an emotionally withdrawn patient (Lane), when she discovers the girl's obsession with Elvis Presley. Though he figures prominently in the plot (he becomes the girl's pen pal) Elvis Presley is seen only in a tiny film clip (a rather curious scene where the girl goes to a theater advertising only "Elvis Presley Film" and sees footage of an old *Ed Sullivan Show* TV appearance.) Background score for this real-life basis melodrama is chiefly an instrumental arrangement of "Love Me Tender."

TRIP, THE (1967)

     D—Color

🎬 Jack Nicholson

🎞 Roger Corman

🎼 Roger Corman

🎫 AIP

● 85m.

✪ Peter Fonda, Bruce Dern, Susan Strasberg, Dennis Hopper, Salli Sachse, Dick Miller

🔵 Sidewalk

A director of television commercials on the verge of divorcing his wife decides to try some acid in the hope it might help him make up his mind. Mike Bloomfield and the Electric Flag supplied the superior score (they're heard almost constantly during the film) for this landmark slice of psychedelic Americana. Avant-garde filmmaker Bruce Conner—whose faster-than-the-eye-can-see style cutting is adapted here by Corman to his own designs—can be seen passing a joint in one of the film's party scenes.

TROUBLE MAN (1972)

D—Color
- John D.F. Black
- Ivan Dixon
- Joel D. Freeman
- TCF
- 99m.
- Robert Hooks, Paul Winfield
- Tamla

Hooks is a good guy private eye, and Winfield is the gang chieftan who tries to frame him for the murder of a rival racketeer in one of the better "blacksploitation" features. The soundtrack album (and the title tune) was a big seller for the composer of the film's score, Marvin Gaye.

TROUBLE WITH GIRLS, THE (1969)

M—Color
- Arnold Peyser, Lois Peyser
- the book *The Chattaqua* by Day Keene, Dwight Babcock
- Peter Tewksbury
- Lester Welch
- MGM
- 104m.
- Elvis Presley, Sheree North
- RCA

Elvis plays a 1920's Chattaqua circuit manager in his last film musical. Film's big production number is "Clean Up Your Own Back Yard." ELVIS #31.

TRUCK TURNER (1974)

D—Color
- Oscar Williams, Michael Allin
- Jonathan Kaplan
- Fred Weintraub, Paul Heller
- AIP
- 91m.
- Isaac Hayes, Yaphet Koto
- Enterprise

Exceptionally bloody black action film stars Hayes as a strong-armed sleuth who wages a personal war against the pimps and pushers who murdered his best friend. "Black Moses" Hayes also penned the score.

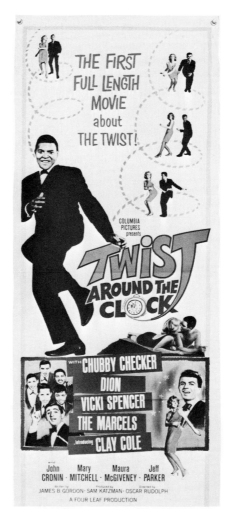

TWIST AROUND THE CLOCK (1961)

M—B/W

- James B. Gordon
- Oscar Rudolph
- Sam Katzman
- COL
- 86m.
- Chubby Checker, Vicki Spencer
- Dion, The Marcels, Clay Cole

The birth of the twist as told through the eyes of Hollywood, as twist prophet Checker comes down from the mount to spread the gospel of the latest dance craze to urban swingers. With this film producer Sam Katzman proved, five years after his phenomenal success with *Rock Around The Clock,* that he still had the magic touch and could ride the crest of a craze with the best of 'em. This formula quickie cleaned up at the box office quite nicely. Chubby sings "Twistin' U.S.A.," "Don't Twist With Anybody Else But Me," the title tune and several others; Dion does "The Wanderer" and The Marcels reprise their "Blue Moon."

200 MOTELS (1971)

M—Color
- Frank Zappa, with additional material by Mark Volman & Howard Kaylan
- Frank Zappa, Tony Palmer
- Jerry Good, Herb Cohen
- UA
- 99m.
- Frank Zappa and the Mothers of Invention, Mark Volman, Howard Kaylan, Keith Moon, Ringo Starr
- UA

Surrealistic fable of musicians' life "on the road" details frantic goings-on as Zappa and the Mothers touch down in "Centerville, U.S.A." Zappa employed all the state-of-the-art video equipment he could lay his hands on for this cartoony tale. Computer graphics, animation (the self-enclosed seg "Dental Hygene Dilemma" is a knockout) and the purposely flat stage sets combine to make this film totally infectious and engaging. The nearly non-stop score, much of it played by the Royal Philharmonic Orchestra and Chorus, was all written by Zappa. Big things were expected for *200 Motels* when it was released, but it came and went very quickly.

TWO-LANE BLACKTOP (1971)

D—Color
- Rudolph Wurlitzer, Will Corry
- Monte Hellman
- Michael S. Laughlin
- UI
- 101m.
- James Taylor, Dennis Wilson, Warren Oates, Laurie Bird

Taylor is a race car driver; Wilson is his mechanic. Together, along with a girl they pick up along the way, they engage in a cross-country race with another driver, played by Oates. And that's just about the extent of the plot, except for some usual "road"-as-metaphor goings-on dreamed up for them by writers, Wurlitzer and Corry. Neither rock star, Taylor, nor Beach Boy Wilson warble so much as a note in this much-heralded (but overly arty) enterprise.

UNDERGROUND U.S.A. (1980)

M—Color
- Eric Mitchell
- Eric Mitchell
- Eric Mitchell, Erdnor Raushalle
- New Cinema
- 85m.
- Patti Astor, Rene Ricard

A clef version of Warhol superstar Edie Sedgewick's life has music by James White and The Blacks and The Lounge Lizards.

UNION CITY (1980)

D—Color
- Mark Reichert

■ the Cornell Woolrich story, *The Corpse Next Door*
■ Mark Reichert
▦ Graham Belin
✿ Kinesis Ltd.
● 87m.
✪ Debbie Harry, Pat Benatar, Dennis Lipscomb

Debbie Harry plays the wife of a milquetoast who impulsively kills a man, and then proceeds to keep the body hidden in an adjacent apartment. Failed Fassbinder-ish version of a Cornell Woolrich story, features a decent dramatic debut by the lead singer of Blondie. That group's Chris Stein also did the music. Pat Benatar appears in a brief role.

UNTAMED YOUTH (1957)

D—B/W
▬ John C. Higgins
■ Howard W. Koch
▦ Aubrey Schenck
✿ WB
● 80m.
✪ Mamie Van Doren, Eddie Cochran

Predictable "expose" of the exploitation of teenage migrant workers. Ms. Van Doren bends over a lot. Eddie Cochran sings "Cotton Picker" as well as taking on some dramatic chores. Music: Les Baxter.

UP THE JUNCTION (1967)

D—Color
▬ Roger Smith
■ the novel by Nell Dunn
■ Peter Collinson
▦ Anthony Havelock-Allan, John Barbourne
✿ PAR
● 119m.
✪ Suzy Kendall, Dennis Waterman
◐ UA

Desirous of seeing "how the other half lives," a young middle-class woman leaves her safe British existence and moves in with two factory workers. Manfred Mann sang and co-wrote (with Mike Hugg) the music for this kitchen sink saga of lower class comings and goings.

UP TIGHT (1968)

D—Color
▬ Jules Dassin, Ruby Dee, Julian Mayfield
■ the novel *The Informer* by Liam O'Flaherty
■ Jules Dassin
▦ Jules Dassin
✿ PAR
● 104m.
✪ Raymond St. Jacques, Ruby Dee, Frank Silvera, Julian Mayfield, Roscoe Lee Browne
◐ Stax

Back in the 30's, director John Ford made a movie classic of Liam O'Flaherty's tale of an I.R.A. informer on the run. By transposing the action from the Irish "troubles" to the black urban ghettos of the 60's, director Jules Dassin ended up diluting the story's impact. The score, by Booker T. and The Mg's, however, worked well.

URGH!—A Music War (1981)

R—Color
Derek Burbidge
Michael White
Lorimar
123m.
The Police, Wall of Voodoo, Toyah Wilcox, John Cooper-Clarke, Orchestral Manoeuvres in the Dark, Chelsea, Oingo Boingo, Echo and the Bunnymen, Jools Holland, XTC, Klaus Nomi, Athletico Spizz '80, The Go Go's, Dead Kennedys, Steel Pulse, Gary Numan, Joan Jett, Magazine, Surf Punks, Au Pairs, The Cramps, Invisible Sex, Pere Ubu, Devo, The Alley Cats, John Otway, Gang of Four, 999, Fleshtones, X, Skafish, Splodgeness Abounds, UB40
A&M

Showcasing 33 acts in 123 minutes, this rockumentary shot at concerts in Los Angeles, New York, England and France offers a "Whitman's Sampler" of some of the leading lights of 80's punk, new wave, techno-rock, reggae and ska. Without any narration or specified context, the makers of this film clearly mean for the music to "speak for itself." Unfortunately with each act allowed only one number (with the exception of The Police) they have some difficulty in doing so. With the camera mostly sticking to the performers in medium shot (there are very few views of the audience) *Urgh!* often appears as austere as *Go Go Mania.* Highlights include Toyah Wilcox singing "Dance" (a highly theatrical and effective Bowie-inspired turn), avant-garde pop sounds from Pere Ubu ("Birdies"), Gang of Four ("He'll Send In The Army") and X ("Beyond and Back"), science-fiction vaudeville bits from Gary Numan ("Down In The Park"), Devo ("Uncontrollable Urge") and Klaus Nomi (the black-haired, white-faced, high-pitched, robot-like creature who, with white industrial jump-suited back-up players, entertainingly, twitches his way through "Total Eclipse") and professional "power pop" sounds from The Police ("Driven To Tears" and Roxanne") and Au Pairs ("Come Again").

VALLEY, THE (1972)

D—Color
Paul Gegauff, Barbet Schroeder
Barbet Schroder
M. Chanderli, Stephane Tchalgadjieff
Lagoon
114m.
Jean-Pierre Kalfan, Bulle Ogier
Harvest

Enigmatic story of a French woman (Ogier) who travels to New Guinea in search of native arts and crafts. This hyper-exotic epic about what finally turns into a quest for a *magic feather* has an appropriately trance-like score by Pink Floyd.

VAN MORRISON IN IRELAND (1980)

- R—Color
- Michael Radford
- Rex Pyke
- Bill Graham Presents
- 60m.
- Van Morrison

Concert material from 1979 dates in Belfast and Dublin, plus interviews with the singer and on-the-road footage combine for an interesting musical portrait of Welsh rocker Van Morrison. Songs include: "Gloria" and "Bright Side of the Road."

VANISHING POINT (1971)

- D—Color
- Guillero Cain (Guillermo Cabrera-Infanta.)
- Richard C. Sarafian
- Norman Spencer
- TCF
- 107m.
- Barry Newman, Cleavon Little, Severn Darden
- Delaney and Bonnie

A nameless driver (Newman) takes off on an unspecified mission pursued by police and egged-on by a blind disc jockey (Little). Delaney and Bonnie appear as singers in a gospel troupe (belting out "You Gotta Believe") in this very confused post-*Easy Rider* exercise in pop existentialism. Actress Charlotte Rampling appears in some versions of this heavily studio-tampered film, but not in others. Other music by Sam and Dave and Big Mama Thornton.

VELVET UNDERGROUND AND NICO, THE (1966)

- R—B/W
- Andy Warhol
- Andy Warhol
- Filmmakers Co-op
- 70m.
- The Velvet Underground, Nico

Film of The Velvet Underground at sixties scenemaker spa, The Dom, also features appearances by actress Mary Woronov and poet Gerard Malanga.

VILLAGE OF THE GIANTS (1965)

- D—Color
- Alan Calliou
- H.G. Wells' *Food of the Gods*
- Bert I. Gordon
- Bert I. Gordon
- Embassy Pictures
- Tommy Kirk, Johnny Crawford, Ron Howard, Beau Bridges
- The Beau Brummels, Freddie Cannon, Mike Clifford

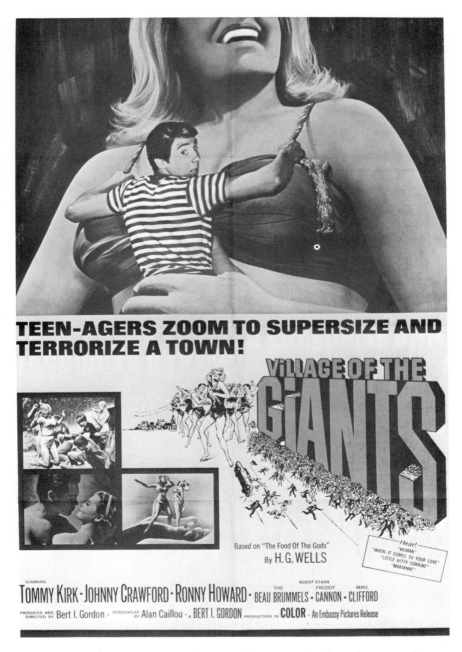

TEEN-AGERS ZOOM TO SUPERSIZE AND TERRORIZE A TOWN!

ViLLAGE OF THE GiANTS

Based on "The Food Of The Gods"
By H.G. WELLS

Hear!
"WOMAN"
"WHEN IT COMES TO YOUR LOVE"
"LITTLE BITTY CORRINE"
"MARIANNE"

STARRING
TOMMY KIRK · JOHNNY CRAWFORD · RONNY HOWARD · GUEST STARS THE BEAU BRUMMELS · FREDDY CANNON · MIKE CLIFFORD

PRODUCED AND DIRECTED BY Bert I. Gordon · SCREENPLAY BY Alan Caillou · A BERT I. GORDON PRODUCTION IN **COLOR** · An Embassy Pictures Release

A gang of teens grow six times their normal size, runs amok and terrorizes a town after quaffing a mysterious potion invented by mad teen scientist, Howard. Director Gordon loosely remade this film in 1976, using the original title of the source material, H.G. Wells' *Food of the Gods*. Appearances by The Beau Brummels, Mike Clifford and Freddie Cannon, who plays and sings "Little Bitty Corrina." Score by Jack Nitzsche.

VIVA LAS VEGAS! (1964)

M—Color
- Sally Benson
- George Sidney
- Jack Cummings, George Sidney
- MGM
- 86m.
- Elvis Presley, Ann-Margret
- RCA

"It's That Go-Go Guy and That Bye Bye (Birdie) Gal in the Fun Capital of the World!" Elvis in yet another role as a race car driver who, this time out, succumbs to the tight curves of Ann-Margret. This is Presley's last good musical, thanks to the contributions of the sensational A-M, and director Sidney. Even here the boy from Tupelo looks a trifle tired, but when Ann-Margret flings down the dancing gauntlet in their duet on "C'mon Everybody," Elvis (as of yore) rises to the occasion. Other songs include: "If You Think I Need You," "What'd I Say" and the title tune. ELVIS #15.

WANDERERS, THE (1979)

D—Color
- Rose and Philip Kaufman
- the novel of the same name by Richard Price
- Philip Kaufman
- Martin Ransohoff
- WB
- 117m.
- Ken Wahl, John Friedrich, Karen Allen

Three members of the "Wanderers," a sixties era Bronx street gang, fight off competition from the "Baldies" and the "Ducky Boys" while going through the usual pangs of adolescence. Philip Kaufman's thinking man's gang movie was the first victim of the fallout over *The Warriors*. Warner Brothers gave it only limited release, changing its ad campaign practically on a daily basis to de-emphasize gang violence connotations and bring the film closer to a safe *American Graffiti* image. There's lots of rock in these young and restless lives—Wahl and Frederich crooning "Stranger Girl" at one point. Other soundtrack sounds include "Walk Like A Man" by The Four Seasons, "Soldier Boy" by The Shirelles, "You Really Got A Hold On Me" by Smokey Robinson and The Miracles, "Do You Love Me" by The Contours, "Shout" by The Isley Brothers, and Bob Dylan's "The Times They Are A-Changin' " (in a scene where the boys visit a Greenwich Village coffee house).

WARRIORS, THE (1979)

D—Color
- David Shaber and Walter Hill
- the novel of the same name by Sol Yurick
- Walter Hill
- Lawrence Gordon
- PAR
- 94m.
- Michael Beck, James Remar, Deborah Van Valkenburgh
- Dot

Teenage gangs fight their way across the landscape of New York city in a highly stylized retelling (with more than a nod to *A Clockwork Orange*) of the retreat of Xenophon's army following their defeat at the hands of the Persians in ancient Greece. When this flashy, visceral youth gang flick first opened, fights broke out in theatres among gang members who had come to see their fictional representatives on screen. It was a predictable situation, but the film industry panicked. Teen violence films already in the can were given limited release or shelved outright. Plans for making more were quickly dropped. The golden age of Motown classic "Nowhere To Run" figures prominently in the plot of this enjoyable if somewhat pretentious thriller—it's played over the radio by a gang-wise female dee-jay." Unfortunately the version used is not the Martha and the Vandellas original, but a new one by Arnold McCuller. Other songs include "Last of The Ancient Breed" by Desmond Child and Rouge, "Echoes of My Mind" by Mandrill, "In The City" by Joe Walsh, and others by Frederick LaPlano, Genya Ravan, The Mersh Brothers, and Eric Mercury. Score by Barry DeVorzon.

WATTSTAX (1973)

	R—Color
≊	Mel Stuart
◼	Mel Stuart
▦	Larry Shaw, Mel Stuart
⚡	COL
●	98m.
✪	Isaac Hayes, Rufus Thomas, Carla Thomas, Kim Weston, The Emotions, Johnnie Taylor, The Dramatics, The Staple Singers, The Bar Kays, Jimmy Jones, Albert King, Little Milton, Luther Ingram
➔	Richard Pryor
◐	Stax

Film of 1972 L.A. Coliseum benefit concert for the community of Watts by Stax Records artists. Richard Pryor is on hand as one of the emcees of the event. Much of *Wattstax* is given over to docu footage of Watts. Musical highlights include Hayes' "Shaft" and Rufus Thomas' "Funky Chicken."

WAVELENGTH (1967)

	D—Color
≊	Michael Snow
◼	Michael Snow
▦	Michael Snow
⚡	Filmmakers Co-op
●	45m.
✪	Hollis Frampton, Amy Tauben

In a New York loft some people move a large cabinet, then leave. A few minutes later two women enter and play The Beatles' "Strawberry Fields Forever" on a record player, and leave. Much later a man enters and collapses on the floor. More time passes, then a woman enters and looks at the man. She makes a phone call to someone named "Richard," telling him she thinks the man, who she doesn't know, is dead and that she'll be waiting outside. She leaves. All this time, the camera—filming the action in one continuous shot—has been ever so slowly zooming across the room towards the wall on the other side. At the film's end it has reached its destination—a black and white photograph of ocean waves. Michael Snow's experimental classic is either totally absorbing or totally exasperating—depending on your disposition. The use of the Beatles song is highly ritualistic in a manner that earned much comment at the time of the film's first release.

WELCOME TO L.A. (1976)

D—Color
- Alan Rudolph
- Alan Rudolph
- Robert Altman
- UA
- 106m.
- Keith Carradine, Sally Kellerman, Geraldine Chaplin, Harvey Keitel, Lauren Hutton, Viveca Lindfors, Sissy Spacek
- Richard Baskin
- Arista

Centering on a singer-songwriter (Carradine) arriving in Los Angeles to cut an album, this loosely-structured film frequently segues into the lives of his friends and casual acquaintances. The charm of the performers (especially Chaplin) is the only relief from the post-existential gloom of this look at what one of the film's songs calls "the city of one-night stands." More revealing than it knows of the pretensions of certain aspects of the music scene, *Welcome To L.A.*'s score (by Richard Baskin) is cut from the same post-psychoanalytic cloth as Dory Previn's urban *angst* toe-tappers. Songs (sung mainly by Baskin—though Carradine chimes in from time to time) include "Where The Arrow Flies," "The Best Temptation of All," and "After The End."

WELCOME TO MY NIGHTMARE (1975)

R—Color
- David Winters
- Key Films
- 84m.
- Alice Cooper

Concert film of Cooper during a mid-seventies swing through Britain. The clown prince of shock rock is also seen in staged studio surroundings, but by the time this film was made Cooper's novelty act had lost most of its edge. The movie's blurry look (16mm blown up to 35mm) doesn't help.

WHAT'S NEW PUSSYCAT? (1965)

M—Color
- Woody Allen
- Clive Donner
- Charles K. Feldman
- UA
- 108m.
- Peter O'Toole, Peter Sellers, Woody Allen, Romy Schneider
- UA

Zany farce of a Don Juan (O'Toole) who finds difficulty making it down the aisle with the one woman he truly loves (Schneider). Sellers, in one of his finest and funniest performances, complicates matters even more as a quack psychiatrist, "Fritz Fassbender," whom O'Toole turns to for help. Tom Jones singing the title song; Manfred Mann doing "My Little Red Book;" and Dionne Warwick's version of "Here I Am" (all by Burt Bachrach and Hal David) are the soundtrack highlights of this Woody Allen-scripted comedy. Score by Bachrach.

WHAT'S UP, TIGER LILY? (1966)

 M—Color
- Woody Allen
- Woody Allen
- Henry G. Saperstein
- AIP
- 80m.
- The Lovin' Spoonful
- Kama Sutra

   Consists of Allen's taking an absolutely wretched Japanese sub-James Bond action film and re-dubbing it with quips, zaps, one-liners and amiably zany witticisms. He yanked the original score and replaced it with an appropriately breezy one by The Lovin' Spoonful, who also crop up on the screen at the most marvelously incongruous moments. Songs include: "Pow," "Respoken" and "Gray Prison Blues."

WHEN THE BOYS MEET THE GIRLS (1965)

 M—Color
- Robert E. Kent
- the musical *Girl Crazy*
- Alvin Ganzer
- Sam Katzman
- MGM
- 97m.
- Connie Francis, Harve Presnell, Sue Anne Langdon
- Herman's Hermits, Sam The Sham and The Pharoahs, Louis Armstrong, Liberace
- MGM

   Sam Katzman's reworking of George and Ira Gershwin's *Girl Crazy* is a quasi-surrealist affair with Francis and Presnell trying to pass themselves off as college students on a dude ranch populated by the likes of Sam the Sham and the Pharaohs (singing "Monkey See"), Herman's Hermits ("Listen People") and Louis Armstrong ("Throw It Out of Your Mind"). Several Gershwin classics from the original *Girl Crazy* score also get sandwiched into the action—not to mention "Aruba Liberace."

WHERE THE BOYS ARE (1960)

 M—Color
- George Wells
- Henry Levin
- Joe Pasternak
- MGM
- 99m.
- Connie Francis, Yvette Mimieux, Paula Prentiss, Dolores Hart
- MGM

   Four young women (*near*-teenagers) visit the Ft. Lauderdale Easter vacation revels and test reality during their first time away from school and family. No rock and roll here, unless one charitably counts Francis as a rocker, but this MGM first-of-its-kind big budget musical proved that there was an endless supply of gold to be mined from the youth movie market. The lesson learned was that the more money you put in, the more you take out at the box office; for this film was a huge hit. Soon everybody re-thought their approach to kids and movies, and rock films began to take on a whole new, more expensive look. Connie sings the title tune.

WHERE THE BUFFALO ROAM (1980)

M—Color
- John Kaye
- the writings of Hunter S. Thompson
- Art Linson
- Art Linson
- UI
- 96m.
- Bill Murray, Peter Boyle
- MCA

The wild antics of "gonzo" journalist Dr. Hunter S. Thompson (Murray) create havoc during his coverage of political events. Hunter Thompson's life and times would appear to be ideal material for an *Animal House* for grown-ups, but this film is strictly sub-adolescent and—worse still—unfunny. Still while moviegoers stayed away, rock fans bought the soundtrack album and made it a modest hit. The main theme is Neil Young's guitar variations on the classic folk ballad "Where The Buffalo Roam." Other songs by Jimi Hendrix ("Purple Haze," "All Along the Watchtower"), Bob Dylan ("Highway 61"), The Temptations, Credence Clearwater Revival and The Four Tops. Bill Murray sings "Lucy In The Sky With Diamonds."

WHITE ROCK (1976)

R—Color
- Tony Maylam
- Tony Maylam
- Drummond Challis
- EMI
- 76m.
- James Coburn
- A&M

"Official film of the XII Winter Olympic Games," this sports documentary features a score by Yes' Rick Wakeman, who also appears from time to time letting loose on the synthesizer, organ and other instruments. Coburn as narrator and M.C. gives us more information than we *really* need to know about the various sports on view.

WHO'S THAT KNOCKING AT MY DOOR? (1969)

D—B/W
- Martin Scorsese and Betzi Manoogian
- Martin Scorsese
- Joseph Weil and Betzi and Hank Manoogian
- Joseph Weil Films
- 90m.
- Harvey Keitel, Zina Bethune

A young man (Keitel) is shocked by his girlfriend's (Bethune) revelation that she was once raped. Very powerful early Martin Scorsese drama about the Italian-American male's virgin-or-whore view of women. Extremely effective use of rock oldies on the soundtrack (years before this practice became fashionable) including "I've Had It" by The Bellnotes, "Jenny Take A Ride" by Mitch Ryder and The Detroit Wheels, and "Shotgun" by Junior Walker and the All-Stars.

WILD ANGELS, THE (1966)

D—Color
- Charles B. Griffith
- Roger Corman
- Roger Corman
- AIP
- 82m.
- Peter Fonda, Nancy Sinatra, Bruce Dern, Michael J. Pollard, Gayle Hunnicut
- members of the Hell's Angels motorcycle club.
- Tower

Loser (Dern), a Hell's Angels member, is fired, brawls with a Mexican gang, is shot by the police and finally dies with his club members at his side who've been rumbling orgiastically right along with him. "There's nowhere to go," the group's leader Heavenly Blues (Fonda) says thoughtfully at fadeout. Taking *The Wild One* at least several steps further, this is the film that practically wrote the manual for all the "chopper" sagas of the sixties—*Angels From Hell, The Savage Seven, and,* most important of all, *Easy Rider.* Music written by future California Lieutenant Governor, Mike Curb, played by David Allan and the Arrows.

WILD FOR KICKS (*orig.* BEAT GIRL) (1962)

D—B/W
- Dail Ambler
- Edmund T. Greville
- George Willoughby
- Times Film
- 92m.
- Adam Faith, Noelle Adam
- Christopher Lee, David Farrar
- Columbia (England)

Middle-class British teenager (Noelle Adam) gets in a real *pet* when her dad remarries. Before it's all over she experiences (this film's wacked-out *ideas* of) the lowest forms of personal degradation, i.e. drag racing ("Go man, go like a race track—voom!"); chicken on the rails ("Here comes the train—let's play.") *and* an "uninhibited" Soho striptease ("Melt! Melt! Melt!"). Music by The John Barry Seven for this great and goofy British "J.D." melodrama sounds remarkably similar to The B-52's. Occasional warbling by British rocker, Faith, and the pouty posturings of Mlle. Adam mark *Wild for Kicks/Beat Girl* as a definite *must* for scholars of teen attitude and rock-to-punk evolution. Songs: "Made You," "I Did What You Told Me," "The Stripper," "It's Legal" and "Beat Girl"—some of which are performed at "Wild Parties in Back Street *Sin Cellars.*"

WILD IN THE COUNTRY (1961)

D—Color
- Clifford Odets
- Philip Dunne
- Jerry Wald

⌾ TCF
● 114m.
✪ Elvis Presley, Tuesday Weld, Hope Lange, Millie Perkins

Rebel without a pause Presley is involved with THREE love interests in this story of a "misunderstood" youth who gets back on the right track with the help of one of his *amours,* psychologist Lange. Weld plays gal friend number two, a high school hellcat, and Perkins is the girl-next-door. The film started out as a well-intentioned one, with a Clifford Odets class-act script, but by the time "Fox" moguls got finished tampering with it, all the toughness was beaten out. Songs were added ("I Slipped, Stumbled and Fell," "Lonely Man," "In My Way" and the title tune), and the film ended up trying to function both as a high fallutin' drama *and* as a standard Presley musical. One of the most confused and *confusing* of all of the singer's movie efforts. ELVIS #7.

WILD IN THE STREETS (1968)

　 D—Color
⚏ Robert Thom
▮ based on his own story
▮ Barry Shear
▦ James H. Nicolson and Samuel Z. Arkoff
⌾ AIP
● 96m.
✪ Christopher Jones, Shelley Winters, Diane Varsi, Hal Holbrook, Millie Perkins, Richard Pryor, Kevin Coughlin
⤵ Melvin Belli, Walter Winchell, Dick Clark, Pamela Mason and Army Archerd
◑ Tower

Pop singer Max Frost (Jones), realizing that 52% of U.S. populace is under 25, launches a campaign to lower the voting age and get himself elected to the presidency. After a series of violent nation-wide demonstrations, the age limit is lowered, Frost is in the White House and everyone over 30 is being carted off to a "retirement" home to be force-fed LSD. Frost faces problems from a new source as the story ends—the under-10's want *their* chance to take things over. Robert Thom's gleefully outrageous script needed a more imaginative director than Barry Shear, but *Wild in The Streets* is still wonderful Pop-Swiftian fun—*The Greening of America* meets *1984* as it were. Jones, yowling out "Fourteen or Fight" (which like all the film's songs was written by the team of Barry Mann and Cynthia Weil) is just O.K. The film's real action is supplied by Winters as his overwrought mother, and Diane Varsi as the most flipped-out of his many girlfriends. Pryor, playing Jones's sidekick, is very subdued in this early film appearance. Other songs include "The Shape of Things To Come" and "Listen To The Music."

WILD ON THE BEACH (1965)

　 M—B/W
⚏ Harry Spalding
▮ Maury Dexter
▦ Maury Dexter
⌾ TCF
● 77m.
✪ Frankie Randall, Sherry Jackson
⤵ Sonny and Cher, The Astronauts

Nearly unbearable stuff about a housing shortage on a college campus. Musical appearances by Sonny and Cher and The Astronauts. Songs include: "The Gods of Love," "House on the Beach," "Little Speedy Gonzales," "Drum Dance" and "The Pyramid Stomp."

IF YOU'RE THIRTY, YOU'RE THROUGH!

This is the story of Max Frost, 24 years old...President of The United States...who created the world in his own image. To him, 30 is over the hill. 52% of the nation is under 25...and they've got the power. That's how he became President.

This is perhaps the most unusual motion picture you will ever see!

SHELLEY WINTERS · CHRISTOPHER JONES · DIANE VARSI

STARRING IN

WILD IN THE STREETS

WILD, WILD WINTER (1966)

M—Color
David Malcolm
Lennie Weinrib
Bart Patton
UI
80m.
Gary Clarke, Chris Noel
Dick and Dee Dee, The Beau Brummels, Jackie and Gayle, Jay and The Americans
Decca

Low budget affair ($214,000 to be exact) about the goings-on at a rockin' rollin' ski lodge, featuring *The Virginian's* Gary Clarke. Director Weinrib *(Beach Ball, Outta Sight)* specialized in quickly made rock movies of this sort, and *WWW* is no better nor worse than any of the others. The Beau Brummels sing "Just Wait and See."

WIZ, THE (1978)

M—Color
Joel Schumaker
the Broadway musical of the same name
Sidney Lumet
Rob Cohen

♋ UI
● 133m.
✪ Diana Ross, Richard Pryor, Michael Jackson, Lena Horne
◐ MCA

All-black musical version of *The Wizard of Oz,* by L. Frank Baum. Quincy Jones served as musical director for this filmization (one of the most expensive film flops of all time) of the hit Broadway quasi-rocker. Ross is Dorothy; Jackson is the scarecrow and Pryor plays the wonderful Wiz. Not nearly so good as the MGM musical, for it is just too big, loud and splashy, but all the principals try hard and Horne, as Glinda the good witch, comes off especially well. Music and lyrics by Charlie Smalls.

WONDERWALL (1968)

    D—Color
➖ Guillermo Cain (Guillermo Cabrera-Infante)
◼ a story by Gerard Brach
🎬 Joe Massot
🎦 Andrew Braunsberg
♋ Cinecenta
● 92m.
✪ Jack MacGowran, Jane Birkin, Irene Handl, Iain Quarrier
◐ Apple

An old professor living in an apartment next to a young model becomes involved in her life when he begins to spy on her through a hole he discovers in his wall. Beatle George Harrison wrote the original musical score for this off-beat semi-fantasy.

WOODSTOCK (1970)

    R—Color
◼ Michael Wadleigh; Asisstant Director: Martin Scorsese
🎦 Bob Maurice
♋ WB
● 184m.
✪ Joan Baez, Joe Cocker, Country Joe and The Fish, Crosby, Stills, Nash and Young, Arlo Guthrie, Richie Havens, Jimi Hendrix, Santana, John Sebastian, Sha-Na-Na, Sly and The Family Stone, Ten Years After, The Who
◐ Cotillion

AND FEATURING! a half-million young, mud-covered, blissed-out, free-loving charter members of what would come to be called "the Woodstock nation." Documentary of the 1969 Woodstock Music Festival—actually called a "music and art fair," though hardly anyone remembers it by that name. Almost everybody recalls the facts arising out of the fest, however, i.e. "x" amount of births, deaths, traffic jams, o.d.'s, etc. Easily the most publicized media event since the birth of Little Ricky Ricardo, this celluloid memento, highlighted by split-screen techniques, superimpositions and ear-splitting stereophonic sound *could* be described as *The Triumph of The Will* of youth culture. The Who's *Tommy* medley and Hendrix's "Star Spangled Banner," both preserved here, are great moments in rock on film in an over-three-hours extravaganza that also features Joe Cocker singing "With a Little Help From My Friends," "Higher" by Sly Stone and CSN&Y doing Joni Mitchell's "Woodstock." Note: A shortened and bowdlerized version of this film, entitled *Woodstock Remembered,* began appearing on TV in 1981.

M—Color
Richard Christian Danus and Marc Reid Rubel
Robert Greenwald
Lawrence Gordon
UI
93m.
Olivia Newton-John, Gene Kelly, Michael Beck
The Tubes
MCA

Goddess in a Venice (California) wall mural (Olivia) comes alive and helps a young painter (Beck) and an old hoofer (Kelly) open a roller disco. A sort of remake of the old movie fave *Down To Earth* (1947), *Xanadu* comes out looking like what one Hollywood wag called—*Midnight Special—The Movie*. Beautifully photographed and edited, this *chocolate mousse* of a film almost defies description. By turns dumb and intelligent, inert and alive. The producers *began* with music tracks by Olivia Newton-John, Cliff Richard and the Electric Light Orchestra (the latter two heard but not seen in the film), and then proceeded to construct the vaguest wisp of a story around this material. The visuals consist of enough glitz and optical effects to sink the Queen Mary—with The Tubes' appearance in a "battle of the bands" night club production number (*Dancin'*) a high point. Many top twenty records came from the soundtrack including: the title tune, *All Over The World*, *I'm Alive, Suddenly*, and *Magic*, but ironically, moviegoers stayed away in droves.

YELLOW SUBMARINE (1968)

- M−Color
- Lee Minoff, Al Brodax, Jack Mendelsohn, Erich Segal
- the songs of John Lennon and Paul McCartney
- George Dunning
- Al Brodax
- Apple Films
- 85m.
- Apple

The Beatles to the rescue as the mythical kingdom of Pepperland is invaded by the Blue Meanies, who want to purge the world of fun and music. The speaking voices of JPG&R dubbed by actors in this elaborate animated feature produced by Apple Films—but the music is pure Beatles. New songs written expressly for the project: "Only a Northern Song," "Altogether Now," "Hey, Bulldog," "It's All Too Much," plus previous Beatle hits like "All You Need Is Love," "Nowhere Man," and "Lucy In The Sky With Diamonds," served up with appropriate images designed by master animator, George Dunning. Additional musical score by George Martin. Note: "Hey Bulldog" dropped from final American release print.

YESSONGS (1973)

	R—Color
■	Peter Neal
▦	Brian Lane
●	75m.
✪	Yes

Rick Wakeman, Jon Anderson, Steve Howe, Chris Squire and Alan White (Yes) filmed in concert in 1972 at London's Rainbow Theatre. Film has an overly fussy look, but this shouldn't faze fans of such songs as "All Good People," "The Clap," "Roundabout," "Wurm (Starship Trooper)," "Yours Is No Disgrace" and "Close To The Edge."

YOU ARE WHAT YOU EAT (1968)

	M—Color
■	Barry Feinstein
▦	Peter Yarrow, Barry Feinstein
✇	Commonwealth-United
●	75m.
✪	Tiny Tim, Peter Yarrow
⮑	The Electric Flag, Barry McGuire, Paul Butterfield, Harper's Bizarre, John Simon, David Crosby, Rosko, The Family Dog
◐	COL

Hippie attitudinizing, sketches and musical interludes are the main ingredients in this wayward docu of sixties counter-culturedom. The editing scheme of this disjointed collage of performances and flower power raps might well have been determined by a toss of the "ching." Songs include: "Memphis Tennessee" and "Be My Baby" (sung by Tiny Tim), Van Dyke Parks' "Come To the Sunshine" (Harper's Bizarre) and "Silly Girl" and "Moments of the Lost Persuasion" (sung by Yarrow).

YOUNG SWINGERS (1964)

	M—B/W
✍	Harry Spalding
■	Maury Dexter
▦	Maury Dexter
✇	TCF
●	71m.
✪	Molly Bee, Rod Lauren
◐	Gene McDaniels

Perky, plucky Bee struggles to keep faltering rock club afloat for her star attraction, Gene ("Hundred Pounds of Clay") McDaniels.

YOUNGBLOOD (1978)

	D—Color
✍	Paul Carter Harrison
■	Noel Nosseck
▦	Nick Grillo, Alan Riche
✇	AIP
●	90m.
✪	Lawrence-Hilton Jacobs, Bryan Bell
◐	UA

Ghetto youths stage an anti-drug vendetta in this drama with a score by the group War.

YOU'RE A BIG BOY NOW (1966)

D—Color
- Francis Ford Coppola
- the novel by David Benedictus
- Francis Ford Coppola
- Phil Feldman
- WB
- 96m.
- Peter Kastner, Geraldine Page, Rip Torn
- Kama Sutra

A young man (Kastner) coming of age in the sixties struggles to get out from under the influence of his overprotective parents and deal with first love—both sacred (Karen Black) and profane (Elizabeth Hartman). Score by John Sebastian (played by The Lovin' Spoonful) for this second Coppola feature. Songs heard in this amiable comedy include the title tune and "Darlin' Be Home Soon."

ZABRISKIE POINT (1969)

D—Color
- Michelangelo Antonioni, Fred Gardner, Sam Shepard, Tonio Guera, Clare Peploe
- Michelangelo Antonioni
- Carlo Ponti
- MGM
- 112m.
- Mark Frechette, Daria Halpern
- MGM

A radical student (Frechette) is falsely suspected of shooting a policeman, and as he flees from authorities his travels constitute a kind of psychedelic version of *Don Quixote*. Both original music by Pink Floyd ("Heart Beat Pig Meat," "Crumbling Land" and others) and recycled recordings fill the air incessantly in this not always successful attempt to pin down the *significance* and *meaning* of the hippie movement. Shot in and around the Los Angeles area (as well as in Death Valley), also heard are the group Kaleidoscope, The Rolling Stones ("You've Got the Silver"), The Youngbloods ("Sugar Babe"), The Grateful Dead ("Dark Star") AND the singin' rage, Miss Patti Page.

ZACHARIAH (1971)

M—Color
- The Firesign Theatre
- George Englund
- George Englund
- ABC Films
- 93m.
- John Rubenstein, Pat Quinn
- Country Joe and The Fish, Doug Kershaw, The James Gang, New York Rock and Roll Ensemble, Elvin Jones
- Dunhill

Rock and Roll western movie satire with a script by members of The Firesign Theatre. Billed as "the first electric western," *Zachariah* contains musical performances by its featured rock groups, decked out in cowboy drag.

INDEX
MUSICIANS, MUSIC INDUSTRY FIGURES, ROCK MOVIES AND SIGNIFICANT SONGS

Numbers in **bold face** indicate a film listing.

Some have to dance... some have to kill!...

ROCK ALL NIGHT

See and Hear THE PLATTERS
and THE BLOCKBUSTERS

A SUNSET PRODUCTION starring

DICK MILLER · RUSSELL JOHNSON · ABBY DALTON

Produced and Directed by ROGER CORMAN · Executive Producer: JAMES H. NICHOLSON · Screenplay by

CHARLES GRIFFITH · AN AMERICAN-INTERNATIONAL PICTURE

ABOUT
THE AUTHORS

BILL REED has written extensively on rock music for *Rolling Stone, Fusion* and other journals. Most recently he has written for television, including the hit series *One Day At A Time.* He also reviews books and concerts for the *Los Angeles Herald Examiner.*

The 35-year-old West Virginia native is a former newspaper reporter, C & W disc jockey and rare book dealer. His likes include Peter DeVries, John Cale, Betty Carter, Rex Stout, Plan Nine, Jane Pauley, The Rolling Stones, Donald Westlake, Marianne Faithfull and TV dinners. He lives in Los Angeles and hates driving.

DAVID EHRENSTEIN is presently a film critic and reporter for the *Los Angeles Herald-Examiner,* and many of his contributions to that paper have been syndicated by King Features. His work has also appeared in such publications as *Film Culture, Film Comment, Film Quarterly,* the *Village Voice, Rolling Stone,* and the E.P. Dutton anthologies *The New American Cinema* (edited by Gregory Battcock) and *Jean-Luc Godard* (edited by Toby Mussman).

Born and raised in New York City, the 33-year-old writer has made Los Angeles his home for the past three years. His two favorite films are *I Was Born But...* and *Hercules Conquers Atlantis.*